"Before I started the RAVE Diet, my weight was 183. In four months, I had lost 38 pounds. And my total cholesterol had dropped to just 138." - Matthew Israel, Ph.D.

"I have been following the RAVE diet since October 30, 2003. I am a 42-year-old police officer and was up to 360 lbs and at 6'3"...well you know. The kicker is that heart disease runs in my family and my father and grandfather both died in their early 50's. My mother died of cancer at 70.
"Today I was 304 lbs. (56 lbs. in 44 days)
"Because of your video, because of your kindness to answer all of my questions and because of the motivation that you have given me, I am succeeding where I have failed in the past." - Mike Salvati

"In just a few months, I have lost 32 pounds, my medications have been cut in half and my blood sugars, blood pressure and cholesterol have all dropped dramatically." - Sirmirrion English

"I have successfully lost 33 pounds since starting this program. I have more energy and feel the best I have since my early 20's." - Bob Bruno

"My cholesterol dropped from 221 to 184. My blood pressure is 130 over 80, down from 150 over 98. My B-12, iron, sugar, calcium etc. were all perfect, and as an added bonus, I have lost 26 pounds over the course of the past 10 months. These are the best results I have ever had." - AnnMarie Iasimone

"I have lost 47 pounds over the past 12 months by changing my entire way of eating and following the RAVE Diet. This has helped me to not only lose the weight, but has also helped me to significantly lower my cholesterol, control my blood pressure, and better my self-esteem." - Albert J. Tarrano

"When I was 11 years old, I was diagnosed with cholesterol of 550. I have been to many different doctors and tried every kind of cholesterol lowering medication, but nothing worked. After following the RAVE diet, my cholesterol dropped to 400 points in just a few months. That is the lowest it has ever been – and without any medication. I was amazed! I've also lost 15 pounds and have never felt better." - Emily Burke

What viewers are saying about the enclosed DVD, *Eating*.

After viewing this video, I switched to the RAVE Diet the very next day. I have lost 25 pounds in six weeks and my whole body has undergone some incredible changes, all of which are extremely beneficial. I can't begin to express my gratitude in having this video pass through my hands. I had been searching for something for a long time, and the information it contained was just what I needed.

Although I had heard much of the contents many times before, nothing ever made an impact as this did. I was stunned. There are no words to express how I felt. A great spiritual teacher said we cannot grow unless we are willing to be embarrassed when our ignorance is revealed, and to sincerely regret past ways of thinking. At 63, I suffer from the typical ailments you mentioned and look forward to changing my diet and the almost certain benefits. Thank you so much for being an instrument of such goodness.

We were overwhelmed by this beautiful, comprehensive piece of work. Thank you for creating such a wonderful gift for humanity. Sometimes I get so discouraged at the lack of interest people show toward not only themselves but also their loved ones. Then along comes someone like you sharing wondrous gifts.

Just want to thank you again for opening my eyes and educating me on things that should have been obvious. Watched the video again last night with my husband, it had even more impact. He did not want to watch it. He agreed to 20 minutes and then he could not turn it off. He was so surprised on how informative it was--he watched the entire video very intently and wants to change his way of eating. He is a southern cracker and was raised on barbecue so I was very surprised it affected him so. Can't wait to see how good we are both going to feel in a few weeks.

I have to say that your video blew me away, even though I'm already extremely familiar with the subject matter. I was struck by the clarity and simplicity with which you explained the various concepts, and I learned quite a few new facts. I just kept thinking about how much I want my various relatives to see it.

I have just watched "Eating" for the second time. What a powerful thing you have done! I am deeply sobered, powerfully moved, and most importantly, clearer still about so many things. Thank you.

What reviewers are saying about the enclosed DVD, *Eating*.

"Rivet yourself to your chair and watch Eating, a mind-blowing video experience that will forever change the way you think about food."
  Joel Fuhrman, M.D., author of Eat To Live

"Eating is a brilliant program. It provides an easy and engaging path to health through good food. I highly recommend it."
  Neal Barnard, M.D., author of Breaking the Food Seduction

"I want both to congratulate and to thank you. You've done us all a major service."
  John Robbins, author of Diet For a New America

"A professionally executed, powerful and moving film."
  Reuben Allen, VIP Magazine

"The best tape on the subject I have ever seen."
  Hesh Goldstein, Health Talk Radio

"A compelling and often shocking look at the standard American diet. Asserts that following federal nutrition guidelines can kill you."
  American Library Association, Booklist, July 2003

"With the ever-growing popularity of programs like the Atkins diet, seeing what commercially produced animal fat and protein does inside of you is a true eye opener."
  Bobbie Willis, Eugene Weekly

"I'm in full agreement with your points and give my endorsement. I was pleased that you identified USDA price supports as a major cause of disease in the US."
  William Harris, M.D., author of numerous books and articles

The RAVE Diet
&
Lifestyle

Mike Anderson

Published by
www.RaveDiet.com

International Standard Book Number (ISBN)
0-9726590-4-8

First Edition: August 2004

Printed in the United States of America

For Harold, Virginia, Harvey and Reva, who have suffered greatly from diet-related diseases, simply because they did not know any better.

Acknowledgments

There were many individuals who contributed to the making of the enclosed film, *Eating*, and this book. I would like to thank the following individuals who volunteered their time and talented efforts to make both possible.

Reuben Allen
Zel Allen
Jesica Baker
Suzanne Cozens
John Hoffman
Matthew Israel
Valorie Kleiman
Jennifer Lee
Mark Lanier
Pedro Morales
Karen Porreca
Robyn Roth
Terry Wayne
Judy Weber

Disclaimer

If you have any medical condition, you should change your diet only under the care of a physician. Neither the author nor any nutritional advisors for this book make any representation or warranty of any kind whatsoever regarding the appropriateness of this program for any individual. The information presented herein is not medical advice and is not given as medical advice. If you need a physician to work with you, please visit our web site at www.RaveDiet.com.

Forward

I got interested in diet many years ago, quite by accident. I had always thought I was eating a healthy diet, as did my family. Then some tragic events began to unfold. First, my father died of cancer. Next, my stepfather died of heart disease. My mother broke one hip and we discovered she had severe osteoporosis. Shortly thereafter, she broke her other hip. A friend of mine, who ate a "healthy" diet, discovered she had breast cancer. Just one year later, she suffered a heart attack.

As I moved into my late forties and passed the age of 50, it seemed like all my friends, family and relatives were suffering from one chronic disease or another. At that time, I more or less shrugged my shoulders and accepted this as a normal part of aging. Unfortunately, as I was to learn, it *is* a normal part of aging – but doesn't have to be.

At about the time I turned 50, I happened to pick up a book that declared, in no uncertain terms, that the major diseases in this country could be prevented and often reversed through diet and lifestyle changes. The corollary of that statement was that all our major diseases were *caused* by diet and lifestyle.

I thought this was a pretty radical statement, but I was curious enough to read further and check out references that were provided with the book. One book led to another and another. In fact, I spent over two years, full-time, researching this subject and I've continued that research ever since.

Before my plunge into diet-related literature, I had always considered myself fairly well read yet I kept asking myself, "Why isn't this information more widely known?" The information linking diet and disease not only comes from people with the highest credentials, but they have irrefutable evidence to back up their claims. "Why doesn't mainstream health authorities tell us about this? Why am I not reading about this in the newspapers?" Unfortunately, after years of research, I have the answer to that question, and it's not a pretty picture.

This information is so powerful that I felt compelled to share it with others, so they can make their own decision based on all the facts. The first thing I did was to produce a film, entitled *Eating*, which is included with this book. It turned out to be a powerful piece and has received much praise and attention. In fact, it is a life-changer for most people who watch it. There were many people, however, who needed more information and I received numerous requests that I write a companion book that would provide more details about the subjects covered in *Eating*. The end result is this book, *The RAVE Diet & Lifestyle*.

In the course of my research, I discovered there were a set of basic rules doctors used when arresting and reversing diseases with diet. These rules form the acronym RAVE. Doctors who reverse diseases with diet have their individual preferences and will emphasize certain foods over others, but all their diets – particularly those used to reverse heart disease – fall within the RAVE concept.

Heart disease is the most documented and easily reversed disease in the books. But it's not just heart disease. Our common cancers, including breast and prostate cancers, have not only been reversed, but can be totally prevented by following the RAVE Diet. Adult onset diabetes is a snap. One doctor gets 90 percent of his patients off insulin within a month by prescribing simple changes in diet. There are literally hundreds of other diseases, ranging from arthritis and autoimmune diseases, to rheumatoid arthritis, spinal disc deterioration and varicose veins that can be arrested and reversed by following the RAVE Diet.

One of those diseases includes obesity, and it's precursor, being overweight. I emphasize weight loss in this book because being overweight has, unfortunately, become "normal" in America. In fact, we've literally lost sight of what normal weight should be. It's become so bad that most people would consider someone at their ideal weight to be skinny. Being overweight is a platform from which many diseases spring, so focusing on weight loss can bring a multitude of health benefits in its wake.

I know what some of you may be thinking. Reversing serious diseases with something as simple as diet may sound ludicrous. If you are thinking this, you're wearing the same shoes I found myself in years ago. I could not believe it either – which is exactly why I felt compelled to get this information out.

Some will consider my message radical, particularly if your dietary habits are within the mainstream. The irony is that I now consider "healthy" mainstream diets to be radical. After all, heart disease and our common cancers are the biggest killers in America today and they are the direct result of eating what most would consider a "healthy" mainstream diet. From the perspective of human history, the RAVE Diet is not a radical message at all. To advise that you follow a diet that reverses heart disease and prevents cancer is hardly radical. It's the most natural thing in the world. Hopefully, you won't consider my message radical either when you finish watching the film and reading this book.

The reason I decided to put this information in a film and book is to present an easy-to-digest summary that will motivate people to change their diets and realize the dramatic health benefits that can result from such a simple, although ultimately profound, change in their lives. All families in America are being torn apart by diseases caused by the foods they eat. These diseases can not only be prevented, but also reversed, by simply changing diet. Hopefully, you will try the RAVE Diet and reap the same health benefits many others have, which will turn your life into a happier existence, not only for yourself, but your family, your friends, and the world we all live in.

Mike Anderson

Introduction – The Tortoise and the Hare

"If everyone is thinking alike, then no one is thinking." – Benjamin Franklin

"Food is cheaper now by a long way, more abundantly available, more highly refined and more pressingly sold to us by very clever advertising companies and techniques. The remarkable thing is how anybody stays thin." – Dr. Andrew Prentice, London school of Hygiene and Tropical Medicine

Only in America do people order double cheeseburgers, large fries and a <u>diet</u> coke.

We live in a strange world when it comes to weight loss. Imagine if you will, someone who's overweight giving advice on how to lose weight. Sounds ridiculous, right? Yet, what we have today are a bunch of fat doctors telling people how to lose weight. In fact, the most successful Diet Doctors seem to be the most overweight.

In the year 2000, long before the controversy about his weight after his death, Dr. Atkins, exceeded federal guidelines for being overweight. One doctor, who saw him many times over the decades, estimated he was 40 to 60 pounds overweight.[1]

Barry Sears, Ph.D., author of the hugely popular Zone diet, was also overweight in the year 2000. Sears even states he's overweight in his own book![2] Yet despite this admission, millions of copies have been sold. Am I missing something? How can people who want to lose weight follow the advice of someone who proclaims, in his own book, that he's overweight?

Perhaps the answer lies in some of the statements Sears makes, such as "You can burn more fat watching TV than by exercising"[3] and "About one-third of Americans are ... suffering from protein malnutrition."[4] The last statement[5] is like saying Americans are suffering from *fat* malnutrition. As a matter of fact, the average American eats enough protein to fuel a champion weight lifter. (See *Notes – Protein.*) But burning fat while watching TV and getting too little protein are the things Americans love to hear because it justifies eating the very diet that has made us the heaviest nation on the planet.

Recently, we have Dr. Phil, who at 6 foot 4 inches and 240 pounds is at the upper-end of the overweight category and teetering toward obesity, according to Harvard's Body Mass Index (BMI). And yet, he claims he's at an appropriate weight for his age and height.[6] By whose standard? And stating his weight is "age appropriate" implies that humans are supposed to gain weight with age, an obvious invention by Dr. Phil and his publicity machine. Of course, Dr. Phil also states that just about everyone can benefit from the supplements he's selling, particularly Dr. Phil.

Then again, there are other Diet Doctors who are just plain terrified of their own diet. Look at Dr. Agatson, for example, author of the best-selling South Beach Diet. Here's a cardiologist who admits to taking an aspirin, fish oil capsules and a statin drug *every day* to prevent a heart attack.[7]

Imagine, if you will, a cardiologist who cannot even design a diet that will free him of drugs that treat a disease he's supposed to be an expert at preventing; a cardiologist who's incapable of designing a diet to lose weight *and* prevent heart disease. A cardiologist who says that eating a candy bar is healthier than eating a potato.[8] And while he tells his readers "Don't even think about limiting the amount of food you eat," his menu plans are, in fact, severely restricted in phase one. But, of course, if you start to gain weight in the later phases, you have to go back to his more restricted diet. In other words, he has a built-in yo-yo cycle within his own diet. And, there are no secrets. It's a simple calorie restriction diet, as are the Zone and Atkins diets. As Dr. Marion Nestle has stated, "What it comes down to is that this is a standard 1,200- to 1,400-calorie-a-day diet, so of course people are going to lose weight."[9]

Parenthetically, if you follow the South Beach Diet like it's author, it's going to cost you some $3,000 just in heart medicines, not to mention the aspirin and fish oil tablets. There are many doctors who design heart-healthy diets, they keep their total cholesterol well below 150 and they *do not* take aspirin, fish oil or any heart medicines, all of which can have serious side effects. Their healthy hearts are due solely to diet, not drugs. You can achieve far better results with diet than you can with drugs when it comes to heart disease, because no drug has ever *cured* heart disease whereas the RAVE Diet has.

There are a number of things these popular diets have in common. Among them, they promise *immediate* weight loss. We're talking over a pound a day. Now, if that doesn't get the attention of someone desperate to lose weight, nothing will. And these books always have some unique, clever scheme, which is apparently unknown to the rest of the scientific world.

Unfortunately, the real world doesn't work that way. Despite claims that you can eat all you want, if you calculate the menu plans of these popular diet books, they're *all calorie restriction diets*!

After you get past the smoke and mirrors, it boils down to calories in, calories out. After an exhaustive analysis of some 107 diets, the American Medical Association found that all these popular diets had nothing to do with restricting carbohydrates and had everything to do with restricting calories.[10] Recently, a study confirmed what everyone should have known in the first place: the thinnest people in the world eat the highest amount of *complex* carbohydrates and the fattest people eat the highest amount of animal protein.[11]

Of course, these popular diets *do* work in the short-term. But then again, *any* calorie-restriction diet will work in the short term. You could eat nothing but lard and if you had fewer calories coming in than going out, you'd lose weight. The problem boils down to sticking with these bizarre diets in the long haul.

It seems when the going gets tough, doctors write diet books in order to make money. Every few years, the public is subjected to yet another "miracle diet" with some "secret" that will cause effortless weight loss. You purchase the book, follow the restricted dietary regimen and – almost miraculously – you're losing weight. Voila!

You're so proud of yourself, you tell your friends. And they're so impressed with your weight loss, they go out and buy a copy of the book, the supplements and whatever other gimmicks they're offering, all in an effort to save their waists and hiplines from seemingly perpetual expansion. And soon they begin telling all their friends about the miracle diet that (finally!) took off those stubborn pounds. And so the circle of dieters grows as fast as the wallets of the Diet Doctors.

Now fast-forward just three years.

No one's talking any more.

In fact, 95 percent of the people who thought they had been saved from everlasting weight gain are off these strange diets.[12] Not only did the weight return, but they're heavier now than when they started the diet and they've increased their percentage of body fat to boot.

Some miracle.

They would have been better off had they never started the diet in the first place. In fact, research shows that dieters gain more weight in the long run than those who don't follow any weight-loss diet at all.

Now fast-forward just five years.

Virtually everyone who started the miracle diet is off the diet. In fact, it's a miracle they could put up with these eating regimens for so long.

The yo-yo diet cycle is nothing new. The first popular "high-protein" diet book was published in 1864 by an English casket maker named William Banting.

During this same era, P.T. Barnum told Americans "There's a sucker born every minute," and the casket-maker's diet did, among other things, prove P.T. Barnum right. The Atkins Diet, Zone Diet, South Beach and other "high-protein" diets all have their roots in, appropriately enough, a casket maker's diet because they all contribute to heart disease, kidney disease, osteoporosis and our common cancers, not to mention the constipation, gastrointestinal difficulties, bad breath and other symptoms that are the result of "high protein" diets. Little wonder the American Dietetic Association has described these diets as "a nightmare."[13] The phrase "high-protein" is simply a euphemism for "high-fat" to disguise the fact these diets are plowing an incredibly unhealthy diet down your throat, with the Atkins diet being up to 60 percent fat.

The fact Banting's diet was all the rage in the late 1800's and Atkins-like diets are now the rage over 100 years later shows 1) how little progress we have made in making people understand such quick fixes don't work; 2) the power of advertising; and 3) how such diets come into vogue when the price of meat is cheap. People think Atkins has come up with something new in the diet field. All he did was popularize a failed diet that was over 100 years old.

Now, take a deep breath because I want you to think about something. Don't you think it's strange – perhaps more than a little embarrassing – that none of these diet plans work in the long term, yet we keep shelling out money only to prove that history does repeat itself – at least when it comes to diet plans? Have Americans become so desperate that common sense has totally gone out the window?

Think about it. We're in such pathetic shape that the most educated population on the face of the earth now needs a doctor to tell them how to eat. In the meantime, billions of "uneducated" people throughout the world are in better health than most Americans, keep slim figures and many have never even seen a doctor. It's only a slight exaggeration to say that people were getting better advice about what they should eat when they were seeing witch doctors.

The goal of weight loss is to reduce the percentage of body fat and you cannot lose body fat quickly. Any program that promises quick weight loss is not losing fat, but simply water. Losing weight is not complicated at all. In fact, it's quite simple and the Diet Doctors have done more to confuse the issue than anyone else. (See *Notes - Problems With the Glycemic Index*, for one example.) But there's a method to their madness: the more complicated dieting seems, the more money there is to be made from all the confusion. And although these diets don't work – even for the Diet Doctors – the good doctors are more than willing to accept your money for the advice they're selling, advice they can't even follow themselves.

Why are things so insane? In a word: money. Selling food, supplements and diet plans is big money. Selling the easy way out is big money. Telling people they can lose more weight watching TV than exercising is big money.

Once all the fog has lifted, you'll see just how simple it is to lose weight. You won't have to buy expensive supplements or special foods, join programs, make yourself miserable or participate in any of the money-making schemes designed to impoverish you. Americans are now spending over $40 billion dollars a year in their desperate efforts to shed pounds and get thin. What diet ads should say is "I lost $350 in two week! Ask me how!" And the vast majority of these bucks flows into the pockets of people with an M.D. or Ph.D. behind their names – and most should be ashamed of themselves for not telling people the truth about weight loss, but instead perpetuating a self-enrichment scam.

Weight loss involves much more than counting calories and eating the right foods. Losing weight is not about the body – it's about the mind. It's about changing the way you think about food. It's also about changing the way you think about life. Your weight is the most visible reflection of who you are and losing weight involves nothing short of fundamentally changing your life. Change your life first, then the weight will come off naturally – and stay off.

We all know the story of the tortoise and the hare. Popular diets are about the hare that loses weight very fast, but ends up losing the race because the pounds return over time. The tortoise, on the other hand, is slow but steady and ends up winning the race by losing weight slowly and surely – and keeping it off for a lifetime.

The RAVE Diet & Lifestyle is a long-term health regimen designed not only to lose weight, but also to enhance your health, energy level and prevent (and even reverse) the common diseases that are ravaging Americans today. Most diet plans start off with a bang and have you lose 20 pounds in a few months. I would rather you change your eating habits first and gradually lose those 20 pounds over the course of a year so they will stay off the rest of your life and never come back.

If you're reading this book because you've tried the Diet Doctors and failed, take heart because the road to success is usually paved with failure. I believe that knowledge is power. Just as a good stockbroker uses his knowledge of stocks to make you a profit, knowledge of food will make you thin and give you all the benefits that come with such a lifestyle.

Being overweight affects all aspects of your life and it becomes cumulative. Your self-respect declines, you stay in more, you become more sedentary, you eat for comfort and end up putting on even more weight. If you're going to achieve success in weight loss, you are going to have to take an honest look at yourself, what you're eating and how you're living. The purpose of this book is to help you do just that.

We're in a state of denial about our weight and as our waistlines expand, we've lost sight of what normal weight is. We keep growing bigger and bigger and think it's normal because we've become used to it. Unfortunately, what's normal to Americans in the 21st century is fat. Have you ever looked at those old-time pictures of working class people living in the 1800s from a weight perspective? Then compared their bodies to ours now? The only fat people you will see in those old pictures are wealthy people, who could afford to eat much like Americans eat today. The average working class American back in those times was thin because they were doing two things correctly: eating the right foods and getting exercise.

Being overweight – and especially being obese – can lead to a host of diseases, among them heart disease. The only scientifically proven diets to reverse heart disease are RAVE Diets. In fact, the RAVE Diet is a friendlier version of other diets that are used to reverse heart disease. No other diet can show actual proof of heart disease reversal. None. And if you eat to prevent heart disease, you will also prevent the other major chronic diseases that are plaguing Western nations, including diabetes, our common cancers, as well as hundreds of other diet-related diseases.

In other words, you will get much, much more out of the RAVE Diet than just permanent weight loss. You'll get a lifetime of good health.

Diet, Disease & Weight Loss

Most people don't let their children smoke, yet they regularly take them to fast-food restaurants and that's just as risky, in terms of cancer, as if they had bought them a pack of Marlborough cigarettes. – B .A. Stoll

"There is only one major disease and that is malnutrition. All ailments and afflictions to which we may fall heir are directly traceable to this major disease." – D.W. Cavanaugh, M.D., Cornell University

There is an old Indian legend in which six blind men come across an elephant. Having no idea what an elephant was, they moved in close and started to feel it.

One touched it's leg and described the elephant as a pillar. Another touched its tail and declared an elephant was a rope. The third touched its ear and said the elephant was like a big fan. And so on. The blind men then began to argue about what an elephant was, based on their experiences – with each insisting he was correct. The problem, of course, was that none of the blind men could "see" the entire elephant, only parts of it.

Many of the problems Americans have with understanding the relationship of diet to disease is analogous to this story. Unfortunately, the inability to see the whole picture is greatly reinforced by so-called "scientific" studies because they only look at specific parts of the entire picture.

Take alcoholic beverages, for example. Recently, there have been waves of studies purporting that wine is good for the heart. This is because these studies are focusing only on a small part of the wine, the antioxidants, which originally come from grapes. What such studies cannot "see" is the alcohol in the wine. When you step back and look at the whole wine beverage, including alcohol, it not only harms the heart, but the brain, nervous system, liver and other organs – and generally devastates the entire body. Instead of saying that wine is good for the heart and ignoring what it does to the rest of the body, the "scientists" should have been saying this study confirms that the antioxidants found in grapes are good for the heart, without endorsing wine as a healthy beverage. Instead, what we have is a bunch of blind scientists stating that wine is a health drink because they are only "seeing" the effects of a specific ingredient on the heart, not what the whole wine package does to the rest of the body.

We have known that antioxidants are good for the heart for decades. And we have known that grapes are good for the body for centuries. What such "scientific" studies are doing is turning bad foods into good foods for the sole benefit of those who sell bad foods. (Don't get me wrong. If you want to get tipsy or even drunk, there's no better beverage than wine – just don't call it a health drink!)

Of course, the "scientific" approach fits very nicely into the marketing plans of food industries and, in fact, virtually all of these "scientific" studies are funded by food industries. These days, if a product has even a tiny bit of good in it, food industries will hire a team of "experts" from a prestigious university to do a study specifically designed to turn an unhealthy product into a "healthy" product. They will then put out press releases and unleash their marketing team to "milk" as much news coverage from the study as they can get. The public then reads the news report and thinks, "Ah ha! Wine is good for me, after all!" and they run to the nearest liquor store and start drinking like fish.

After a 60 Minutes show ran a story on the so-called French Paradox, which made the ridiculous claim that wine was responsible for the deceptively low rate of heart attacks in France, wine sales increased by a whopping 40 percent. What was lost in all the hoopla was the fact that the French Paradox is a mirage. The French have different methods of classifying deaths, which make it appear that deaths due to heart disease are lower in France than other Western nations. When statistical methods are standardized, however, it turns out the French die of heart disease at rates comparable to other Western nations. And regardless of how you view the statistics, heart disease is France's number one killer, just as it is in other Western nations who eat comparable diets.[1]

The dairy industry is famous for sponsoring "scientific" studies showing the benefits of consuming their products due to the calcium content. And because the dairy lobby has many politicians in their pockets, our official calcium requirements are now absurdly high. Surprisingly, no one has ever thought to ask why we need ever-higher amounts of calcium in our diet when there has never been a single recorded instance of calcium deficiency of a dietary origin in the history of the human race![2]

Despite this fact, the dairy industry – backed by the authority of the USDA – has scared the wits out of women who think the calcium in dairy products will somehow magically bind to their bones, make them strong and prevent osteoporosis. (See *Notes - Osteoporosis* for more on this subject.)

What the dairy industry does is simply hire a bunch of blind scientists and instructs them to focus on a single ingredient in order to turn an incredibly bad food (high levels of sodium, cholesterol, saturated fat and animal protein) into a good food. Recently, they funded a study which made the ridiculous claim that calcium was the key to losing weight![3]

We could go down the list of so-called scientific studies which purport to show the benefits of a single ingredient in a food (e.g., the "good fat" in vegetable oils, the "good fat" in fish, flavonoids in chocolate candy bars), while ignoring the package of bad ingredients these good ingredients come in. These studies, of course, are nothing but marketing tools employed by food industries working on a gullible public trying their best to find a healthy meal somewhere in America.

In the meantime, Americans get sicker from eating bad foods the scientific community has declared "healthy." Of course, the sicker they get from eating bad foods, the more it feeds into a bottom-feeder – the pharmaceutical industry. In an effort to counteract a bad diet, we end up taking medicines to treat symptoms of diseases that are the result of eating bad foods – primarily because a bunch of functionally blind scientists told us these bad foods were good for us to eat.

During the 1800s, there was a doctor who followed the medically approved bleeding and drugging procedures of the time, but eventually lost confidence in these procedures because he saw that the health of his patients was not improving. In fact, he found that his patients started to get much better when he prescribed fewer or no drugs. Following a hunch, he decided to eliminate the drugs altogether and give his patients placebos, or sugar pills, instead. At the same time he gave them advice about improving their diet.

The key to this approach was that he told his patients *the pill would not work unless they followed the diet he prescribed.* Well, his patients followed his dietary advice to the letter, thinking the pill would not work unless they followed the diet, and much to their surprise, the "pill" worked! The diseases in his patients quickly vanished and the good doctor's fame spread rapidly. He soon became known as the greatest healer of his time – for all the wrong reasons. No one talked about the diet he prescribed and all his patients could do was blather about his wonderful magic pills.[4]

It's been estimated that 70 to 85 percent of all hospital patients suffer from illnesses associated with diet-induced diseases.[5] This should not come as a surprise. Humans evolved primarily on a diet of whole, natural plant foods. Today, whole plant foods constitute *only seven percent of our diet!* 42 percent of our calories come from animal foods and a whopping 51 percent of our calories come from refined foods.[6]

Evolutionary Percent of Calories

Animal foods	5 percent [7]
Refined foods	0 percent
Whole plant foods	95 percent

Current Percent of Calories

Animal foods	42 percent
Refined foods	51 percent
Whole plant foods	7 percent

In other words, animal and refined foods – which contain neither fiber nor cancer-fighting or heart-healthy nutrients – make up a whopping 93 percent of the calories we consume today. It doesn't take much imagination to see how our diet is driving us into hospitals.

We began our evolution some five to six million years ago. During that period, humans ate 95 percent of their calories from whole plant foods. The precipitous fall in whole plant food consumption began only a century ago.

It should be obvious that disease would follow our switch from a plant-based to an animal- and refined-foods-based diet and this accounts for the explosion of the chronic, degenerative diseases and common cancers which are currently affecting every family in America today. Here is a brief summary of the differences between plant foods and animal and refined foods.

Plant Foods	Animal Foods	Refined Foods
Fiber	No Fiber	No Fiber
Cancer fighters	No cancer fighters	No cancer fighters
Anti-oxidants	Oxidants	Oxidants
Low fat	High fat	High fat
Low saturated fat	High saturated fat	High saturated fat
No cholesterol	High cholesterol	High trans fat
Low pesticides/toxins	High pesticides/toxins [8]	High sugar
No hormones	High hormones [9]	

The Magic Of Whole Plant Foods

The best, simplest and most cost-effective way Americans can vastly improve their health and prevent our major diseases is to radically increase their consumption of whole, natural plant foods. Unlike foods that may have a single "good" nutrient that comes in a package of bad nutrients, whole natural foods do not have such tradeoffs. Whole foods are good for the whole body. They are not just "heart healthy," they are healthy for the heart, the brain, the arteries and all the organs – the entire body.

How good are whole foods? We are just at the beginning of our understanding. Let me give you an illustration. In the 1970s, there was a study conducted in which animals were fed two percent of their diet from red dye, sodium cyclamate or an emulsifier. The animals that were fed just one additive showed no harmful effects at all. The animals that were fed two of the additives showed balding fur, diarrhea and retarded weight gain. But the animals that were fed all three additives were dead within two weeks.[10]

In a similar fashion, it was recently reported that Parkinson's disease has been linked to the exposure of not one, but a combination of pesticides, namely paraquat and organophosphate.[11]

What this illustrates is that toxins, when taken together, <u>amplify</u> their toxicity in a synergistic and logarithmic fashion.

In a similar – but beneficial – way, nutrients work together in the same way, e.g., calcium with magnesium, vitamin E with selenium, protein with B6 and so forth. There are also thousands of antioxidants that work together in a synergistic fashion that multiplies and enhances their health-enhancing effects. A tomato, for example, contains over 10,000 different phytochemicals. The possible combinations and permutations of nutrients once inside the body are simply mind-boggling. And, at this point, we have only a child-like understanding of how these nutrients work together in thousands of combinations.

There have been a number of studies that show when a single chemo-preventive nutrient is fed to animals it had no effect on the incidence of cancer. But when two or more nutrients were combined, the cancer growth was sharply cut.[12] What these studies examined was just a few nutrients, not the thousands and thousands of combinations that go on inside your body every day in the real world.

Remember when vitamin C was the rage? Everyone was taking vitamin C tablets like they were going out of style. Then it was discovered that vitamin C wasn't very well absorbed unless a couple of bioflavonoids were present (hesperidin and rutin). So the manufacturers re-tooled and added these bioflavonoids to the pills and everything was supposed to be Ok again. Except it was later discovered that despite the presence of these bioflavonoids, the body couldn't absorb vitamin C very well unless calcium was present as well. So the pills were re-formulated with bioflavonoids *and* calcium. So, while the public remained confused – but nonetheless kept swallowing their vitamin C tablets – they continued to overlook a source of vitamin C that had *all* the elements together and allowed optimal absorption of the vitamin: citrus fruits, such as oranges and grapefruits – and other plant foods bearing vitamin C! While "blind" scientists were baffled trying to come up with one or two or three key ingredients that would allow the body to effectively absorb vitamin C in pill form, people forgot that nature had already come up with a solution to this problem in the form of whole plant foods, which contain thousands of nutrient profiles scientists are still in the dark about. [13]

The point is this: when scientists try to isolate a single nutrient or even a handful of nutrients, this is not only overly simplistic, but doomed to misleading results and failure. In fact, this kind of analysis is like the six blind men trying to understand the nature of an elephant. While science will continue to identify key nutrients in foods, it is a certainty that science will never understand how the millions of nutrients interact with each other. The mathematical possibilities are simply too immense.

When I say there is "magic" in whole foods, I'm talking about what we do not understand about whole foods – and that is far more than we do know.

What we *do* know, however, is that they are good for us – in fact, far and away much better for us than anything ever created by science. What we do know is that we should eat a wide variety of foods because each food has it's own nutrient profile and this profile will interact with other foods containing their own profile and together, they will multiply – in logarithmic fashion – each other's protective benefits.

When a diet is practically devoid of whole plant foods, only trouble can result. In such a situation, Americans are turning to supplements in order to bolster an inadequate diet – but supplements cannot possibly replace the potency of whole foods containing a multitude of nutrient profiles we haven't even a clue about. In every study ever conducted, which compared supplements with whole plant foods, supplements could not hold a candle to the power and potency of whole foods. A recent study showed that taking supplements containing lycopene from tomatoes, did *nothing* to lower the risk of prostate cancer, whereas whole tomatoes, containing a complex profile of nutrients, did lower the risk.[14] How it lowered the risk, scientists haven't a clue because nature is far too complex to be understood with our crude tools. And, once again, this illustrates the failure of trying to isolate a single nutrient as a cure to a disease and sell it to the public as "magic bullet."

The bottom line is that no matter how hard they try, scientists cannot capture the "magical" nutrient profiles of whole foods in a pill and that magic can only be passed into your body by eating them.

A Diet of Disease

No matter how strange something is, if you give it enough time, it becomes normal. Americans have now accepted heart disease, cancer and other degenerative diseases as a normal part of the American way of life.

One could not design a diet more efficient at clogging arteries than the American diet. Between animal foods and refined foods, our arteries don't have a chance. What amazes me is that everyone doesn't die of heart disease.

The war on cancer does not take place in hospitals or laboratories. It takes place inside you and battles are being won or lost every day, depending on your diet.

"Each patient carries his own doctor inside him. We are at our best when we give the doctor who resides within a chance to go to work." Albert Schweitzer, Nobel Prize Winner

The Laws of Heart Disease

Before 1900, heart disease was virtually unknown and so rare it wasn't even included in standard American textbooks.[15] Today, heart disease (cardiovascular disease) is the scourge of the nation. Practically everyone has heart disease, children are now taking heart medicines, and it's the biggest killer in the nation – killing half the population – yet it's the single most preventable major disease in the books. Heart disease has become so prevalent that drug makers are now working to make cholesterol lowering drugs non-prescription so taking them will be as easy as taking an aspirin. They've already made it that way in Britain.

While everyone is concentrating on selling drugs that *treat* heart disease, no one is talking about *curing* the disease. And almost everyone ignores the fact that a disease that kills half the population and maims even more is solely the result of a bad diet.

Heart disease is a totally benign disease and can be easily cured with a change to the RAVE Diet. Heart disease isn't just preventable – it's *reversible*, no matter what your age. As the film *Eating* so clearly demonstrates, heart disease immediately responds to changes in diet, as the body begins to heal itself from the onslaught of bad foods.

According to William Castelli, director of the famous Framingham Heart Study, entire populations have reversed heart disease by a change in diet. Before World War II, about three-quarters of the people in Belgium suffered from heart disease. During the German occupation, however, soldiers trucked every scrap of meat and all the livestock out of Belgium to Germany. Within two years, heart disease had disappeared from the Belgium population, *because they had no meat to eat.* Heart disease also disappeared in every other country where Germany removed livestock, including Holland, Poland, Norway and in northern France. Unfortunately, as farm animals returned to these countries after the war, so too did heart disease.[16]

Incredulous as it may seem, advocates of high-fat diets will argue that meat-based diets can prevent and even reverse heart disease. The problem such an argument is that there has never been a single human being who has ever arrested or reversed heart disease on meat-based diets.

Reversing heart disease is actually a very simple and inexpensive thing to do and there are literally millions of Americans dying to have their heart disease reversed on meat-based diets. Since there are so many people on "high-fat" diets, such as the Atkins diet, one would think that out of those millions, just one person would have reversed his or her heart disease – even by accident.

You have to ask yourself, "Why haven't the Atkins people recruited someone with severe heart disease and reversed it?" If they had just a single individual who reversed heart disease on their diet, he or she would become the poster boy for that diet overnight – and their publicity machine would have a field day. Why hasn't this been done? It would only take six months and they would have publicity to last them years. Then everyone could eat steak and eggs for breakfast.

I say to these people, stop the arguments and stop citing so-called "scientific" studies. Show me a real human being who has reversed heart disease on anything other than a RAVE Diet.

Long silence.

In fact, no one has ever arrested or reversed heart disease on anything but a RAVE Diet.

Of course, trans-fats or hydrogenated oils can also be a cause of heart disease. Those who promote high-fat diets have seized on this fact and cite trans-fats as the main cause of heart disease. This argument not only ignores clinical studies and over 50 years of solid medical research, but common sense. When cows are fed meat, for example, they develop heart disease – just like we do – and no cow that I know of has ever eaten an Oreo cookie. Similarly, autopsies of prehistoric humans who ate meat-heavy diets in certain areas of the world have shown heart disease in 25 year olds. And to my knowledge, they never had Krispe Kreme donuts for breakfast while sitting around the campfire. There are also cases where people have actually reversed heart disease following a RAVE Diet, but then returned to eating meat – and their heart disease returned as well. When an animal-based diet is introduced to populations who never had heart disease in their history, heart disease becomes their number one killer. And when meat is taken away from populations, such as those cited above during World War II, heart disease is reversed.

To blame this disease on trans-fats, while saying it's Ok to eat high levels of saturated fat and cholesterol, high-fat advocates are providing people with very dangerous advice. It simply boils down to yet a diversionary tactic to keep people on a meat-based diet and keep the revenues of high-fat diet programs, fat.

Another, related, argument of the high-fat set is that during the last 20 years, Americans are eating *less* fat, yet getting fatter, so lowering dietary fat doesn't result in weight loss. The conclusion: it isn't the fat that's making us fat, but the carbs, so follow a low-carb diet. As appealing as this argument may seem, it is completely false. In fact, Americans are now eating more fat than ever. The basic problem is that they are also eating more *calories* than ever. As a result, the *percentage of fat* from total calories has declined, but the total fat in our diet has actually *increased*.[17]

The arguments of the high-fat priesthood are not only lame and deceptive, but also there are big differences in honesty between high-fat and low-fat advocates, as illustrated in how the deaths of Dr. Nathan Pritikin and Dr. Robert Atkins were handled. Pritikin, who followed a RAVE Diet when he reversed his own heart disease, stipulated in his will that he should be autopsied and the results published, regardless of the outcome. Following his will's directives, his body was autopsied and it was found he had the heart and arteries of a young man, which were completely clear of any signs of heart disease, or atherosclerosis. He had, indeed, totally reversed his heart disease with diet and the results of his autopsy were published in the New England Journal of Medicine.[18]

In stark contrast, everything possible was done to conceal the health of Dr. Atkins before and after his death, despite claims by the Atkins people his diet was "heart healthy" and despite decades of solid medical research showing such a diet to be stupendously heart un-healthy. In fact, a recent study has shown that the Atkins diet reduces blood flow to the heart by 40 percent after just one year.[19]

High amounts of any kind of fat, be it vegetable fats or animal fats, decreases the amount of oxygen delivery to the body. After a high-fat meal, doctors can actually see blood sludging in the whites of patients' eyes, due to the high concentration of fat.[20] A blood sample taken from a man a few hours after eating a cheeseburger and shake revealed that *half* of the blood sample consisted of fat.[21] American blood is so thick with fat that doctors are now scrambling to put millions of patients on aspirin therapy in an effort just to thin their blood.

Some people try to justify a 30 percent fat diet by pleading we *need* lots of fat in our diet. But, in fact, the amount of fat you *need* is tiny – just 3 to 4 percent of total calories from fat.[22] In other words, a 30 percent fat diet (what mainstream medicine calls a low-fat diet) is giving you 10 times the amount of fat that you actually need – and most Americans eat a 40 percent plus fat diet. In fact, there has never been a recorded case of fat deficiency of a dietary origin in the history of mankind. Even prisoners of war do not suffer from too little fat in their diets! That Americans should worry about getting enough fat in their diet is a sad commentary on how we've been hoodwinked by high-fat food industries and the U.S. government that supports them.

With respect to heart disease, there are two "laws" that are, to date, irrefutable.

1) Heart disease can only be reversed on a true low-fat diet (10% of total calories).
2) Heart attacks do not occur with people having total cholesterol levels under 150.

The RAVE Diet will show you how to achieve a 10 percent fat level with delicious foods so you can reverse heart disease – and if you eat to prevent or reverse heart disease, you'll be preventing all the other degenerative diseases that are making Americans sick and causing them to die prematurely. That is the ticket the RAVE Diet has for you on the health train.

On a heart disease prevention diet – as opposed to a reversal diet – the maximum fat level is 20 percent of total calories. Since most adult Americans already have heart disease, you should try to reverse it as much as possible by getting your fat level down to 10 percent and strictly following the RAVE Diet.

While medical authorities are fiddling with LDL and HDL levels and ratios, your goal should not be a ratio, but a total cholesterol level below 150. If you do that, you'll never have to worry about having a heart attack again. And you simply cannot get your cholesterol level below 150 unless you adopt a RAVE Diet.[23]

People like to scoff at the idea that diet is so powerful, preferring to take expensive medicines instead. They will point to studies that show a change in fat levels does not have an effect on diseases. The problem with these studies is that they make small dietary changes. For example, they may reduce a 40 percent fat diet to a 30 percent fat diet and say the dietary fat level does not make a difference. That's like switching from regular cigarettes to light cigarettes and that won't prevent anything.

What you have to do is make *big* change before you'll be able to reverse and prevent our diet-related diseases. What medical authorities have to do is reduce dietary fat from 40 percent to 10 percent before they will see a difference – and it will be a *huge* difference. It's also been shown that a diet of 10 percent fat is far more effective than heart disease medicines in lowering LDL cholesterol levels – and it doesn't carry any side effects.[24]

Following mainstream advice to eat more fruits and vegetables simply will not get the job done. It's a bit like adding a couple of raisins to a chocolate bar and declaring that chocolate bar to be healthy. In order to realize the healing effects of plant foods, you have to make a complete switch and do it in an uncompromising fashion. The RAVE Diet & Lifestyle shows you how to do just that.

The Laws of Cancer

We have spent over 30 years and countless billions of tax dollars trying to find a cure for cancer, yet Nature has been solving the dilemma from the beginning. The cure for cancer is right inside all of us and it's called your immune system.

Your immune system is your internal body armor. Picture your immune system as being like the front defensive line of a football team. The mission of this defensive line (your white blood cells) is to stop the other team (cancer cells) from getting through and scoring points. If the defensive line, your immune system, is weak or injured the other team gets through causing damage and scoring points. How do you build up your defensive team? The *only* way is through diet.

For years Japan had the highest per capita consumption of cigarettes, yet the lowest rates of lung cancer in the world, because Japanese smokers had strong immune systems due to their low-fat, plant-based diet.[25] Of course, now that the Japanese diet is becoming Westernized, they are compromising their immune systems and cancer is on the rise. Cancer is scoring points.

With respect to cancer, there are four "laws" that are irrefutable.

1) Your immune system is the only cure for cancer.
2) A weakened immune system is the biggest cause of cancer.[26]
3) The higher the dietary fat, the more the immune system is weakened.
4) The only foods that contain immune-strengthening and cancer-fighting nutrients are plant foods.

Your eating habits can either strengthen or weaken your immune system. If you are not eating enough plant foods, you will be deficient in antioxidants that feed an army of immune system cells that defend the body against cancer. Your immune system has been trained over millions of years to recognize and selectively kill cancer cells and is a million times smarter at killing them than sledge-hammer-like conventional treatments, such as chemotherapy or radiation, which indiscriminately kill cancer cells while also killing the only cure for cancer – your immune system cells.

In every population throughout the world eating an animal-based diet, cancer is the second leading killer, after heart disease. Among other things, due to the high-fat content, animal-based diets suppress the immune system by killing off immune system cells.

Imagine what an oil spill in the ocean does to the marine life it encounters. Most are killed, some are maimed. Birds covered with oil cannot fly. This is what happens when high amounts of fat hit your blood stream. Immune system cells die off, those that survive cannot "swim" in your blood stream, they become blinded and as a result cannot recognize and kill cancer cells. Now imagine eating three high-fat meals a day. Americans have created a constant oil slick in their blood streams that is caused by breakfast, lunch and dinner.

The higher your intake of fat, the more your immune system is weakened, which leaves you open to infections and diseases. We have an epidemic of immune system impairment and this accounts for many of the diseases we are suffering from, especially cancers. In fact, we've become so used to a suppressed immune system that we now think it's normal. We also think that dying of cancer is a normal part of the human condition. It is not.

Any kind of fat will compromise the immune system, even so-called "good fats" containing Omega-3 fatty acids. In addition to being an oil slick, it's been found that Omega-3's that come in concentrated forms, such as fish and vegetable oils, are composed of highly unstable molecules which decompose and unleash dangerous cancer-causing agents (free radicals), and cause damage to cells that can lead to cancer. Such fats also suppress natural killer cells and the production of immune substances, which are important not only for cancer protection, but protection against viruses, bacteria and parasites.[27]

High concentrations of Omega-3's also promote the spread of cancer cells. This is thought to be due to the production of free radicals, suppression of the immune system and changes that are caused in small hormones that promote tumor growth.[28]

Unlike concentrated fats in fish and vegetable oils, the Omega-3s found in natural, whole foods are <u>stable</u> and do not produce free radicals. Thus, if you want Omega-3s, get them from whole plant foods, not vegetable or fish oils.

Eating concentrated sources of "good fat" really boils down to getting too much of a good thing. Just as a modest amount of sunlight can actually prevent cancer,[29] too much sunlight can cause cancer. Just as we need a little saturated fat in our diet, too much can clog up our plumbing. When vegetable oils are made, thousands of nutrients, as well as the fiber, are removed and all that's left is 100 percent fat, or empty calories. This is an extremely concentrated form of fat and too much of a good thing, which will cause bad things to happen, like an oil slick in your blood. (For more on vegetable oils, see *The RAVE Diet & Lifestyle: No Vegetable Oils*.)

The high-fat content of animal-based foods significantly suppress the immune system, so it's little wonder that heart disease and cancer are America's two biggest killers. Lowering the fat in your diet is not only the best thing for your heart, but it's also the single best way to strengthen your immune system. Instead of a steady stream of fat, the RAVE Diet will lower your fat intake and give you a steady stream of cancer-fighting nutrients that will feed your immune system and keep it strong.

Hormonal Cancers: Breast and Prostate

Excessive dietary fat not only suppresses the immune system, but it also stimulates the production of abnormally high sex hormones, which greatly increases the risk of developing hormone-related cancers, such as breast and prostate cancer. Any time you take a bite into a hamburger, hot dog, chicken leg or any other high-fat meal, you're not only weakening your immune system, but you're getting a hormone adjustment as well.

A young girl raised on a typical high-fat Western diet has much higher estrogen levels and begins her menstrual cycle at a much younger age than one eating a RAVE Diet. In just 140 years, the average age of puberty in US girls has dropped from 17 to 12 – and menopause starts four years later. In other words, women on high-fat diets have added nine years of menstrual cycles to their lives. How do we know diet causes this? Because women throughout the world, including those in the US, raised on RAVE Diets reach puberty at the normal age of 16 or 17.

When woman experience tenderness in their breasts each month, it's because estrogen is stimulating breast cells to divide and that's when a mutation, or cancer cell, is most likely to appear. If you have more menstrual cycles and more stimulation from higher levels of estrogen, there's a much greater chance you'll not only develop breast cancer, but other hormone-related cancers.

Milk is full of *bovine estrogen* from cows, so it's little wonder that dairy products have been strongly linked to breast and prostate cancer. Body fat also stimulates the production of estrogen, so the more body fat you have, the higher your estrogen levels will be. This is the reason overweight women have higher cancer risks.

Pesticides and other chemical toxins also raise estrogen levels because these chemicals mimic sex hormones once they are inside the body. Since 95 percent of the pesticides Americans consume are in meat and dairy products – not plant foods – you're getting a double-boost to your hormone level when you eat animal foods.[30]

Breast cancer thrives in an estrogen-rich environment and estrogen levels for American women are up to twice as high as women around the world eating low-fat, plant-based diets. The problems American women experience with menopause is due to the *dramatic drop in estrogen levels*. If you get rid of this sharp drop, you get rid of the problems. By changing to the RAVE Diet before you reach menopause, the drop in estrogen levels will be smooth and you will eliminate the problems. The Japanese, for example, don't even have a word for "hot flash" simply because Japanese women eating traditional, plant-based diets do not experience hot flashes – or other problems associated with menopause.

Eating a high-fiber diet is important because fiber removes excessive sex hormones from the body and lowers estrogen levels, greatly reducing your risk of cancer. If these hormones are not carried out by fiber, they are recycled back into the blood, which drives up hormone levels even further.

Men who eat high-fat diets also reach puberty earlier and have abnormally high levels of male sex hormones. Many studies have linked high testosterone levels to prostate cancer, but the most revealing fact is that prostate cancer simply does not occur in eunuchs, men castrated at an early age. Nor does it occur with men throughout the world who are eating low-fat diets because they have normal levels of testosterone. Incidentally, you'll never see a bald eunuch because hair loss is also related to testosterone levels. Although a tendency toward hair loss is genetic, you can significantly delay its onset and slow or arrest its spread by getting your testosterone level back to normal with a change to the RAVE Diet. In some cases, a change in diet has actually resulted in the re-growth of hair.

Prostate reduction is also linked to a low-fat, plant-based diet and prostate cancer is rare in populations that eat such a diet. Most prostate cancers have decades of slow growth before a tumor develops. This is the time when a change in diet can be most effective in strengthening your immune system and killing those cancer cells. And getting your testosterone level back to normal will not affect your manliness — only your chances of getting cancer – and perhaps going bald before your time.

Eating any farm animal today adds to your hormone overdose because large corporate farms use hormones to increase animal growth and output – and these hormones are passed on to us when we eat these animals or their products. Since 1995, Europe has banned the use of hormones on farm animals because of the links to human cancers. Europe has also banned American beef from its shores because of our continued use of hormones on livestock.

The modern cow produces 25 times more milk than a cow did just 50 years ago. A good part of that increased production is due to drugs, antibiotics – and artificial hormones. In fact, milk turns out to be a hormonal delivery system as it contains over 50 hormones. Numerous studies have shown links between the hormones in dairy products and the development of hormone-related cancers. In populations eating low-fat RAVE diets, breast, colon, prostate and other cancers are rare or non-existent.

The link between fat and cancer has been observed by the Surgeon General, who said that in comparing populations, "…death rates for cancers of the breast, colon, and prostate are directly proportional to estimated dietary fat intakes."[31]

There are many "experts" who dispute the link between fat and cancer, citing studies in which dietary fat was cut from 40 percent to 30 percent and this had no effect on the incidence of breast cancer. Of course it didn't! A 30 percent fat diet *causes* breast cancer. You will not prevent the incidence of breast – or our other common cancers – until you cut dietary fat intake down to ten percent of total calories – the same dietary fat level that reverses heart disease.

Conventional Cancer Treatments

The medical profession looks quizzically on "spontaneous" cancer remissions, cancers that have disappeared for no apparent reason. But upon close inspection, it's been found that almost 90 percent of these "spontaneous" remissions occurred after people made big changes to their diets, [32] that strengthened their immune systems.

Conventional treatments do not cure cancer. In fact, they severely damage your only hope of curing the cancer – the immune system. Following conventional treatments, cancer remains in the body. When the doctors say they got all of it, they are not telling you the whole story because there can be over a *million* cancer cells in your body they cannot detect, just waiting for an opportunity to regroup and multiply in order to resume their lethal march. The fact they did not get it all is the biggest reason for such a high rate of cancer recurrence. Only the immune system is smart enough to selectively recognize cancer cells and completely cure cancer, without impairing the immune system. After conventional treatments, however, the immune system is so damaged, it shouldn't be surprising that cancers re-emerge so frequently.

Despite what you've read in the news, the success rate for breast cancer, for example, *has not changed over the last 80 years*. Women with breast cancer do not live longer, after they have been diagnosed, than they did in the 1920s – and over 90 percent of the women diagnosed with breast cancer will die of breast cancer. Despite ever-aggressive treatments and early detection, the expected increase in life expectancy with conventional treatments is close to zero. In fact, when conventional treatments are used, only six percent of women have their lives extended – and the longest those women had their lives extended was a mere 14 months – compared to those who did not receive treatment. [33]

The cancer success rates you hear about in the news are due primarily to statistical manipulation as a result of increases in "five-year survival" rates. This increase, however, is due solely to early detection – which simply means that the clock measuring "five year survival" starts running sooner, *not that patients live any longer*. In other words, the improvement in survival rates is merely a statistical deception. The patient "lives longer" within the five-year clock, simply because the clock starts sooner due to early detection.

The cancer industry becomes giddy as the media promotes early detection because the earlier the detection, the greater the five-year survival rates will be, which makes the cancer industry look as if it is actually helping people. But, in fact, all the cancer industry has done is made people's lives miserable by putting them through surgery, chemotherapy, radiation and other invasive treatments – and created a living hell for patients through nausea, vomiting, infections and damage to their internal organs – while pocketing billions of dollars. And after all this "treatment," they have not extended the lives of their patients one iota. In those few "successful" cases, most cancer patients die of a later recurrence of cancer or a disease brought on by the chemotherapy or radiation treatments themselves. In fact, if you add in all the people who have died of another disease because of the side effects of chemotherapy and radiation (e.g., died of pneumonia due to a weakened immune system), conventional treatments have done far more harm than good.

In plain English, cancer victims would have lived the same number of years without conventional treatments. The next time you hear about improvements in cancer treatments, ask for improvements in life expectancy rates, not five-year survival rates. You could survive conventional treatments for five years and die in the sixth year and the cancer industry would consider their treatments a success – and record it as such. Don't fall for this statistical lie.

The origins of chemotherapy are found in chemical warfare agents, such as mustard gas, and chemotherapy is just as toxic to the patient as it is to the enemy soldier it was intended for. All the cancer industry did was turn chemo-warfare into chemo-therapy and coin the term "war on cancer."

Regardless of the name (Tamoxifen, etc.), all chemotherapeutic treatments do much more harm than good for the body and they have not proven to be successful in either curing cancer or extending lives. In fact, an article in the *Scientific American* showed that chemotherapy was able to "save" the lives of, at most, just three percent of cancer patients.[34]

Much the same can be said for radiation treatments, which are also extremely toxic to the body. Does it not seem strange to you that we are trying to cure a cancer with a treatment that has proven to cause cancer?

Instead of allowing the body to take care of cancer cells naturally by strengthening the immune system, we assault the body with invasive and destructive agents of war. Our current arsenal of cancer treatments is the modern equivalent of bloodletting because in these cases, the "cure" is all too often worse than the disease. The truly remarkable thing is how the body can survive these treatments at all. Even the medical establishment has acknowledged the failure of cancer treatments. In the February 9, 1994 issue of the *Journal of the American Medical Association*, the "War on Cancer" was declared a failure.

What would I do if I had cancer? I would investigate every natural cure for cancer that strengthens the immune system and cleanses the body of toxins. I would never subject myself to conventional treatments that destroy the only hope of curing cancer – the immune system. To be sure, there are people running cancer-cure scams, but there are also legitimate institutions, which take patients who have been given death warrants by conventional medicine – and these institutions have brought patients back to robust health and long lives.

Why doesn't mainstream medicine embrace these treatments, despite their successes? Simply because natural treatments are not attractive candidates for investment, due to the fact they are *not patentable* and therefore *not profitable*. Sadly, when natural treatments score solid cancer successes and have a strong track record, they are dismissed as dubious quackery. When an extremely toxic drug can show only marginal rates of success within just a few years, however, it will easily enter the realm of "acceptable treatments" within the cancer industry.

If you are skeptical that profitability is the prime decision-making criteria for mainstream cancer treatments, please pick up a copy of *Reclaiming Our Health* by John Robbins and read Part Four, which reviews the origins and miserable state of conventional approaches to cancer treatments.

Also, check our web site for a current list of institutions that treat cancers naturally. (www.RAVEDiet.com) The web site also contains many personal stories of people completely curing life-threatening cancers, as well as other diseases, by adopting a RAVE-like diet and lifestyle.

Take the case of Anthony Sattilaro, M.D., who contracted prostate cancer, which rapidly spread throughout his body. He was just 46 years old when his oncologist told him the cancer had gone too far, there was nothing he could do, and Dr. Sattilaro should get his affairs in order and prepare to die.

A few days afterwards this pronouncement, Dr. Sattilaro happened across two young men looking for a ride and he decided to give them one. In their discussion, Dr. Sattilaro mentioned the death sentence he was facing. The two men happened to be attending a macrobiotic cooking school and told him that if he changed his diet, the cancer would go away.

Needless to say, you can imagine how an M.D. would feel about getting cancer advice from two young kids! The boys asked for his address and later sent him more information. The information could not satisfy his scientific standards, but he was driven by a combination of curiosity and desperation. After all, conventional medicine had given up on him. What did he have to lose?

He went to a meeting and decided then that he would adopt the diet. The tastes were different than what he had been used to, but he decided to stick with the diet because of one significant thing, which started happening very soon after he switched his eating habits: *the terrible pain he was suffering started to diminish!* He found he needed less pain medication and *in just three weeks* his cancer pain was completely gone. His energy returned and he was able to work again. He continued on what was essentially an Asian peasant's diet with large amounts of brown rice and vegetables, while strictly avoiding all dairy, meat and refined foods.

A year later, he went to his doctor and asked to be re-tested for cancer. When the results came back, his doctors were shocked. The cancer was gone. It was no longer in his bones, his spine, his skull nor anywhere else in his body.

For the next ten years, Dr. Sattilaro led a life that was cancer free. He got so involved in diet that he wrote a book about his experience, entitled *Recalled by Life*. Then something unfortunate happened. After ten years of a cancer-free existence, he decided to re-introduce fish and chicken into his diet. Shortly thereafter, the cancer returned, along with the pain. Despite ten years of being declared free of cancer, after his change in diet, his medical mind was still not totally convinced the diet had made the difference. As a result, he continued eating chicken and fish, was forced to resume taking his narcotic painkillers – and soon the cancer killed him.

A woman contracted breast cancer and cured it by using natural treatments and adopting a plant-based diet.[35] Years after her cancer was gone – thinking she was somehow now immune from cancer – she decided to return to her previous diet – of chicken and fish. Just like Dr. Sattilaro, soon after she changed back to her old diet, she contracted breast cancer for the second time. Unlike Dr. Sattilaro, however, she switched back to a RAVE-like diet and underwent natural treatments for a second time. Fortunately, her breast cancer vanished once again. She had learned her lesson about the power of diet for the last time.

These are just two stories, but there are thousands more, which demonstrate just how *powerful* a change in diet and lifestyle can be.

Within the next few years, cancer is expected to eclipse heart disease as the number one cause of death in America. It is already the number one fear, and rightly so because we have no effective treatment for cancer and no medical cure.

The average American has six bouts with serious cancers during their lifetimes. Those with healthy immune systems won't even know about the battle their bodies are waging with cancer. Those with weakened immune systems will find out about their battle in the hospital.

Each and every immune cell is made from the food you eat. A deficient diet means a deficient immune system. Nurture your immune system with the RAVE Diet & Lifestyle and it will protect you not only against our common cancers, but our other major diseases as well.

Other Diet-Related Diseases

There are a host of other diseases that can be cured with simple changes in diet. One lady recently adopted the RAVE Diet and her arthritis was completely gone after just three months. And so were the drugs she had been taking for decades. Did her doctor ever mention a change in diet to her? Of course not. He was totally baffled. He wasn't even aware diet could do this – until *she* told him.

The problem with modern medicine is that our authorities are totally unaware of the power of diet. As mentioned previously, studies will change the fat content of diets from 40 percent to 30 percent with no effect. But small changes like this will not cure anything. And based on such worthless studies, medical practitioners will tell you diet plays no role in diseases.

Unfortunately, these studies have not gone far enough and the medical establishment simply doesn't get it. Woman eating RAVE Diets do not get breast cancer. Men eating RAVE diets do not get prostate cancer. Nor do they get any of the other common eating-related cancers or other diseases, such as heart disease. They don't become overweight, and they don't get diabetes, arthritis or hundreds of other diseases now plaguing Americans.

Adult onset diabetes is ravaging the nation and even children are now being diagnosed with *adult* diabetes. Dr. Joel Fuhrman reports that over 90 percent of his patients who were on insulin at the time of their first visit, were taken *completely off their medications within the first month*! [36] In fact, he has called insulin the worst thing to ever happen to diabetics because it keeps them on an eating habit that caused the disease in the first place.

The vast majority of adult-onset diabetes cases can be completely reversed with diet – and most within a matter of months. Even the few who cannot get off their medications can benefit from the RAVE Diet because their medications will be drastically reduced. Even Type I diabetics can have their medications reduced by a third following the RAVE Diet. [37]

Check our web site (www.RAVEDiet.com) because it has many personal stories of people curing life-threatening diseases by adopting a RAVE Diet & Lifestyle. Diseases ranging from rheumatoid arthritis to lupus to cancers have all been reversed following this diet.

Due to the long time span involved in degenerative diseases, researchers are still trying to unravel the causes, but diet is at the heart of all of them. Take a simple condition such as acne, which affects up to 95 percent of all American teenagers. Currently, the medical profession confidently states that diet plays no role in acne. However, there are many studies of teenagers *in other countries* who eat native diets of whole plant foods where acne is simply unknown. *Not a single teenager gets acne.* [38] Western medicine needs to cast its net wider and look at people eating non-Western diets before they conclude that diet plays no role in diseases.

Weight Loss Using Old-Fashioned Foods

The fundamental trick to successful weight loss is to figure out a way to eat fewer calories, while feeling full and satisfied.

The problem with modern diets is that we consume far too many calories before we feel full. We then try to reduce calories by reducing portion sizes, which makes us feel deprived, if not downright depraved. This is precisely why modern diets fail in the long run. Yes, you can lose weight by reducing portion sizes, but you don't feel quite human doing it day-in and day-out, year after year. There is something intrinsically wrong with this approach and the reason modern diets are such failures. Among many other things, it sets up the yo-yo cycle of dietary restriction, then failure and binge eating, so you end up gaining more weight than if you had never started dieting in the first place.

The RAVE Diet approaches diet in a different manner. In the first place, the root of the word "diet" means lifestyle and since your body is the most obvious and visible feature of your life, if you want to change your body, you're going to have to change your life – and change it for good. By following all aspects of the RAVE Diet, your life will be transformed.

The RAVE Diet is also linear in that most people will start out eating what I call "transition" or substitution foods (see *Substitution Guide*) until they fully adopt the RAVE Diet. This allows a smooth transition into the full-blown RAVE Diet, and hopefully avoids the yo-yo syndrome. This is not a crash diet to lose lots of weight in three weeks (although it can be, depending on you), but a gradual approach to changing your eating and living habits so you can not only live with the foods you eat, but live with yourself. The rate of weight loss really depends on how much you have to lose. If you are interested in losing weight fast, see *Accelerating Weight Loss*.

Remember the hare and tortoise story in the beginning? The tortoise always wins when it comes to losing weight. The RAVE Diet will accommodate lapses in eating because it requires that you change your *attitude* about eating and that's what the film *Eating* is intended to do. Once your attitude has changed, you may fall off the horse occasionally, but you'll have the knowledge and confidence to know you'll get back on it and ride again.

The RAVE Diet is really a throwback to the old-fashioned diets our ancestors ate. Before the early 1800's, modern refined foods were not readily available (read *refined* carbohydrates), yet today, refined foods occupy over 50 percent of our calories. Eating animal foods, including dairy products, was a very occasional event due to a lack of availability (no refrigeration and high cost). Today, animal foods constitute a whopping 40 percent of our total calories. Taken together, *over 90 percent of the calories we consume today are from foods that were either non-existent back then or were eaten only on special occasions*.

Today, only seven percent of our calories come from natural, whole plant foods, yet these were the foods where the bulk of our ancestors calories came from, in the form of whole grain breads, potatoes, brown rice, corn, oats, rye, barley meals, beans and other vegetables, fruits and whole grains.

When the eating habits of numerous populations are compared, the results are strikingly consistent: as the consumption of natural plant foods declines, there is a corresponding rise in diet-related diseases, including weight gain.[39] When almost all their calories came from natural, whole plant foods, there was almost never a problem with weight, nor diet-related diseases. The one exception was the wealthy, which could afford to eat the way Americans eat today.

In other words, the RAVE Diet calls upon you to look back at the foods your ancestors ate – and make their past habits, your future habits. Old-fashioned foods are better because whole foods fill you up on fewer calories, whereas modern foods require that you eat excessive calories before you feel full – the reason we're gaining weight.[40]

Of course, you could run 10 miles a day and you would lose weight no matter what kind of diet you were eating. But would you be healthy? You might *look* healthy, but despite your weight loss, you might not be healthy on the inside. We all know the famous cases of long-distance runners who dropped dead of heart attacks. That's because their coronary arteries were clogged due to their diets. In the case of Jim Fixx, for example, his coronary arteries were plugged solid with atherosclerosis. One was 99 percent blocked, another 80 percent, and a third 70 percent. Losing weight isn't a problem. Losing weight and staying healthy is.

This old-fashioned RAVE Diet will fill you up without restricted portions, reduce your caloric intake gradually, never leave you hungry and always leave you healthy. The only things you'll be deprived of on this diet are the major diseases that are wreaking havoc on American health.

Why Doesn't The Government Promote This Diet?

There is an overwhelming amount of scientific and other data that tells us The RAVE Diet is the healthiest diet on the planet. With Americans getting sicker each day from the foods we eat, you might be asking, "If this diet is so great, why doesn't the government promote it?"

Good question. First of all, the government "does" promote it, but in a very miniscule way. If you compare what the government spends promoting whole plant foods versus what it spends promoting animal and refined foods, I doubt it would amount to a tenth of one percent. Compared to the billions of dollars spent subsidizing the meat, dairy, egg and sugar industries, for example, fruits and vegetables destined for human consumption receive zero subsidies. Even feed crops destined for *farm animal* consumption receive subsidies, but those destined for human consumption do not. This, of course, is the result of meat and dairy industry lobbying.

When the US changed to an animal-based diet early in the 1900s, everyone thought animal foods (meat, egg and dairy products) were nutritionally beneficial foods. In fact, the government got behind meat and dairy farmers and started promoting these foods to help farmers out which were, at the time, very small businesses. One of the key missions of the U.S. Dept. of Agriculture is, in fact, to promote meat and dairy products and it continues to do so to this day. The "Got Milk?" and "Beef, it's what's for dinner," and "Pork, the other white meat," as well as a myriad of other advertising campaigns, are all government-sponsored programs. The federally-funded school breakfast and lunch programs are simply subsidized dumping grounds for unhealthy food designed to put money into farmers pockets regardless of what it is doing to the health of the school children forced to eat this garbage.

Today, small farmers have been displaced by huge agri-businesses that receive almost all agricultural subsidies – and reap almost all the profits. And to ensure that the tradition of political support and rich subsidies continues uninterrupted, agri-businesses funnel millions of dollars into the pockets of politicians every election.

With the democratization of animal foods (and refrigerators), everyone thought Americans had the best darn diet on the planet because rich foods were affordable and everyone could eat animal products on a regular basis. At mid-point in the century, however, something started to happen to Americans – they were suddenly dying of heart attacks and cancer was starting to spread like wildfire.

Since we had the best diet on the planet, no one suspected that eating animal foods had anything to do with these two health epidemics. Medical researchers searched high and low for an explanation and came up empty-handed – until a few researchers started looking into our change to an animal-based diet.

Once the investigation into diet showed promise, massive efforts were employed in an attempt to find out what it was about our diet that caused disease. Over 50 years later, we are literally buried in scientific papers linking animal foods to the leading causes of death and disability in this country.

"Ok," you might be saying. "But with all this evidence, why doesn't the government do something?" In a phrase, money and politics. The meat and dairy industries are a huge part of the economy. They contribute massive amounts of campaign finance money in very successful efforts to purchase politicians. The politicians think this is good not only because it allows them to get re-elected, but also because these food industries employ people, which helps keep our economy going. So our politicians continue to subsidize these industries that would, in fact, go bankrupt without these subsidies. Ironically, the meat, egg and dairy industries are the same people who tout freedom of the marketplace and want *no* government interference in their businesses, except when it comes to receiving subsidies or promoting their products. In that case, government intervention in the marketplace is quite all right.

Along with our change in diet, came a change in taste, which has continued through the generations. Americans now crave animal foods. When meat prices go up, as they did during the Nixon administration, there is a howl of protest from consumers, who demand that politicians do something.

The end result is a joining of several forces that effectively block any attempt to change things. Consumers love their meat and politicians love the money they get from agri-businesses. The government gives only lip service to healthy foods because, quite frankly, there is no profit – or political payoff – in such foods. In addition, the pharmaceutical and medical industries would not be the giants they are today were it not for our diet. In other words, these industries have no incentive to change things either – and both contribute heavily to our politicians.

The last time we saw a report on Nutrition and Health by the Surgeon General was back in 1988. It was supposed to be updated every two years, but the report's damnation of dietary fat created so much furor with food lobbies that our politicians effectively censored any further reports from that office.

Despite the Report's indictment of animal fat, people who worked on the report were told, in no uncertain terms, that the report's recommendations could not say, "eat less meat."[41] So instead of saying, "eat less meat," agencies found a way to water down their recommendations by saying, "eat less saturated fat." This was acceptable to the meat lobby because it means far less to the consumer than saying, "eat less meat." This language compromise has led to a great deal of confusion in the public mind. Health agencies would like to say, "eat less meat," because that has meaning to consumers, but their hands are tied by food industry influence. This is the primary reason you see health authorities today saying "eat less saturated fat" – because it is politically correct and does not threaten their own sources of income from food industries.

The influence of food industries spreads much further than Washington. In fact, food industries deliberately contribute money to health organizations in order to water down their nutritional recommendations. In fact, it's now become a part of their marketing strategy, just like advertising. The health organizations food industries contribute to include the likes of the American Cancer Society, the American Heart Association and the American Dietetic Association,[42] as well as individual health authorities who have any influence over the public. In addition, food industries contribute millions of dollars every year to universities that do studies for them that are designed to sell their products.

Food industries spend a tremendous amount of money on advertising not just in television and print media, but medical and nutritional journals. As a result, their editorial influence is pervasive in terms of what gets said and printed in the media. These industries also employ an army of professional writers who are skilled at writing letters to the editor. It's more than likely the next time you see a letter to an editor touting the benefits of one animal food or another, that letter was written by a hired gun from a food lobby.

Some public figures will rail against any government interference when it comes to food choices and shout there must be "freedom of choice" when it comes to food. In fact, however, we have no freedom of choice because politicians in Washington have already decided Americans are going to eat. By subsidizing the animal and refined food industries, the heavy hand of the government has already interfered in the marketplace and made hamburger – one of the most expensive and resource-intensive foods on the planet – cheaper than raspberries. Until such subsidies are gone and the government gets out of food price-fixing, the "freedom of choice" argument is empty. We have no free market or freedom of choice when it comes to food.

The only way we are going to make Americans eat healthy food is by letting the free market determine the price of food. That means taking away all subsidies food industries receive. That would make unhealthy foods so expensive, only the wealthy could afford to eat them on a regular basis. If those subsidies could be "willed away" overnight, our eating habits would be back in the 18th century and our diets would resemble the old-fashioned diets of our ancestors, who did not suffer from the diet-related diseases that are ravaging us today. Heart disease would vanish from the landscape, just as it did when the Nazis removed animal foods from the countries it occupied and our common cancers would begin their retreat overnight.

Of course, you don't have to wait for the government to do this. You can do this yourself by simply following the RAVE Diet.

I was recently at an American Heart Association fund-raiser. I really wasn't surprised when I found out the main course was veal (I opted for their meat-less entrée). Serving veal or prime rib or some other form of meat is typical of "health" organizations. Why do they serve such unhealthy fare? Because they are trying to raise money – and unwittingly – bring more heart patients into the hospital because the more heart patients in hospitals, the more money they will raise for research into treating a disease that could be completely cured by simple changes in diet. In fact, we do not need any further research into heart disease. We already have a cure for heart disease. It is diet.

Baseline Measurements: Countering Skepticism

"You can fool some of the people all of the time, and all of the people some of the time, but you cannot fool all of the people all of the time." - Abraham Lincoln

It's difficult to convince many people that diet can be so powerful. Most eating diseases are like nutritional time-bombs that take decades to develop, so people may feel healthy now, but they no doubt have heart disease and cancers slowly growing in their bodies.

I remember talking to a woman who was very skeptical of the RAVE Diet. She said, "Look at me! I'm healthy and I eat whatever I want!" She, like so many other people, considered herself to be as healthy as her peers. Unfortunately, being as healthy as one's peers in American is not being healthy at all. She was grossly overweight (she called it a few extra pounds) and I could tell by just looking at her – and generally knowing what she ate – that she suffered from at least heart disease and no doubt other diseases were at work inside her body. A few years after our brief conversation, I learned she had a heart attack. Don't let *your* skepticism keep you from this diet just because you're as healthy as your peers. Our norms for what is healthy have steadily deteriorated over the years and these norms are killing people.

There are many claims being made by various diet plans, which would make anyone skeptical. If you are a "normally healthy" – and skeptical – person and want to try the RAVE Diet, what I would suggest is that you test your own skepticism by getting a few tests done *before* you start the diet, then re-test in six months (or earlier). That will be a measure of just how healthy your skepticism really was.

A friend of mine was on the Atkins diet for many years and was very skeptical of the RAVE Diet. He did lose some weight on Atkins, but it crept back over the years until he was back where he started. He continued with Atkins until his doctors discovered his coronary arteries were blocked. They put a stent in, which served as his wake-up call, so he finally started the RAVE Diet. He's lost 80 pounds and he's never felt better. His test results are now the best they have ever been in his life and his total cholesterol is now at 116. His cardiologists are amazed and somewhat baffled. He now thinks they are incompetent. I would not go that far. They are very skilled at manipulating drugs, performing surgeries and providing temporary fixes for a broken heart. But the typical cardiologist does not have a clue how to actually *cure* heart disease. Sadly, by the time you finish this book, you'll know more about curing heart disease than your doctor does.

The RAVE Diet heals internally and aside from weight loss (if you're overweight), you won't be able to "see" how your body is healing without these tests. Once your test results come back, you'll not only be amazed, but your doctor will too. Another friend of mine adopted the RAVE Diet and her cholesterol dropped 60 points in just three weeks. All her doctor could say was "I don't know what you're doing, but keep doing it." The truly sad part is that the doctor should have given her this dietary advice, not me.

The following should be goals to make sure you are heart-attack proof. And these are goals that should be met without any medication.

Total Cholesterol:	below 150
LDL:	below 90
Triglycerides:	below 150
Homocystein:	below 10
Blood Pressure:	110/70 – 125/80
Weight:	Ideal/Good

Don't worry about your total cholesterol getting too low. Despite what you may have heard, this has never happened to any human being. The typical rural Chinese peasant has total cholesterol levels around 80 – 90 and they would consider a total cholesterol level of 150 to be very high. Of course, with the introduction of American food in Chinese cities, Chinese cholesterol levels are skyrocketing, along with their diet-related diseases.

Despite the efficacy of these tests, they are still only markers, i.e., they do not measure the blood flow to the heart. For those truly concerned about their heart condition, you can get any of a number of tests that measure blood flow to the heart, e.g., a Thallium stress test or MUGA scan. Your doctor can tell you which is the best for you.

Note: In the beginning, your HDL ("good cholesterol") will go up because you are getting rid of excess cholesterol and clearing your arteries. HDL is a measure of the cholesterol leaving your body. Over time, however, the HDL will go *down* because there will simply be less cholesterol to get rid of, since you are not consuming it, nor high levels of saturated fat, and you are clearing your body of excess cholesterol. Ideally, the ratio of total cholesterol to HDL should be less than 3. (Divide your total cholesterol by your HDL, e.g., 150 total cholesterol / 50 HDL = 3.) [43] The point is, you should really be more concerned about your LDL ("bad cholesterol"), not HDL. This is the reason HDL is not listed as a measure.

Weight Measurements

Your current weight is the single best indicator of what your future health is going to be like, so it's important to get it under control. Below are general weight tables for people between 4'10" and 6'3". The ideal weight ranges are best for preventing disease, living at optimal health and adding years to your life. For every pound you are above your ideal weight, your risk of developing diseases rises accordingly.

These are very general ranges for _all_ body frames, including men and women. If you want to fine-tune your weight, use a Body Mass Index (BMI) calculator that can take into account frame size. Also, use a BMI calculator to look up your weight if you're outside the height ranges shown here. Healthy weights will also vary depending on your body-fat mass and lean body mass, i.e., if you have a high ratio of lean muscle to fat, you can be above these ranges and still be within your targeted weight range.

The first reaction by many people is that the ideal weight ranges are too "skinny." Quite honestly, this is because we're used to seeing fat people and our perception of what is attractive has changed as the majority of Americans have become overweight. As you lose weight and move close to your ideal weight, your friends will likely be concerned that something is wrong with your health. Actually, it's just the opposite. Something is wrong with _their_ health and it revolves around their weight. When I first started doin' the RAVE, I lost 35 pounds in six months and received similar reactions. But while friends were fretting about my "skinny" appearance, they were also full of envy as they peppered me with questions about _how_ I lost so much weight – and kept it off.

Ideal

4'10"	91–105	5' 7"	121–140
4'11"	94–109	5' 8"	125–144
5' 0"	97–112	5' 9"	128–149
5' 1"	100–116	5'10"	132–153
5' 2"	104–120	5'11"	136–157
5' 3"	107–124	6' 0"	140–162
5' 4"	110–128	6' 1"	144–166
5' 5"	114–132	6' 2"	148–171
5' 6"	118–136	6' 3"	152–176

Good

4'10"	105–119	5' 7"	140–159
4'11"	109–124	5' 8"	144–164
5' 0"	112–128	5' 9"	149–169
5' 1"	116–132	5'10"	153–174
5' 2"	120–136	5'11"	157–179
5' 3"	124–141	6' 0"	162–184
5' 4"	128–145	6' 1"	166–189
5' 5"	132–150	6' 2"	163–194
5' 6"	136–155	6' 3"	176–200

Overweight

4'10"	119–143	5' 7"	159–191
4'11"	124–148	5' 8"	164–197
5' 0"	128–153	5' 9"	169–203
5' 1"	132–158	5'10"	174–209
5' 2"	136–164	5'11"	179–215
5' 3"	141–169	6' 0"	184–221
5' 4"	145–174	6' 1"	189–227
5' 5"	150–180	6' 2"	194–233
5' 6"	155–186	6' 3"	200–240

Obese

4'10"	143+	5' 7"	191+
4'11"	148+	5' 8"	197+
5' 0"	153+	5' 9"	203+
5' 1"	158+	5'10"	209+
5' 2"	164+	5'11"	215+
5' 3"	169+	6' 0"	221+
5' 4"	174+	6' 1"	227+
5' 5"	180+	6' 2"	233+
5' 6"	186+	6' 3"	240+

If your doctor thinks these goals are not realistic, you're seeing the wrong doctor. Go to our web site and see our current list of Healthcare Providers, who can achieve these goals solely through diet and exercise, not drugs.

Practically all adult Americans – and most school children – have heart disease and most adult Americans have cancers slowly growing inside them that can't be detected yet. You can start to reverse these and other diseases by following the RAVE Diet on your own. If you want to treat a serious disease with diet, again see the list of Healthcare Providers at our web site (www.RaveDiet.com) who regularly heal patients with a wide range of diseases by simply using diet and exercise.

The RAVE Diet & Lifestyle

The Best Health Insurance You Can't Buy

"It turned out to be a lot easier than I had expected. In fact, it felt rather natural. I discovered a new world of foods that were very tasty, diverse, and satisfying. I never felt deprived and, unlike my experiences with other "diets" I had been on, I never felt hungry. Gradually my tastes and orientation to food changed and my desire for the higher-fat foods I had been used to went away." - Raymond Kurzweil, The 10% Solution

21 Days To a New You!

The RAVE Diet is not about restricting food portions, but *changing food choices* and breaking through the vicious eating cycles that are making people sick and overweight. Many people will look at the RAVE Diet and make a snap judgment that it's difficult to follow. It only seems that way. Some of our greatest skeptics decided to try it and found the diet not only easy to follow, but satisfying and delicious.

When we say "21 days to a new you!" we're not talking about losing 21 pounds in 21 days, but *changing your tastes for food in just three weeks*. That's how long it takes for most people to make a complete switch in their taste buds. The problem is that we've lost our taste for natural foods because most of the food we eat today is smothered with salt, fat, sweets and chemicals. As a result, our taste buds have become warped as we crave the "highs" of sugar, fat and salt that have become a standard part of the typical American diet. In other words, our taste buds are really what's packing on the extra pounds.

By following the RAVE Diet, your taste buds will be "re-trained" and the cravings you have for bad foods will be replaced with a desire to eat good food. This is the essence of the RAVE Diet: simply re-training your taste buds to enjoy the foods nature provided for us during the millions of years of our evolution. Once your taste buds are re-oriented, weight loss and all the other health benefits of this diet will fall into place automatically as your body begins to heal itself.

Many people made a switch from whole milk to skim milk. Do you remember how terrible skim milk tasted when you first tried it? After you got used to it, and you tried whole milk again, remember how awful it tasted? Too heavy, too greasy and too fatty. You will experience similar changes in taste when switching to the RAVE Diet. The highs of sugar, fat, sweets and chemical additives will be replaced by more subtle tastes, along with the aromatic flavors of herbs, spices and sauces. Food will taste so much cleaner – much like the difference between spring water and a syrupy soda.

The RAVE Diet is actually pretty simple in terms of re-training your taste buds because we're already familiar with most of the foods in the diet. The big difference is that we have to eat more of them, then gradually try out unfamiliar foods and discover interesting new tastes.

Your tastes for food will change with this diet and you'll find you prefer the "cleaner" taste of natural foods. After eating this way, you'll find that high-fat foods will taste heavy and greasy. Many people have told me that when they do eat high-fat foods, their entire system slows down and they feel sluggish.

Stick to the RAVE Diet for 21 days and you'll find you won't want to go back to the heavy, calorie-dense foods you've been eating. In just 21 days, your tastes will change, you'll be on your way to permanent weight loss and you'll be feeling better to boot!

"Progress is very important and exciting – in everything but food." Andy Warhol

Imagine moving to a country where everything is pretty much the same as what we have here – all the modern conveniences, technology, transportation, nice housing, and so forth. But there is one big difference. The way people eat is old-fashioned. They don't have refined foods. They don't allow fiber and cancer-fighting nutrients to be removed from foods. They don't squeeze fruits and vegetables in order to eat concentrated oils from them, while throwing away the rest. And they don't eat the animals they live with. As a result, people live long, healthy, high-quality lives. If you can imagine such a country, it's possible to live there without even moving – by simply adopting the RAVE Diet & Lifestyle.

Today, scientists, pharmaceutical companies, doctors and laymen are all looking for magic pills that will prevent the major diseases of our time. Pop a pill and you can keep living that self-destructive lifestyle we call the American way of life. Unfortunately, it doesn't work that way and never will. "Lifestyle" is the key word because preventing (and reversing) diseases involves the interaction of many different factors and they can all be boiled down to how you live your life. And that can't be put in a pill.

At first glance, the RAVE Diet may sound like a negative, restrictive eating regimen, but nothing could be further from the truth. What it does is direct your eating habits away from heavily advertised, health-destructive foods and toward foods humans have eaten for millions of years. These foods have proven their success over eons in protecting humans from the diseases that have emerged as our biggest killers in just the last 100 years. These are clean-burning foods that will strengthen your entire body. The goal is to eliminate foods that interfere with or impair the body's immune system, while increasing foods that strengthen the body's ability to heal itself.

You'll find you actually have a wide range of food choices "doin' the RAVE," and in the process you'll discover just how narrow your old eating habits actually were. In essence, what we're doing is eliminating the foods most people did not eat before the 20th century and most people throughout the world still do not eat today. It's an old-fashioned diet, but with some significant improvements. Think of it as an adventure, not only in food, but also in health that will have a profound payback over the years.

The RAVE Diet is uncompromising and strict adherence to it won't be possible for many. If that is the case for you, it should be thought of as an ideal diet – something to strive for – because the closer you follow it, the better the results. When followed to the letter, it works and works wonders.

The word RAVE is a simple acronym used to help people remember the rules. It is based on the guidelines used by doctors to treat and reverse diseases. This is what RAVE stands for:

No R efined foods
No A nimal foods
No V egetable oils
No E xceptions
   & Exercise

Although many of the reasons for each term are explained in the film *Eating*, as well as previous text, the following also provides a succinct explanation.

No Refined Foods

"Unhealthy food is available everywhere all the time, like never before in history. Gas stations, drug stores, schools…" – Dr. Kelly D. Brownell, Yale University

Hunters are using candy as bear bait. After gorging himself on candy, "One bear was just started walking around in circles…. Among the deleterious health effects: cavities, hair loss and lethargy." If it does that to a 500 pound bear, just imagine what it does to humans. – Newsweek, November 3, 2003

Refined foods are plant foods that have been denatured and stripped of their fiber, vitamins, minerals, antioxidants and other nutrients. These foods are lifeless imitations of the vibrant products found in nature. They are devoid of any nutritional value and are usually transformed into dull, man-made foodstuffs that do not satisfy hunger, wreak havoc on your health and generally don't require teeth to eat them. Sadly, about *half* of the total calories in a typical American diet come from refined foods.

Refined foods are simple carbohydrates such as white flour, wheat flour, refined sugar, pastries, white pasta, white semolina, white bread, white rice, French fries, chips of any variety, cakes, soft drinks and similar junk foods. You know the foods I'm talking about – foods that have been transformed from their natural state into man-made products. (See *Reading Labels & Ingredients*.)

Because refined foods have no fiber, they spike your blood sugar, cause insulin surges, stimulate your appetite, accelerate the conversion of calories into body fat and promote many diseases. From your body's perspective, eating refined foods is, for all practical purposes, the same thing as eating refined sugar straight out of the box. From a weight loss perspective, refined foods do not fill you up, so you'll soon be hungry after eating them, which means you'll have to eat even more calories to feel full.

Many people think they are eating a plant-based diet because they are eating foods that do not contain animal products. Refined foods are every bit as bad for your body as animal foods and should be completely eliminated from your diet. A plant-based diet is about eating natural, whole plant foods. The health benefits of this diet (including weight loss) will be greatly diminished if refined foods are not eliminated from your diet.

Food manufacturers have spent billions of dollars researching ways to mix the right ingredients in order to "seduce" you into eating bad foods. Scientists have found that chocolate, for example, reaches its point of "maximum irresistibility" with a mix of 50 percent sugar and 50 percent fat.[1] But it doesn't stop there. Ingredient profiles have been created that are targeted at genders and age groups in order to make refined foods as addicting as possible. If this reminds you of cigarette companies, you're thinking in the right direction.

Americans now spend about 90 percent of their food budget on refined foods. As a result of processing foods, the natural flavor is destroyed and has to be replaced with chemical additives. In fact, the heart of food flavor in America is not found in natural foods at all, but in the refineries and chemical plants that dot an industrial corridor along the New Jersey turnpike.[2]

Chemical flavoring not only accounts for the flavor in refined foods, but also most of the meat Americans consume. Eric Schlosser documents this flavoring via chemistry with the following account:

> "After closing my eyes, I suddenly smelled a grilled hamburger. The aroma was uncanny, almost miraculous. It smelled like someone in the room was flipping burgers on a hot grill. But when I opened my eyes, there was just a narrow strip of white paper and a smiling flavorist."[3]

Ninety percent of the money Americans shell out for food buys a mix of chemistry and fiber-less, processed foodstuffs devoid of any real nutritional merit. This is how removed we have become from real food. We have not only lost our taste for real food, but we've come to prefer the taste of chemicals.

As opposed to the *simple carbohydrates* found in refined foods, *complex carbohydrates* are found in natural, whole foods, such as whole grain foods, vegetables and fruits. These are the good carbohydrates that keep your blood sugar level on an even keel, promote health and keep you feeling full longer because they contain their natural fiber and all the nutrients nature gave them.

Always use *whole* wheat pastas or *whole* wheat breads because they kept their fiber on the way to the grocery store. Make sure the label says whole wheat, *not* wheat flour. With grain products, the first ingredient should always have the word "whole" in it, sprouted wheat or organic rolled oats. Don't let the words "hearty wheat," "stoned wheat," or "multigrain" on the package fool you. This is just healthy sounding advertising because these ingredients are made from refined white flour. And there is no difference between white flour and wheat flour. Wheat flour has some caramel coloring so it looks brown and sounds healthier, but it's the same as white flour.

Those who complain about carbohydrates are complaining about *refined*, or simple, carbohydrates, not the *complex* carbohydrates found in whole, natural foods. Those in pursuit of weight loss on "low-carb" diets are trading one set of problems for another because their diets are lacking in nutrients, particularly antioxidants and vitamins, which are essential for good health and can only be found in whole plant foods. (This is one reason why many low-carb diets recommend that people take supplements – in order to make up for the poor nutrition of such diets.)

Plant fiber does a number of miraculous things for your health, but one thing it does best is remove toxic substances from your body so you can flush them down the toilet. Fiber even removes heavy metals such as mercury, which you probably have in your body as a result of eating fish – or farm animals that were fed fishmeal. Fiber also removes cholesterol – the reason a fiber-rich diet will lower your cholesterol. In addition, fiber binds with sex hormones, such as estrogen, and removes them from your body. In the case of estrogen, American women have very high levels of estrogen due not only to our high-fat diet, but also due to the lack of fiber in our diets. Fiber also slows down glucose absorption and controls the rate of digestion, making food act more like a time-release pill, *which will keep you feeling full longer.*

Think of plant fiber as your intestinal broom because it will clean out a dirty bowel and prevent bad things from happening, like colon cancer. One of the major reasons refined foods and animal foods are not part of the RAVE Diet is because they do not contain fiber.

If you don't think you're eating much refined food now, I have a small experiment for you. Almost all refined foods come in some kind of packaging. Every time you eat any refined food, keep the packaging it came in and put it in a bag. Do this for a week and at the end of the week inspect the contents of the bag. That should be enough to scare you into eliminating refined foods from your diet.

No Animal Foods

When we kill animals to eat them, they end up killing us because their flesh, which contains cholesterol and saturated fat, was never intended for human beings, who are natural herbivores. - William Clifford Roberts, M.D., Editor-in-Chief, American Journal of Cardiology

"No one can contemplate directly eating 13 pats of butter, but they essentially do when they eat a cheeseburger." - William Connor, M.D., The New American Diet

Animal foods are excluded for all the reasons discussed in the film, *Eating*. If you are worried about not getting enough protein as a result of excluding animal foods from your diet, please see *Notes – Protein*, as that should set your mind at ease.

The only thing you'll miss from eating animal foods is the saturated fat, cholesterol and animal proteins – as well as the diseases these ingredients bring to your body. When you come right down to it, all our nutrients are ultimately obtained from plant foods. Meat-eating animals (including humans) feed off plant-eating animals, which really amount to storage systems for plant nutrients. The problem, of course, is that the plant nutrients in animals are delivered in a package of saturated fat and cholesterol. So why eat animals when you can get everything you need directly from plants – without the cholesterol – and in a low-fat package with healthy fiber and cancer fighting chemicals to boot?

And calorie for calorie, plant foods are far richer in nutrients than animal foods, with green vegetables being the most nutrient-rich foods on the planet.

From a weight loss perspective, many studies have confirmed that over time, the more people eat meat, the more they gain weight. The more people eat whole plant foods, the less likely they are to gain weight. In a recent multi-nation study, it was found that <u>without exception</u>, the thinnest people ate a *complex carbohydrate* diet, while the fattest people ate a meat-based diet.[4] Eliminating meat from your diet is essential if you want to achieve your ideal weight, reverse heart disease and protect yourself against cancers and our major degenerative diseases.

From your heart's perspective, the difference between "lighter" meats and red meat is insignificant and much like the difference between regular cigarettes and "light" cigarettes. All meats – from red meat to chicken to turkey to fish to liquid meat (dairy products) cause heart disease, as well as many other diseases.

As the film *Eating* points out, there is no difference between red meat and white meat of any variety, be it chicken, pork or fish. A three-ounce piece of skinless chicken contains 72 mg of cholesterol, while a three-ounce piece of steak contains 75 mg. In other words, they are both chock full of cholesterol and saturated fat, the two deadliest ingredient in the American diet.

The so-called "good fat" in fish just temporarily thins your blood, while the saturated fat and cholesterol in fish promote heart disease. The hype in the press regarding fish is about treating a symptom of heart disease – and prolonging the disease – not preventing, arresting or reversing it. The next time you read about the benefits of fish oil, all you're doing is reading about the benefits of eating plant foods because the original source of the "good fat" in fish comes from the plants fish have eaten. Get your "good fat" directly from the source without the mercury and other toxins that come with fish products.

The one sure way we know that animal foods harm us is that our bodies start clearing out our arteries the minute we stop eating them. Dr. Nathan Pritikin, who pioneered heart disease reversal with diet, did not experience success in reversing his heart disease until he completely eliminated animal products from his diet.[5] By following the RAVE Diet, we can return our arteries to the state they were in when we were 21 years old, just as Dr. Pritikin did, as well as Dr. Neal Pinckney – who describes his experience in the film *Eating*.

The animal package doesn't get off the hook with just heart disease, because every population that has adopted an animal-based diet has also adopted cancer as their second leading cause of death. One of the most interesting studies ever done in cancer research showed that when rats were fed a diet of 20 percent protein, they all developed cancer. Of the rats that were fed a five percent protein diet, *none* of them developed cancer. In subsequent tests to confirm the validity of the initial tests, it was found that it was not protein, per se, but animal protein that was the culprit in promoting cancer.[6] In yet further tests on dairy products, it was found that casein, the primary protein in all dairy products, was the most aggressive cancer promoter of all.[7]

Cancer has always been prevalent in populations eating an animal-based diet. In fact, back in 1892, Scientific American made the following observation: "*Cancer is most frequent where carnivorous habits prevail.*" The studies cited above suggest that animal protein may be one of the reasons why cancer is so prevalent among populations eating animal foods.

The protein requirement for normal adults is only two and a half percent of total calories. Mother's milk is five percent protein and that is at a time when the body is growing at its highest rate. More than five percent protein is not only unnecessary, but also potentially dangerous. Just one reason "high protein" diets should be avoided like the plague. (For more discussion of protein, see *Notes - Protein*.)

Bottom line: Animal foods cause disease, and cardiovascular diseases in particular. Not a single human being has ever failed to improve their health when they stopped eating animal foods. The evidence is simple, and simply overwhelming.

If you feel you cannot eliminate animal foods completely, try using them as condiments for flavoring only or limit your consumption of animal foods to the bare minimum until you can wean yourself off them completely.

No Vegetable Oils

Strictly speaking, vegetable oils are part of the Refined Foods group because they contain no fiber, they're devoid of nutrients and they are 100 percent fat. They also constitute a whopping 11 percent of the calories Americans consume.[8] Putting two tablespoons of oil in your salad has the fat equivalent of two scoops of ice cream. From a weight loss perspective, eliminating vegetable oils is a very easy – and healthy – way to cut calories.

There are other problems with vegetable oils, however. These oils contain high levels of saturated fat, which is essentially "cholesterol in disguise" because it stimulates your liver to make more cholesterol than your body needs and ends up clogging arteries. In fact, adding <u>any</u> oil to your food will raise your cholesterol level, even more than eating cholesterol itself.[9]

Hydrogenated vegetable oils (trans-fats) are particularly efficient at clogging arteries and depriving your body of oxygen. These oils are found in all kinds of refined foods such as chips, cookies, crackers, cereals, breakfast bars and other baked goods. Every time you eat a bag of cookies it's no different than biting into a piece of meat.

In packaged goods, look for the word "hydrogenated" in the ingredients list and put it back on the shelf. And any food that's deep-fried, such as fast food French fries or donuts, will contain these artery-clogging oils. Most commercial brands of peanut butter will also use hydrogenated oils. Purchase the type where the oil is separated and you have to refrigerate it, then pour off the excess oil on top before stirring it up. Or, better yet, grind your own nut butter at a health food store.

Hydrogenated oils are the "glue" that holds refined carbohydrates together in order to increase shelf life. In fact, the healthy amount of trans fats in your diet should be exactly zero. Ingredients used for longer shelf lives in food translate into longer illnesses and a shorter shelf life for you.

Fried animal foods, such as fried chicken, are probably the *most dangerous foods in existence* because they combine high levels of saturated fat and cholesterol, with hydrogenated oils. In other words, your blood vessels are getting a triple-whammy when you eat fried animal foods.

Even seemingly "innocent" foods such as movie popcorn are dangerous as they are usually popped in coconut or palm oil, both of which are extremely high in saturated fat.

The current rage among some health authorities is olive oil. It's ironic that our health authorities are advising an overweight nation to eat the most concentrated form of fat on the planet, which packs more calories, pound-for-pound, than butter. The basic reason (presumably) is that they are trying to move people away from margarine, although these same authorities (e.g., The American Heart Association and virtually all major health experts) were praising margarine just a

olive oil

few decades ago – and quoting studies purporting to show margarine containing this dangerous oil was heart healthy!

Although olive oil is healthier than butter or margarine, that's not saying much. It's probably the worst way to get heart healthy fats because there's almost no nutritional bang for the calorie buck. In fact, olive and other oils are so nutritionally bankrupt that Joel Fuhrman, M.D., gives oils a score of 1 out of 100, just above refined sweets, which score a zero.[10]

Olive oil is 100 percent fat, contains high concentrations of saturated fat while the fiber, antioxidants, vitamins and minerals of the olive itself have all been stripped away. In clinical studies on humans, olive oil has been shown to be as bad for the heart as eating roast beef.[11]

In addition, the Omega-3's in vegetable oils are highly unstable and tend to decompose and unleash free radicals that cause damage to cells. Vegetable oils have also been implicated in several different studies with cancers.[12]

Vegetable oils also suppress the immune system and actually promote the spread of some cancers.[13] Simply put, olive and other vegetable oils are bankrupt foods that have little nutritional value, a very high caloric cost and actually do damage to your body. If you're after the good fat in olives, get it from the olives themselves, not the denatured oil.

Some highly questionable studies[14] claim to show a "slower progression" of heart disease when people consume olive oil, but having a slower progression of heart disease hardly makes the case that olive oil is heart healthy, assuming such a causal relationship exists in the first place. Other studies have shown it is not the olive oil at all, but the high fiber content in a traditional Mediterranean-type diet that accounts for lower rates of heart disease.[15] A diet is not heart-healthy unless it arrests and reverses heart disease and only a whole, plant-based diet – which specifically excludes *all* oils – has been proven to do that. Adding oils to such a diet only impairs its effectiveness.

The model for the Mediterranean diet harks back to the 1950's and before when people, especially in the island of Crete, were virtually free of heart disease – despite their indulgence in olive oil. This was not because of the olive oil, but because they ate primarily vegetables and whole grains, a little fish and got lots of exercise. Today, their consumption of olive oil has remained the same (if not increased), but their consumption of whole plant foods has plummeted, as has their exercise. As a result, heart disease and obesity have skyrocketed. Olive oil has nothing to do with preventing heart disease and clinical studies have shown that, in fact, it promotes arterial lesions.[16] It's just another magic bullet that is, in fact, a big, fat fantasy promoted by the olive oil industry determined to get high levels of fat back into our diets.

The leading health authorities in reversing heart disease with diet, including Dr. Caldwell Esselstyn, Dr. Joel Fuhrman, Dr. John McDougall and Dr. Dean Ornish, all agree that vegetable oils should be *excluded* from a heart-healthy diet. These are doctors who actually reverse heart disease, as opposed to those who just talk about it or promote the greasy stuff because of financial ties to the olive oil industry. In fact, there's not been a single case of heart disease arrest or reversal where any vegetable oil was a part of the diet. So, if olive oil is so "heart-healthy," why would doctors who reverse heart disease specifically exclude it? Because they consider vegetable oils to be "heart dangerous" and so should you.

As we saw in *The Laws of Cancer*, even the good fat in oils has been shown to unleash dangerous free radicals and promote the spread of cancer cells, whereas the good fat in natural, whole foods is stable and does not display this behavior. Fat should be released into the blood stream slowly and you can only get that slow release by eating natural plant foods in their natural packages that still contain their fiber.

In a nutshell, here's the argument against oils: *all* dietary fats – be they animal or plant fats of all kinds – at levels above 20 percent of total calories, cause heart disease. This has been proven in many clinical tests.[17] To prevent heart disease, you have to reduce your *overall* fat intake. A diet of 100 percent whole plant foods is as heart healthy as you can get. Why introduce a highly concentrated form of fat, such as vegetable oils, that will surely bring your fat intake level into an unsafe zone?

Oils should be put in vehicles and machinery, not your body. In fact, the original use of Canola oil was to lubricate machinery. Then someone came up with the bright idea that people might actually eat it. (These days, some are even converting their cars to run on vegetable oil.) Flaxseed oil is commonly used as a thinner in paints and varnishes and when consumed in high quantities, can hamper the blood's ability to clot.

Instead of using vegetable oils for cooking, cook at lower temperatures and use water to make your own broth – or use the substitutes below. You'll be surprised at how well they work. And with a little practice, you'll soon find you prefer the cleaner taste. It's like the difference between eating peaches in heavy syrup and eating fresh peaches right off the tree. Once you stop using oils, you will be able to taste the difference and you'll never go back. (Also see *Cooking Without Oil.*)

Oil substitutes for sautéing: apple juice, sherry, vegetable stock, vinegars, wine, beer, low-sodium Tamari (soy sauce)

Oil substitutes in baked goods: applesauce, pureed bananas, pureed stewed prunes (Use non-stick pans.)

For salads, choose a dressing without oil, such as Paula's No-Oil dressings (you can find these at health food stores and increasingly at regular grocery stores) or a vinegar-based dressing, such as a Balsamic or brown rice seasoned vinegar dressing. Or try citrus juices in place of salad dressing. If you don't like the taste of vinegar dressings, try mixing them with a tomato-based sauce to make your dressing. Many people have started off with this diet and could not stand the taste of vinegar – but now prefer it as because their tastes have changed. Your tastes will change if you give this a chance.

Change to the RAVE Diet and you can get off aspirin and other blood thinning medicines. If you're taking these because of a medical condition, work with your doctor to wean you off them.

No Exceptions

"We all agree your theory is crazy, but is it crazy enough?" Niels Bohr, Nobel Laureate

Now, after all these negative "No's", you're probably thinking I'm crazy for also saying "No Exceptions" because everyone is going to have some exceptions in our world of plentiful temptations. That, however, is precisely why I say it. It's right out of the school of if you give them an inch, they'll take a mile.

If you are simply trying to lose weight, as opposed to reversing a disease, then I would say you could apply a "99 percent" RAVE rule, that is, follow the RAVE Diet for 99 percent of your caloric intake. In practical terms, this means having rare exceptions to these rules. Roger Ebert, the film critic, recently lost 89 pounds. He describes rare exceptions like this,

> "I agree with McDonald's that a visit to Mickey D's can be part of
> a responsible nutritional approach. That's why I've dined there
> twice in the last 17 months."[18]

In other words, if you follow Roger Ebert's example and dine at McDonald's every eight months or so, it won't set your weight goals back very much.

If you are fighting a disease, however, the No Exceptions rule should be applied to the letter. In fact, Dr. Nathan Pritikin followed a strict RAVE Diet when he reversed his heart disease. (The printed versions of his diet have made compromises by including animal foods in it.) If you want to prevent or reverse heart disease and the diseases associated with narrowing and closure of the blood vessels throughout your body, you will want to follow the RAVE Diet strictly – or it simply won't work. In fact, success on health issues will correspond directly with how strictly you follow the diet.

Doctors who administer dietary treatments to cure diseases will tell you the No Exception rule is the biggest area of concern. When patients stray from their diets, even a little, it can significantly undermine the goals they are trying to achieve. A friend of mine cured an arthritic knee with the RAVE Diet, but over the Christmas holidays he indulged – and the pain in his knee returned.

I can always tell when someone is not following the diet strictly – they don't lose weight. People who follow this diet without exceptions will lose weight, if they need to. When someone says to me, "The diet isn't working! I'm not losing weight!" I always volunteer to make an inspection of what's in their refrigerators and pantries – and they *always* say NO! That's because their kitchens are full of exceptions – and so too is their diet.

The RAVE Diet is the diet that not only prevents, but has also reversed heart and other diseases. Just eating a little more fruits, vegetables and whole grains won't do much, if anything, for your health. If you want to have a big impact, you have to make big changes.

I'm not a disciplinarian and I think that an occasional indulgence is fine – so long as it is very occasional. For example, you might have a piece of cake during a birthday party or you might indulge in small ways during holiday festivities. This is Ok, so long as you get right back into the RAVE Diet. The biggest problem is that occasional exceptions can easily lead you back into old habits.

Most of us think we can get away with more than just an occasional exception, but there is real pain involved in these exceptions. "Oh, these are only calories," you say. Ah, but they're not. They're usually *empty* calories, which means you'll soon be hungry again and you'll need to consume even more calories in order to feel full.

"So what?" you say. "I'll just work off the calories." Well, first of all, it's a lot easier to say you're going to work them off than it is to actually work them off. To work off a Snickers candy bar, you'd have to spend 51 minutes jogging or two hours walking just to get back where you were *before* you had a few minutes of pleasure eating that candy bar. A 20-ounce Coke will cost you nearly an hour of biking. In other words, these brief moments of pleasure can be very painful over the long run. (To think of it another way, you'd have to eat about three pounds of apples to equal the calories you consume in one five-ounce chocolate bar.)

Second, you can't "work off" cholesterol. The average person can only get rid of 100 mg of cholesterol a day. A single egg contains 213 mg and that excess cholesterol ends up clogging arteries. The only way you're going to get rid of cholesterol is to stop eating it and lower your saturated fat intake so you'll give your body a fighting chance to get rid of the excess. The body's extremely fine-tuned to handle this, but it can't function properly when it's overwhelmed by a bad diet.

You might think of the RAVE Diet as your lifelong marriage partner. You might have an occasional affair with Mr. Sweet or Ms. Fat or Mr. Salt, but these are temporary distractions that can't possibly give you a lifetime of satisfaction and love like your marriage partner can. The best advice I can give you is to stay faithful and monogamous and, like a good marriage, the payoffs will be incalculable.

Finally, your friends may laugh at you for following such a "crazy" diet. But they'll stop laughing when they see your new body and lifestyle. When they're suffering through the anguish of diet-related diseases later in life and you continue to dodge those disease-laden bullets, trust me, you'll have the last, crazy laugh.

Exercise

"The sovereign invigorator of the body is exercise, and of all exercises, walking is the best." – Thomas Jefferson

It always amazes me that we don't have half an hour to exercise, but manage to squeeze in an average of four hours of TV a day.

"What, are they allergic to sweat?" – Richard Simmons

Animals in the wild never get fat. Humans in the wild never get fat. Domesticate dogs, they get fat and diseased. Domesticate humans, they get fat and diseased. Our sedentary lifestyles are simply not suited to our Stone Age bodies.

Exercise is an essential part of the RAVE Diet. As mentioned previously, the root of the word diet actually means "lifestyle" and a change in diet really means a change in the style of your life. Active Americans get a fraction of the cancers and other diseases that sedentary Americans get. Among other things, exercise helps to correct bad health habits by burning up and stabilizing blood sugar levels, improving immune function and lymph flow, getting oxygen to all parts of the body and strengthening bones, while helping us handle stress better and increasing both the quality and quantity of sleep.

Exercise also speeds the passage of carcinogens and toxins from the body and recent studies have shown that exercise keeps your brain as fit as your body as you age. In other words, exercise will not only make you feel fit and improve your appearance, but it will prevent a wide range of diseases.

As your main exercise, choose a regimen that's just the opposite of cancer – one that's aerobic – an exercise that makes you breath and respire to raise the oxygen levels in your blood. Cancer hates oxygen and thrives in areas of your body with low oxygen levels, where the blood supply is limited, due to clogged blood vessels caused by a bad diet. It's no accident that the American Cancer Society recently made exercise a cornerstone of cancer prevention.

Walking is probably the best exercise for all of us. It's easy, cheap and gets you outdoors, which can do wonders for your mental state. It wasn't that long ago that walking wasn't an exercise at all, but transportation for the vast majority of Americans, so try to find opportunities during the day that allow you to walk more, instead of driving to a destination.

Always get at least half an hour of exercise a day, or 45 minutes five times a week. If you've had a busy day, even 15 minutes can be beneficial. Try walking for 30 minutes in the morning and 30 minutes in the evening. I guarantee it will transform your life within a month.

Get out in the sun occasionally. It will bring some perspective into your life, it's the best way to get vitamin D and recent studies have shown that moderate exposure has a protective effect against all sorts of cancers – including skin cancer. Just the opposite of what we've been told for the last 20 years.

And when the brain is producing "happy chemicals" – such those released when you exercise – they actually strengthen your immune system.

The best time to exercise is whenever you can, but most people prefer to exercise in the mornings because it seems to jump-start their metabolism, giving them more energy and mental acuity throughout the day. It's also easier to find the time in the early hours because there are usually fewer demands on your schedule.

Insofar as weight loss is concerned, exercise will reduce fat and build lean muscle mass, which will *increase your metabolism* and that, in turn, will burn more calories. The more exercise you get, the more muscle you gain. The more muscle you gain, the more your metabolism and energy will increase – and the more fat you'll burn.

When you're sedentary, you lose muscle mass. When active, you gain it and that is the key to burning more calories. Don't use the excuse that your metabolism slows down with age. Nonsense. Metabolism is a function of lean body mass, the more you have the higher your metabolism. Get moving, build up your lean body mass and your metabolism will move with you.

There's a secret known to those who exercise regularly: exercise *creates* energy. Don't wait for energy to come to you when you're tired. When you feel that afternoon slump, shake it off and get your body moving. Taking a 15-minute walk will keep you more awake and alert the rest of the day than an afternoon nap – or that cup of coffee.

Humans are naturally lazy because we're programmed to conserve energy. In the past, we were forced to exercise to find food and there was a balance between the calories expended to locate or farm food and the calories we consumed. Today, we have created an incredibly artificial living environment that's designed to conserve energy, so much so that many Americans are so inactive they're practically living their lives in bed rest. Humans in industrialized countries are very much like caged birds, but in our case we're caged in our chairs and couches. Despite our technical advances, we're still trapped in Stone Age bodies and those bodies need to be exercised – just as faithfully as they are fed every day.

The best incentive to exercise is that it simply makes you feel wonderful and alive! But if you need an immediate reason to exercise, here's one you can't resist – you'll enjoy a much better sex life! (For more, see *Sex, Booze, Rock 'n Roll*)

The RAVE Diet Food Pyramid

By now, you may be saying, "What's left to eat?" Actually, there are a wider variety of foods available in the RAVE Diet than what the typical American diet includes today. Let's take a brief tour of the RAVE Diet food pyramid.

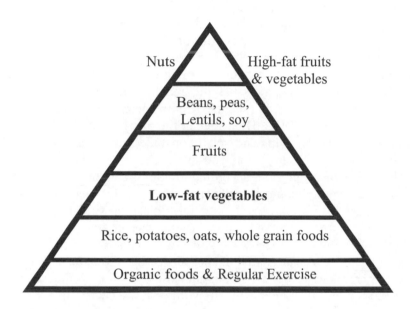

These are the only foods that contain both fiber and cancer-fighting nutrients *in the same package*. At the top are foods with a high fat to fiber ratio. As you move down the pyramid, the amount of fat decreases, relative to the amount of fiber.

At the very top are foods such as nuts, seeds and high-fat fruits and vegetables, like avocados and olives. Great foods, but over 80 percent fat, so go easy on them. (This includes nut butters.)

The higher protein foods tend to be beans, peas, lentils and soy. These are near the top of the pyramid because they are still high in fat content, so you need to watch the proportions. And you don't need to eat these foods to get protein. Both protein and calcium are found throughout the pyramid and you'll get more than adequate amounts of both – as well as all other essential nutrients – by just eating any variety of these foods.

Vegetables and fruits are the two most important food groups for fighting cancer and keeping you looking and feeling young. Optimally, your diet should really be centered on *low-fat vegetables*. In fact, low-fat vegetables can occupy a much larger portion of the pyramid if you want, depending on your food preferences. Leafy green vegetables, for example, can give you practically everything you need in terms of nutrients – that's how good they are. In fact, calorie-for-calorie, green vegetables are the most nutritious foods on the planet.

At the base of the pyramid are rice, potatoes and whole grain foods. Use these as meat substitutes to fill you up. Avoid white rice because the fiber, vitamins and other nutrients have been removed. Choose brown rice instead (or another *whole* grain rice) and always eat potatoes with the skin.

You'll hear some people say to eat fruits and low-fat vegetables exclusively and avoid "starchy" foods at the bottom of the pyramid, as well as the high-fat foods at the top of the pyramid. This is good advice, but not everyone can eat like this and feel satisfied. Rice, potatoes, corn and other whole grain foods serve as "filler foods" because they are satisfying and fill you up. In their natural forms, these foods are very low in fat (potatoes are one percent fat) and rich in nutrients. As you start out on the RAVE Diet, stick to the proportions shown in the pyramid because this diet is satisfying and you'll consume a wide variety of foods eating this way. Your diet will evolve as you learn more about whole plant foods and you can change the proportions according to your preferences and dietary goals.

If you're concerned about an imbalance between Omega-3's and Omega-6's, follow the phrase "more greens, less grains," meaning you should make low-fat green vegetables the predominant part of your diet. If you want extra Omega-3, sprinkle some ground flaxseed on your food. (For more on the benefits of flaxseed, including its cancer-fighting properties, see *Essential Tips & Tricks*.)

Spices, herbs and sauces are throughout the pyramid. Use these to give your food added flavor. Spices and herbs, in particular, are calorie-free, rich in cancer-fighting nutrients and can turn plain-tasting foods into fabulous foods. (See *Rules for Meal Preparation – Flavorings*.) If you're not familiar with spices, you can start with Italian Seasoning, as that is universally liked, and branch out from there. If you think eating a plant-based diet is boring, you'll be pleasantly surprised once you learn how to use spices.

Organic foods are at the base of the pyramid. You should buy certified organic products whenever possible. These foods are grown without the use of chemical fertilizers and pesticides. Pesticides, in fact, reduce the amount of antioxidants in plants, so organic foods have higher cancer-fighting nutrients than conventionally grown foods. The reason for this is that plants use their own antioxidants in an effort to defend themselves against pesticides, thus lowering the antioxidants available to consumers.[19] (For more on organic foods, see *Reading Labels & Ingredients*.)

It's a lot easier than you think to follow the RAVE Diet. All you have to do is choose your favorite foods from the pyramid, follow the proportions – and Bingo! – you're doin' the *RAVE*. It's really as simple as that. Remember, plant foods are medicines. The more you eat, the healthier you're going to be.

For meal preparation guidelines, see *Rules for Meal Preparation*. And if you ever get stumped about what to eat, see *Food Lists*, which shows a sampling of just how many foods are available with the RAVE Diet.

Essential Tips & Tricks

Here are a few simple keys to the RAVE Diet.

The #1 Golden Rule: Always eat foods as close to their natural state as possible. Eat whole foods that come in their natural packages and avoid foods that come in a package or can, unless they are fresh-frozen.

Always eat whole foods: In packaged goods, look for the words "whole," "sprouted wheat" or "organic rolled oats" in the first ingredient, not the second or third. Always eat whole-wheat pastas or whole wheat breads. Make sure the label says whole wheat, not wheat flour. Don't let the words "hearty wheat," "stoned wheat," or "multigrain" on the package fool you. Such ingredients are made from refined white flour and there's *no difference between white flour and wheat flour*. Wheat flour has some caramel coloring and sounds healthier, but it's not.

Eat a wide variety of colorful foods: Always eat a wide variety of foods because each food has it's own special health benefits and cancer fighting profiles – and they work as a team, complimenting, reinforcing and magnifying each other's benefits. This is the new math of cancer prevention and eating a variety of foods actually multiplies cancer-fighting and cardiovascular benefits because they work together synergistically. Along the same lines, most of the antioxidant benefits of fruits and vegetables come from the component that gives them their color, so make sure your plate is full of different colors – *the deeper and darker the colors, the more cancer-fighting nutrients*. The magic is in variety. Get in the habit of chopping up vegetables and putting them in containers, or buying vegetables already chopped up. That way, you can add a variety of foods to your meal very conveniently.

Uncooked Food: Try to eat *at least* half of your food uncooked and without any dips or toppings. Try to eat your food plain. If you buy good tasting products in the first place, you won't need anything on them.

A Salad Is An Ideal Meal: A salad puts into practice the previous four tips about eating. If you find that a salad takes too much time to prepare, simply stop by your local salad bar, be it in a restaurant or supermarket – but bring your own salad dressing, or use vinegar without oil. If you use plenty of sliced beets, the juice from them can serve as a delicious dressing.

Never cook with salt: Natural plant foods contain all the salt you'll ever need. People like to say that salt brings out the flavor in food. Nonsense! All it does is give food a salty taste, camouflage the real taste of food while promoting blood clotting and high blood pressure. Learn to use spices and herbs, instead of salt, to flavor your food. Or try Mrs. Dash or Salt-Free Spike. A few weeks after you stop using salt, you'll find you won't miss it at all.

Take a Multivitamin: Take a good daily multivitamin. This applies to any kind of diet because it's cheap health insurance. Unless you live off the land, like our ancestors did, you'll need vitamin B-12 and you can get it easily this way. B-12 is a bacteria that comes from the soil, not animals. Herbivorous animals happen to have B-12 because they consume soil when they eat plants, thereby storing B-12 in their flesh. A multivitamin will also give you vitamin D if you don't get out in the sun very often, or don't get it in fortified foods.

Ground Flaxseed: A tablespoon of ground flaxseed should be a part of your daily diet. Flaxseed is not only the single best source of fiber in the world, but it has been proven to be very effective in fighting breast cancer and, presumably, other hormone-based cancers such as prostate cancer. In one study, women eating flaxseed muffins every day proved that flaxseed was just as effective as Tamoxifen in shrinking cancer tumors – and without the side effects of an extremely toxic drug.[20] You can purchase a flaxseed grinder (coffee grinders work just as well) or purchase flaxseed meal that is already ground up from health food stores. Sprinkle it over anything and everything, from fruits to salads and oatmeal or any other dish. Avoid flaxseed oil, as it's a refined product and part of the restricted vegetable oil group in the RAVE Diet. (See *The RAVE Diet & Lifestyle – No Vegetable Oils*.)

Snacking: Snacking in-between meals is not bad in and of itself. It all depends on what you eat. Avoid packaged "snack" foods like the plague. Always eat whole plant foods, such as fruit or vegetables. Fruits are the best snack. The high concentration of water and fiber makes them very filling. If you're at work, bring an extra large helping of lunch and snack on that. (See *Fast Food: Meals In Minutes* for quick meal suggestions and *What To Expect* for more on snacking)

Beverages: Water should <u>always</u> be your beverage of choice. Any beverage containing any kind of sweetener is off limits. (See *Reading Labels & Ingredients*.) Any beverage containing a stimulant, such as caffeine, should be avoided as well. Stimulants give you an "artificial" high because when you come down from them, you're at a lower point than you would have been without having taken them in the first place – the reason you need that second cup of coffee. Fruit juices are fine so long as they are unsweetened and contain the fiber, or pulp from the whole fruit. There are no specific rules about fluid intake, except that you should drink as much water as you're comfortable with. If you're trying to lose weight, see the next section, *Accelerating Weight Loss* for additional guidelines on water consumption. Avoid "sport drinks" and any drink that carries a "health" label with it. You're simply wasting your money.

Eating Out: Ethnic restaurants usually have the best food choices, but in any restaurant, just order whatever is on the menu, but ask them to leave out the bad stuff by following the RAVE Diet rules. Simply say you don't eat meat and dairy and ask them to prepare a vegetable plate for you. You can request they not cook it in oil, but American chefs simply don't know how to do that. Steamed vegetables are the best. Look at what they are offering as side dishes and ask that they make a special plate of side dishes for you. Stay away from restaurant pasta. Whole-wheat pasta is rare in restaurants and they all cook pasta with oil. Also, most restaurant pasta is made with eggs. If you're at a steak house, go for the baked potato and vegetable side dishes. Or head straight for the salad bar. When eating at a sushi bar, just order the vegetarian sushi. If it's not on the menu, just request it. Ask for Balsamic vinaigrette to dip your bread in, instead of oil. Better yet, ask for a plate of vegetables, instead of bread, because all restaurant bread is refined. Dip the vegetables in Balsamic vinaigrette.

All airlines serve meals without meat, egg or dairy products. Ask for their Pure Vegetarian or Vegan meals. When you go to a fast food restaurant, you can usually purchase a baked potato and salad. If you don't think this will fill you up, have *two* baked potatoes. And watch the salad dressing. A recent news article reported that McDonald's salads had more calories than their cheeseburgers, due to the dressing, so use it *very* sparingly.

And during holiday gatherings with family and friends, eat before you get there to curb your appetite.

Following the RAVE Diet can be as simple or complicated as you want to make it. If you need recipes, look at the sample recipes in this book and explore the web site recipe links that contain thousands of delicious recipes (See *Recipes On The Web*) – but leave out any refined foods, animal foods and use vegetable oil substitutes. (See *Rules for Meal Preparation – Cooking Without Oil*)

For convenience, use frozen fruits and vegetables. They're almost as good as fresh and may be better in some cases due to modern storage and transportation techniques.

Coffee and many other stimulants - as well as alcohol - dehydrate your body and take more fluid out of it than they bring in. This contributes to cell dehydration, which some experts cite as the cause of premature aging. Avoid these products and make water your beverage of choice – it's the single best thing you can do for dry skin and wrinkles. By the way, dehydration and high blood sugar levels cause hangovers. The best way to prevent a hangover is to drink water before you go to bed. And take a walk the next morning to help burn off the excess sugar in your blood.

I'm sure most of you are thinking, yes, this all sounds good, but if I eat according to this pyramid, what a sacrifice! Actually, it's just the opposite. This diet is very indulgent because there are no restrictions on portion sizes.

Many people will agree with the health aspects of the RAVE Diet, but simply can't change their eating habits. First of all, everyone already eats plant foods. Rice, potatoes, lettuce, tomatoes, fruits, bread and so forth are all part of our diets and we all eat a wider range of plant foods than we realize, just too little of them. All you have to do is substitute that slice of steak or chicken on your plate – with *more* plant foods. You'll feel full and just as satisfied as you would with your standard American diet. Many studies have shown that potatoes are just as satisfying as meat – to meat-eaters – and there are hundreds of ways to prepare potatoes.

If you think you "hate" all vegetables, start by simply eating more of the familiar plant foods you do like – such as potatoes and brown rice. There are so many ways to "disguise" the taste of vegetables with seasonings and sauces that this shouldn't be a barrier. (See *Rules for Meal Preparation – Flavorings*.) You just have to get a little creative with your food preparation. This may be a challenge at first, but read up on how to prepare vegetables in this book and also what they can do for your body, which may make them go down a little easier.

Just as your taste for meat and dairy products was acquired, you can acquire a taste for foods you thought would be impossible to eat. Take bread, for example. If you buy good-tasting whole grain bread in the first place, you should enjoy the taste of the bread by itself, without any high-fat toppings. Try it. You can acquire the clean taste of "plain" bread after just a slice or two and you'll love it. Some people "hate" the taste of Portobello mushrooms. Trying grilling them with barbeque sauce or A1 steak sauce. They're delicious and a great substitute for hamburgers. And if you absolutely can't stand mushrooms (or another plant food), put them in food processor, then mix them into a meal.

Your tastes for food will change with this diet and you'll find you prefer the "cleaner" taste of natural foods. After eating this way, you'll find that high-fat foods will taste heavy and greasy and you'll notice that when you do eat high-fat foods, your entire system slows down and you feel sluggish.

Plant foods are bulky, which means you end up eating more food, in terms of quantity, but you'll actually consume fewer calories. One of the biggest problems is convenience in that you usually won't find healthy food at your local convenience store. This diet does not have to be inconvenient, you just have to think ahead and think in terms of whole plant foods. It's easy, once you get used to it. See *Fast Food – Meals In Minutes* for a few suggestions along these lines.

Accelerating Weight Loss

If you want to accelerate your weight loss, follow these rules:

1) Eat only low-fat, plant foods that come in their natural packages.
2) Never skip meals, especially breakfast.
3) Drink at least a full glass of water half an hour before you eat to curb your appetite.
4) Eliminate breads, alcohol and salt.
5) Go light on all grain products and high-fat fruits and vegetables.
6) Go very light on nuts and nut products.
7) Make *low-fat vegetables the center of your diet.*
8) Snack on fruits because they contain water and fiber and are filling.
9) Try to eat at least one full meal salad a day with minimal dressing (make sure the dressing does not contain oil). In fact, a salad a day will not only keep the doctor away, but those pounds as well.
10) Follow the *No Exceptions* rule to the letter.

There is a time lag between the time you eat and the time you feel full. On a typical American diet, you could quickly gulp down 2,500 calories at one sitting – more than enough for a full day – and still not feel full. By taking time to eat, you give your stomach an opportunity to tell your brain that you're full. If you only have 5 – 10 minutes to eat a meal, don't try to feel full by eating more because you'll consume too many calories. You'll feel full in another 15 or 20 minutes. In the meantime, drink water and give your stomach enough time to send its message to your brain.

Also, get as much exercise as you can. Exercise not only does miraculous things for your health, but it will burn off those extra calories and tip your scales in the right direction. There's no better way to lose weight than exercise and healthful eating.

One lady told me she was always hungry eating this diet. Her problem was that she was trying to lose weight the traditional way – by starving herself. She mistakenly felt that if she ate too much food she would gain weight. Eating the RAVE Diet is counter-intuitive because you should always eat when you're hungry. In the beginning, many people find they're eating more food than they ever ate in their lives, yet still losing weight. Don't be afraid to eat natural plant foods because they are very low in calories and fat. As your body adjusts to this new way of eating, you'll find your appetite will adjust too. Just stick to it!

Another lady told me she wasn't losing weight. Her problem was that she was making too many exceptions and loading up on refined foods. If you make exceptions like this — and can't help it — then the only option you have is exercise.

There's no magic bullet that will automatically reverse a sedentary lifestyle. Only you can do it by making exercise a daily part of your life.

Believe it or not, the *biggest* complaints I've had were from individuals who were afraid they were losing too much weight! When you get down near your ideal weight, your weight loss will stabilize and your appearance will be transformed. People may call you "skinny" only because we're used to seeing fat people as the norm. If you want to see someone at his ideal weight, take a look at Kevin Costner in the film "No Way Out." He looks terrific and that's how you can look too, no matter what your age.

Visualizing Your Weight Loss Goal

There is a very simple, yet powerful, trick you can employ that will keep you on the RAVE Diet and enable you to resist temptation. What you should do is close your eyes and visualize what you will look like when you achieve your weight loss goal. Picture yourself running and playing, picture what you will look like in your new clothes, at social occasions and in every different situation you can imagine in your new lifestyle. In addition, visualize everything that you *associate* with your new lifestyle – a new attitude, confidence, new friends and so forth. No doubt, it is a very happy sight.

Spend a few minutes running these visualizations through your mind, then lock in the images. Do this frequently. You simply can't do it too often.

Every time you feel a craving for a food that is off the RAVE Diet, take a deep breath, close your eyes and run those images through your mind.

At the same time, imagine you have to make a journey in order to reach your new lifestyle. You have to walk a long way in order to get to your destination. Picture the food you want to eat as representing an obstacle to reaching your new lifestyle. Picture that food as a river you have to swim, a mountain you have to climb – or simply the most difficult obstacle you can imagine. That food you crave so deeply – that piece of chocolate or cheese – represents a setback that will keep you from reaching the lifestyle you want so badly. Each bite is going to set you back in your journey and make reaching your goal all the more difficult.

Some people make "vision boards" where they cut out pictures from magazines and newspapers and paste them onto a board. It ends up as a collage of images representing what their lifestyle goals are. After they have finished their collage, they hang it up in a place so they will see it every single day to remind them of what they are striving for.

There are an infinite number of variations to this theme. It's simply asserting mind over body in order to get you where you want your body to be. Always keep the positive images in your head. They will steer you in the right direction and keep you moving forward toward your new weight goal and lifestyle.

The RAVE Diet For Kids

The RAVE Diet is excellent for children. The questions and answers parents may have are much too extensive to be covered here and deserve special treatment, so a few references are provided, below.

If you are an expectant mother, breast-feeding is probably the most important single thing you can do for your child. When we are born, our immune systems are weak. Mother's milk gives us the very first boost to our immune system.

Do not feed your child formulas. Breast fed babies are far healthier than formula-fed babies and *only mother's milk has immune strengthening nutrients.* And never, ever feed your child milk from any animal. Mother's milk is species-specific. Nature simply did not design animal milk for humans. Cows milk is designed for baby calves, not humans. The only milk humans are designed to drink is human mother's milk – and then only as a baby.

Here are a few references that will answer your questions.

Books
Healthy Eating For Life For Children, Physicians Committee for Responsible Medicine
Raising Vegetarian Children, Joanne Stepaniak, Vesanto Melina

Web Sites
Vegetarian Baby and Child
    http://www.vegetarianbaby.com/
Articles on Vegetarian Parenting
    http://www.vegsource.com/parent/
Veg Family
    http://www.vegfamily.com/

What To Expect

I spent the last week eating no snacky stuff. I packed two lunches with me to work each day. When I got hungry in the afternoon, I reheated the second lunch and ate that. And I lost 2 pounds! <u>I am really surprised that I can feel full and eat so much food and still lose weight</u>. It's a strange feeling. I really didn't try cutting back on portions or doing anything "diety." My goal was simply to get through each afternoon without eating junk food. So I just took each day one at a time and ate rice, beans, vegetables, and fruits and ate enough to feel full. Thank you for your support and amazing film. Talk about life-changing. Best to you always, Chris (letter to the author)

If I feel any better, I will have to consider additional surgery – a vasectomy! – Everett Ramsay, after leaving the Pritikin Center

Everyone is different and people will react somewhat differently to any new diet they adopt. You'll find you are eating far more food than you ever have in your life – and still losing weight. This is very different than typical dieting plans where you have to restrict portions in order to reduce caloric intake.

Here are just some of the possible changes you might experience when adopting the RAVE Diet.

Baseline Measurements: Eating habits can vary considerably even within the RAVE Diet guidelines, which is one of its strengths in that it can accommodate specialized diets within its overall boundaries. If you have trouble meeting the Baseline Measurement goals, e.g., your triglycerides are too high, always increase your consumption of low-fat vegetables and decrease your consumption of starchy vegetables, fruits and whole grains. In other words, aim toward the middle of the RAVE Diet food pyramid and make *low-fat vegetables* the center of your diet. In short, go for the greens – particularly leafy green vegetables – and cut back on the grains. Try that for a month and your results will improve dramatically.

Cravings: Some people experience cravings for some foods, particularly sweets, chocolate and cheese. Hard as this may be to believe, these are withdrawal symptoms and not totally uncommon when switching to the RAVE Diet. Such foods are actually addictive and food manufacturers have invested heavily in juggling ingredients to make foods as addictive as possible.[21] The problem is that we've lost our taste for real food because most food we eat today is smothered with salt, fat, sweets and chemicals. As a result, your taste buds are currently "warped." It normally takes about three weeks for tastes to change. If you stick with the RAVE Diet, your cravings for the "highs" of sugar, fat and salt will go away as your taste buds return to normal boundaries. If you don't think you can resist these cravings, think of substitutes, such as soy ice cream instead of regular ice cream. (See *Substitution Guide.*) And remember to use the visualization techniques described above to resist temptation. (See *Visualizing Your Weight Loss Goal.*)

Hunger In-Between Meals: Some people get hungry before lunch, others in mid-afternoon, depending on the meal beforehand. This happens most often with people who are trying to lose weight because they will cut back on portions. This is a mistake on the RAVE Diet because all the foods are low calorie to begin with. Some people will eat only fruit for breakfast and get hungry before noon. Add whole grain products to your breakfast, such as oatmeal, and whole wheat bread. (By the way, oatmeal is *the* most filling breakfast food.)[22] If you eat salads for lunch, make it a meal salad (think big!) and add a handful of beans. Or have a baked potato with it or another side dish. If you're at work, bring your own food in plastic containers and make sure you have enough to snack on if you need to. (See *Rules for Meal Preparations – Fast Food: Meals In Minutes.*) At dinner, use brown rice or potatoes to fill you up. Don't be afraid to eat because you'll probably consume a larger quantity of food on the RAVE Diet than you did previously – until your body adjusts. The quantity is not as important as the type of foods you're eating. Remember, this is a long-term diet and it's much better to lose the pounds slowly and comfortably because you're establishing new eating habits for the rest of your life. The hunger, in-between meals, is usually the result of consuming fewer calories – which is, after all, the point of this diet. Your body has to adjust to the caloric decline slowly, so *increase* the portion size at first so you don't get hungry later.

Constipation Cured: A good bowel movement is one of the most under-appreciated aspects of American life. With the RAVE Diet, your constipation will be cured and, for most, this will be the biggest immediate change. You'll not only experience bowel movements like you've never had them before, you'll also be getting rid of toxic substances in your body on a regular basis. And if you're accustomed to reading the newspaper while sitting on the toilet, that pastime will be history because you won't have time! Nor, will you experience the straining you used to put up with (which can result in varicose veins). Some people will find they have two to three bowel movements a day (one after every meal). Far from being abnormal, this is actually the ideal. Parenthetically, constipation (and the accompanying straining) is a common side effect on "low-carb" diets, such as the Atkins, Zone and South Beach diets. It's not surprising that profits of laxative makers skyrocket when low-carb diets are the craze.[23] Our intent is to put these businesses out of business because once you've adopted the RAVE Diet, you'll never have to take a laxative again.

Detoxification: What you will be doing on this diet is a natural form of detoxification. The high fiber content of the diet will bind with many toxins in your system (e.g., mercury) and take them out of your system the same way fiber binds with cholesterol and removes it from your system. A very small percentage of individuals, may feel a lack of energy or fatigue. This is the result of the body detoxifying itself. People who quit smoking often experience exactly the same feelings. Stick with it! This will pass as your body gets rid of toxins and adjusts to this new way of eating. Your energy will return and return at a much higher level than before. Other people have experienced headaches. This is similar to withdrawal from caffeine. Again, stick with it. This is a classic sign of detoxification and the headaches will go away.

Initial Gas: Due to the high fiber content of the RAVE Diet, you may experience more flatulence than normal. As your body transitions to the RAVE Diet, however, that problem will go away and you won't have any more gas than you did on your old diet. A side benefit: the gas from eating plant foods is nowhere near as smelly as the gas you get from eating animal foods (scientific fact). You'll also find that not only your breath, but also your body odor is much sweeter smelling. Parenthetically, refined plant products, such as refined soy products cause more gas than whole, natural plant foods.

Not Eating Animal Food: Some will, no doubt, experience anxiety because they think they're going to miss out on an essential nutrient by not eating animal foods. (See *Notes – Protein*.) This is a measure of the brainwashing we have all experienced, not only from the meat and dairy industries, but also from our own government, doctors and dieticians. Trust me, only good health will result. This is, after all, the way humans have been eating for millions of years. A neighbor of mine told me that he couldn't sleep without having a slab of steak or chicken before he went to bed. He was clinically obese and still is. *You* won't have any problems sleeping on this diet. In fact, I wish I had a dime for everyone who told me how good he or she felt by *not* eating animals. You will too and it just may help you sleep more soundly.

Pleasure Traps: We're living in a sea of food advertisements which constantly tell us it's "Ok" to eat bad foods. During holidays, in particular, your friends will encourage you to eat bad foods and it's difficult to resist these temptations. This is the "Pleasure Trap," and often results in backsliding and getting away from the RAVE Diet altogether. Once you do that, the weight will return and you'll be back where you started. Simply stated, the Pleasure Trap means you will be caught in a trap of immediate pleasure, which undermines the long-term goals you have set for yourself. You'll be sacrificing long-term pleasures (being slim and the lifestyle that goes with that) for the short-term pleasures of high sugar, salt and fatty foods. What to do if you fall off the wagon? The first thing I'd suggest is that you get some blood work done to see how out of whack your measurements are against the *Baseline Measurements* spelled out in this book. That should provide some incentive to get off the animal or refined foods. If you find yourself caught in the Pleasure Trap, here is what I would suggest: Get off the animal and refined foods completely for at least three weeks. The process of withdrawal is not all that different than cigarettes. It takes about three weeks to change your taste buds – roughly the same amount of time it takes for a smoker to really feel he or she is over the nicotine hump. And just as cigarettes will always be a lure to a smoker, so too will animal and refined foods to someone who was once addicted to them. Stay away from these foods for at least three weeks and the cravings should come under control, if they're not gone altogether. Find substitutes in herbs, spices and sauces. As your taste buds get used to these flavors, you will come to prefer them. Get smart and follow the RAVE admonition "No Exceptions" – and stick with it. The long-term rewards are far too great to sacrifice for short-term pleasures that will only wind up on your belly and butt.

Carbophobia Conquered: You'll be able to enjoy carbohydrates of all varieties – so long as they are made from *whole,* natural foods. The carbohydrates you should rightly be afraid of are from refined foods. One misconception about high carbohydrate diets is that they raise triglycerides (blood fats). This is a common misconception based on tests done with *refined* or simple carbohydrates, which will raise triglycerides. If you're eating only *complex* carbs found in natural foods, triglyceride levels will not go up. In fact, the best way to dramatically reduce triglycerides is to follow the full RAVE Diet – the combination of complex carbohydrates and exercise will reduce triglycerides better than any other approach. (In a few people, who are sensitive, any form of fruit will raise triglycerides because the primary sugar is fructose, a simple sugar.) There is so much confusion about carbohydrates, it would take a book to sort them out. Instead, just remember the refined carbohydrates are the bad guys, while whole food carbs are the good guys.

Sniping Remarks From Uninformed "Friends": In social occasions, I normally do not bring up diet, but if you are eating, it's often inevitable. A remark often heard by people is that low-fat diets are dangerous. This is how strange our attitudes toward food are. The fact we consider a diet that actually reverses heart disease to be dangerous is nothing short of outrageous! Yet the diet your friends are on – which causes heart disease – is considered to be safe. People who call low-fat diets dangerous are, in fact, eating the most dangerous diet in the world, which kills half the population with cardiovascular disease – and even more through related diseases. People eating RAVE-like diets are in excellent health throughout the world and are not killed off with cardiovascular disease, our common cancers, diabetes and our other major diseases. A low-fat diet is the healthiest – and safest – diet in the world. There are billions who can attest to that. Unfortunately, very few are Americans and I'm sure very few are your friends.

Better Skin: Because you are clearing out your blood vessels, the blood flow carrying oxygen and nutrients throughout your body will be greatly enhanced and will produce some amazing results. Some people have even had "liver" or "sun spots" disappear from their skin when they adopted this diet. Other people have told me that if they don't consume oils, their skin will dry out. This is a misconception, and a greasy one. Most people have dry skin because they are dehydrated due to their diet. Restrict your consumption of diuretics, which take more fluid out of your body than they bring in – and increase your consumption of plain water and plant foods (which contain high amounts of water). Doing this will keep your skin moist and fresh and do more for your wrinkles than any skin cream on the market. The most common diuretics are coffee, tea and similar stimulants, as well as alcohol.

Better Senses: Largely as a result of opening up your blood vessels, there will be a range of changes you will notice over time, including better hearing, eyesight, taste, smell and touch.

Cheaper Grocery Bill: Many complain about the higher cost of organic foods, but overall, you will save money on groceries. One estimate, made some years ago, pegged the savings at around $1,400 a year. If fruits and vegetables are expensive in your area, use frozen fruits and vegetables instead of fresh. Frozen produce is often packed at the peak of freshness and will also taste better than out-of-season produce. The big savings with the RAVE Diet is not on groceries, however, but current and future health care and medication costs.

Blaming the Diet? Don't blame this diet for coincidental things that may happen to you either physically or mentally. I've heard everything from a man's hair turning gray, to someone's depression blamed on this diet. Don't worry. Your nails, hair and everything else will continue to grow just fine, if not better than ever. The only thing you may experience are anxiety attacks because you think you're not getting enough protein or calcium, especially after you watch the next food advertisement on television. You'll get over it. A year after adopting this diet, you'll have a completely different view of food that will make your doctor smile at your next checkup.

Food Sensitivities/Allergies: In rare cases, the increase in consumption of whole plant foods may trigger food sensitivities or food allergies with certain foods simply because you are eating more of them. In these cases, it is a matter of finding out which foods are triggers and eliminating them from your diet or cutting back on them. For specific information on a variety of "trigger" foods, get a copy of *Foods That Fight Pain, Neal Barnard, M.D.*

If you are already in good health, the changes will be subtle and you will find you will be in even better health over the long-term. If you have an eating-related disease, such as heart disease, the changes can be dramatic, such as those described by Dr. Neal Pinckney in the *Eating* film. Within just two weeks, he cleared up severe angina and the pain was completely gone in just one month. After just seven months, he completed an eight-mile marathon run. And he did this simply by adopting the RAVE Diet.

If you have any one of a myriad of eating-related diseases, these can be treated and cured with diet. Check our web site (www.RaveDiet.com) for a list of health providers who treat diseases naturally using diet.

Sex, Booze, Rock 'n Roll

"I wouldn't recommend sex, drugs or insanity for everyone, but they've always worked for me." – Hunter S. Thompson

The Sex Diet

Now that I have your attention, let me explain that the Sex Diet is very simple and easy to follow. Instead of having a meal, you simply have sex. Anyone who's tried this will tell you it's a great way to lose weight. It not only reduces caloric intake, but burns off those extra calories as well. Naturally, I tried this for a while and must say I had a great time and lost weight, but unfortunately, it can't go on forever. There are, however, many ways in which the RAVE Diet can make your sex life explosive without ever skipping a single meal.

The two key aspects of the RAVE Diet that will revitalize your sex life is 1) by opening up your arteries – yes the ones supplying blood to your genital areas (this goes for both male and female) – and 2) with exercise.

By eliminating animal products and refined foods from your diet, you won't become impotent due to damage caused to the arteries supplying blood to the penis.[1] Men with high cholesterol levels are more likely to experience erectile dysfunction[2] and the high levels of environmental chemicals concentrated in meat[3] wreak havoc on testosterone levels, resulting in decreased ejaculate volume, lower sperm counts, poor sperm motility and infertility.[4]

It's ironic that Viagra was originally developed to treat the pain caused by angina, a condition brought on by the same cause as impotence – a high-fat and cholesterol-laden diet. Viagra, of course, did not help angina, but test subjects found much to their delight – it solved another problem they were experiencing as a result of their diets.

The second element of the RAVE Diet – exercise – will add years to your sex life, improve your self-image, mental clarity, reduce stress, rev up your sex drive – no matter what your age – and will result in better erections.[5]

By opening up your arteries and getting plenty of exercise, you'll find your sex life rising like a Phoenix from the ashes, so to speak. And once that happens, there are a host of benefits from having frequent sex. Here are just a few:

- Improved sense of smell (production of the hormone prolactin surges)
- Reduced risk of heart disease (sex reduces risk of heart attack or stroke)
- Weight loss (hey, if nothing else, it's exercise)
- Reduced depression (who wouldn't be happy after sex?)
- Pain relief (levels of the hormone oxytocin surge)
- Less frequent colds and flu (strengthens the immune system)
- Better bladder control (similar to Kegel exercises)

- Better teeth (seminal plasma contains minerals shown to reduce tooth decay…)
- A happier prostate (lower chance of prostate cancer with more sex)

Insofar as booze is concerned, one of the best things you can do to lose weight is to cut it out because alcohol is nothing but empty calories. Ok, ok. I know it does other things for you besides pack on the pounds. If you're going to drink, drink wine and drink only *before* you have sex.

If you're looking for a truly out-of-this-world sexual experience, there is one absolute best time to drink: *after* you exercise and *before* you have sex because both will get you in the mood. (Trust me, I've done a little study on this.) The combination of exercise and a little booze will do wonders for your sex life, so get exercising, jump into bed and live a little!

And insofar as rock 'n roll goes, well, in this context, no further comment is necessary…

The Pursuit of Happiness

"The goal in life is to die young – as late as possible." – Ashley Montagu

The relationship between diet and disease is as old as the Bible. You may recall the biblical story of Daniel. After suffering through ill health, Daniel made a radical proposal to take the servants off their rich, royal diet and put them on a diet of vegetables and water. In only ten days, the servants looked healthier and better nourished than any of the other men who had eaten the rich, royal foods.

You don't have to eat just vegetables and water to achieve the health of Daniel's servants and the remainder of this book shows you how to eat a wide variety of delicious foods that will do wonders for your health and well-being.

The RAVE Diet is an elegantly simple solution to the health problems that are tearing apart the very fabric of our lives. Instead of complicated drugs and surgery, diet can replace them all and bring simplicity to your health and balance to your life.

Our bodies are incredibly smart. We have over 60 *trillion* cells intricately and automatically coordinating their activities so we can go on with our lives without having to worry about our health. But when we introduce bad foods to our bodies, we start to destroy this finely tuned masterpiece, balance is lost and the preconditions for disease set in. Our bodies scramble to recover and regain balance, but so long as bad food keeps coming in, our bodies will remain out of balance and, over time, disease will set in. Our bodies are extremely forgiving of bad habits – but only up to a point – and when our bodies have had enough, people will get a wake up call like they've never had before.

What most Americans – and medical experts – consider to be a balanced diet today is radically tipped toward heart disease, cancer, diabetes, obesity and all the other health problems we are now experiencing. One of the favorite lines of doctors is that "…as we age, we tend to get…." But this is nonsense. Do you think a large belly is the result of aging? A big butt? Do you think osteoporosis automatically comes with age? Arthritis? Heart disease? Our common cancers? We get these diseases as we age because of a lifetime of bad eating habits, coupled with a sedentary lifestyle.

How many days do you have in your life? If you live to 75, you have about 27,000 days of living on this earth. I used to think 27,000 days was a lot. I also used to think $27,000 was a lot – until I was nearly out of money. Then those last few precious dollars seemed like a fortune. It works the same way with life.

Remember how long it was between the time you were 10 and 20? Imagine adding the same number of high quality years to the end of your life by just changing your eating habits and getting a modest amount of exercise.

The RAVE Diet is not about adding years to your life so much as it's about raising the *quality* of your life by avoiding diseases and making the last third of your life just as vigorous as the first third.

For me, the measure of a good life is how much happiness you get out of it. To me, the pursuit of happiness is really about owning *less* stuff, while gaining *more* purpose in life. "Stuff" brings temporary pleasure. Purpose brings lasting pleasure. People who look outside of themselves for happiness by pursuing "stuff" are always disappointed because long-term happiness inevitably springs from within. The same can be said for your health. Health *always* comes before wealth and you must remind yourself of that when setting your priorities.

Depression is the consequence of seeking excessive stimulation. When you strive to experience extreme "highs," you will inevitably end up depressed when the exhilaration from those highs wears off. Always seek to find your middle ground. Balance your life. Seek purpose in it and go for more than just the temporary, immediate highs life has to offer.

For every immediate pleasure you give up, you gain something more valuable and lasting. The smoker or alcoholic who gives up their destructive habits gain much more than they lose. You will gain much more by giving up the "pleasure traps" of animal and refined foods – without exception. I've seen people transformed by the RAVE Diet. I've seen men, who used to grill steaks on the barbeque during football games, now talking about the best way to make chopped salad. You'll feel good about yourself and what you're doing – not only for your own health, but the world we all live in.

Dare to be different. Change your life and seek long-term happiness from within by adopting a lifestyle that I guarantee will pay countless dividends throughout your entire life.

RAVE Diet Guidelines & Recipes

Reading Labels & Ingredients

Due to food industry lobbying designed to hide bad ingredients and confuse the customer, you almost have to attend night school to understand food labeling. Let's simplify it.

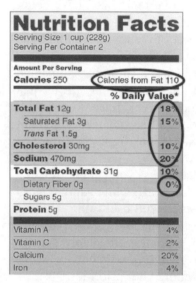

The label to the left is for macaroni and cheese (which you should never eat!) that we can use for illustration purposes. There are three circles you should focus on. The first is "Calories from Fat." Manufacturers rarely do the math for you, but this is 44 percent fat (110 / 250 = .44). Put it back on the shelf. You should ideally find products with zero fat or less than 10 percent fat.

Next are Total Fat, Saturated Fat and Cholesterol, shown as a percent of daily calories. Again, look for zeroes. You will find many choices of packaged products with these numbers at health food stores.

After cholesterol is sodium. This is a big item in packaged products because it's used as a preservative and percentages will vary all over the place. The lower, the better.

Look closely at the serving size because the trend is to make serving sizes smaller in order to disguise just how bad a product really is. Many candy bars, for example, are now two servings!

The last circle is Dietary Fiber, which is of great importance. In this case, the larger the number, the better.

A Simple Rule of Thumb About Fat

If you are trying to maintain a diet at 10 percent fat (which reverses heart disease), anything more than 1 gram of fat per 100 calories is higher than you want. If you are trying to prevent heart disease and do not have any risk factors, then 2 grams of fat per 100 calories is your maximum for a 20 percent fat diet.

Due to food industry lobbying, a product can be labeled "fat free" and it can list zero grams of fat, if the fat content is less than 0.5 grams of fat. This is how foods can have oil or high-fat ingredients listed in their Nutrition Facts label, yet contain "zero" fat. Fat free means less than 0.5 grams of fat per serving. Low fat means less than 3 grams of fat per serving.

When food manufacturers moved to fat free packaged goods, what they did in many products was add more sugar and simple (refined) carbohydrates to replace the fat, so instead of *eating* fat, you're quickly *creating* fat inside your body.

Ingredients

On ingredients lists, the top three ingredients to look for are:

Whole, sprouted wheat or organic rolled oats should be the first ingredient in any grain product, such as bread or cereal.

Hydrogenated oils – never purchase a product that contains the word "hydrogenated" anywhere in the ingredients.

Sugar, high fructose or fructose should never be the first, second or third ingredient. In fact, the best products have none of these ingredients.

Also, never purchase anything with the word "instant" on it, such as instant oatmeal.

There will also be a list of ingredients on the package with names most of us could never pronounce. Here is a *short* list of ingredients you should avoid:

all oils, especially hydrogenated oils
(partially, fully or whatever)
alum (as in aluminum)
artificial colorings (any food dye)
calcium propionate
carrageenan (some are sensitive to this)
caseinogen
casein
collagen
diglycerides and monoglycerides
EDTA
gelatin
glycerin/glycerides
hydrolyzed vegetable protein
hydrolyzed oat flour
hydrolyzed plant protein
hydrolysates
hydrogenated vegetable oils
lactic acid

lactose
lactulose
lard
monodiglycerides
monoglycerides
monosodium glutamate (MSG)
mycoprotein
palmitate
polysorbates
rennet
rennin
sodium caseinate
sodium nitrite
sugar (any form of sugar)
sulfites
tahini
vegetable oils, especially hydrogenated
oils (partially, fully or whatever)
whey

A comprehensive list of ingredients would require a book, so in general, if you can't pronounce it, don't put it in your mouth. When in doubt, your best bet is to put the product back on the shelf and go for natural products that come in their natural packages.

Sticky Labels on Fruit

Ever noticed those little "brand" stickers on fruit? They tell you how the product was grown or "created."

There's a number on the label known as the "price look up" or PLU code that speeds up the check out process. But there's more to the PLU than just price.

For conventionally grown fruit, the PLU code consists of 4 numbers.

Genetically engineered fruit has a 5-number PLU, beginning with 8.

Organically grown fruit has a 5-number PLU, beginning with 9.

Using this system for an apple, the numbering would look like this:

```
 4011 - conventional grown apple
84011 - genetically engineered apple
94011 - organically grown apple
```

Organic Labeling

100 Percent Organic: Must contain only organically produced ingredients.

Organic: Defined by the USDA as containing 95 percent of organic ingredients.

Made With Organic: Must contain at least 70 percent organic ingredients. These foods cannot bear the USDA organic seal.

Some Organic Ingredients: Products with less than 70 percent organic ingredients are only allowed to list the organic items in the ingredient panel on the side of the package. These also cannot display the USDA organic seal.

Don't confuse the label "organic" with the label "natural." Natural is a loose term generally meaning that no artificial ingredients were added in processing and has nothing to do with how the product was grown or raised.

What Organic Means

Organic standards require that the land used to grow organic food go through a three year "transition period" to make sure the crops are free of synthetic pesticides and synthetic fertilizers.

All organic agriculture prohibits the use of synthetic pesticides and fertilizers, irradiation and sewage sludge. In addition, no genetically modified organisms can be contained in anything labeled organic.

Organic standards specify that animals may only be fed plant diets, with no animal by-products, which eliminates the risk of certain diseases, such as mad cow disease.

Organic products are also likely to taste better, be free of artificial preservatives and chemicals and not contain any genetically modified organisms.

Rules for Meal Preparation

One of the beautiful things about the RAVE Diet is its simplicity. There are no complicated formulas or calories to count so you're eating like a human being, not a target of food advertisers.

Here we present a simple meal preparation formula that will provide you with filling meals, made with a wide variety of nutritious foods, which will keep you happy and healthy – and feeling full on fewer calories.

The RAVE Diet food pyramid, shown below, depicts the types of foods you can eat and the proportions. This is a general food pyramid designed to get you started. There are a multitude of different specific diets within the RAVE Diet pyramid that you can follow, depending on your food preferences and dietary goals. For example, some advocate eliminating or greatly reducing grain products. Others advocate making vegetables the bottom rung of the pyramid. The RAVE Diet can accommodate these different emphases, but for most people, the pyramid below will satisfy their dietary goals.

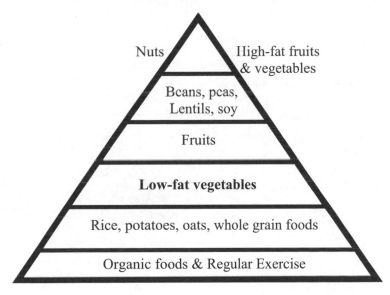

Layering

There is a "layering" logic that conforms to the food pyramid. At the bottom is what I call "filler" foods, that is, rice, potatoes and other whole grain foods such as whole grain pasta, barley, bulgur, corn and oats. You will typically eat more of these foods than any other and they will serve the purpose of filling you up and making you feel satisfied. These are the lowest fat and most satisfying foods in existence. Potatoes are 1 percent fat, brown rice is 6 percent fat, wild rice is 3 percent fat, barley and bulgur are both 3 percent fat. All of the whole-wheat grains are under 10 percent fat. Compare that with typical (non-fried) servings of rib steak (78%), chicken (54%), turkey (42%) or Atlantic salmon (54%), and you can see where we're going with this.

The next layer will be low-fat fresh (or frozen) vegetables. You can actually increase your proportions of these and decrease your proportion of the filler foods. In fact, you can eat an unlimited quantity of low-fat vegetables and eliminate filler foods altogether. It just depends on your taste preferences.

Fresh (or frozen) fruits are the next layer. For breakfast, these are great and they're wonderful for desserts as well in the afternoon or evening.

Beans, peas, lentils, and soy foods are the next layer, followed by nuts and high-fat fruits and vegetables, such as avocados and olives.

In general, the fat to fiber ratio increases as you go up the pyramid, which accounts for the declining proportions. In other words, the higher fat foods are found at the top of the pyramid.

Here are a few simple examples of layering:

Breakfast
    Condiments
    Nuts
    Unsweetened juice/smoothie
    Fruits
    Oatmeal & breads

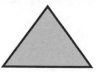

Lunch (salad)
    Seasonings/sauces
    Avocado
    Beans
    Low-fat vegetables
    Green leafy salad vegetables

Dinner
    Seasonings/sauces
    Beans/peas
    Low-fat vegetables
    Rice/potatoes/bulgur, etc.

There are an infinite number of variations on the layering theme and, in this sense, there are no rules. You can tailor the diet to meet your specific tastes and dietary goals. Use the *Mix-Ins/Side Dishes* recipes to mix in your favorite foods with filler foods. The sample recipes contained in this book are just that –

samples – because you will discover what you like and how you like to prepare your food on your own. Don't be afraid to substitute recipe ingredients, add vegetables to recipes or change them around. Everyone has their favorite plant foods and you will be able to fit them into the rules very simply. And don't worry about making a mistake. Too much ginger in a recipe, for example, can be easily covered up by adding other spices.

As a convenience, the only appliance you may wish to consider purchasing is a rice cooker that cooks brown rice. Get the type that will turn off the cooker and keep the rice warm, if you happen to be away. Crock-pots, pressure cookers and other appliances are also nice additions.

Cooking Without Oil

When sautéing, use about twice as much water (or other oil substitute) as you would oil – and add as necessary. This will vary, depending on what you are sautéing, but with a little experience you will get the hang of it. And remember, you can always add more oil substitute if needed. You'll soon discover you don't need even a drop of oil to make your food delicious – and it won't have that greasy taste, but the nice, natural taste of whole foods.

Cook on low or medium heat to avoid the water (or oil substitute) evaporating too quickly. This will take a little longer than a high-heat oil-based sauté, but it's worth the wait because you're not sending the oil to your hips – or waist – and the food tastes so much cleaner! If you need to brown something, just turn up the heat to high at the end of the cooking, stir the food, and the water will evaporate quickly. Believe it or not, you can make delicious browned home fries using just water! The following are oil substitutes for sautéing and baking:

Oil Substitutes for

Sautéing: water, apple juice, sherry, vegetable stock, wine, vinegars

Baking: any pureed fruit, e.g., applesauce, apple butter, pureed bananas, pureed prunes (Use non-stick pans.)

With baked goods, use the same amount of substitute, as you would oil. Many use baby food purees as a convenient substitute. Baby food purees work best if the puree is diluted with a little water.

Pressure Cooker Note: If you use a pressure cooker, many recipes call for added oil to prevent foaming, particularly for beans. You can eliminate the oil by putting a strip of kombu (dried seaweed available at health food stores), which will eliminate the foaming. Just remember to remove the kombu before you serve the dish. Newer pressure cookers do not have a problem with foaming.

Making Plain Foods Taste Fabulous

To most people, natural whole foods taste rather "plain," at least until your taste buds adjust and you come to enjoy the wide varieties of tastes inherent in whole, natural foods. The easiest and most delicious way to make these foods more exciting is to add seasonings and sauces.

I'm often asked, "How do you liven up your food?" It's easy with seasonings and sauces because there are hundreds you can choose from. What follows is a short list to get you started. The flavors of most whole plant foods are very subtle and they will easily take on whatever seasonings or sauces you care to use. Just be careful with commercial seasonings or custom mixes to make sure there is no added salt in them. You should avoid all salt seasonings, except for salt substitutes, such as Mrs. Dash or Salt Free Spike.

And don't by shy when you're dining out. If you eat a food that tastes delicious, ask the chef what seasonings he used with it.

Here is a short list of some of my favorite commercial seasonings:

Coriander
Cumin
Curry
Fajita Seasoning
Hungarian Hot Paprika
Italian Seasoning
Mint
Mustard
Oregano Leaf

Flavorings

The following lists various foods and the seasonings that are typically used with them. We then give a short list of seasonings, sauces, salad dressings, condiments and sweeteners. Of course, if you have a favorite seasoning, it can go with practically anything – because it's *your* favorite.

Seasonings, Sauces, Salad Dressings, Condiments & Sweeteners

Seasonings

Beans
   Avocado, cayenne, chili, cumin, epazote, Mexican oregano, parsley, pepper, savory, sage, thyme
Breads
   Anise, basil, cardamom, cinnamon, coriander, cumin, dill, garlic, lemon peel, orange peel, poppy, seeds, saffron, thyme, rosemary
Fruits
   Anise, black pepper, cardamom, cinnamon, coriander, cumin, ginger, mint
Potatoes, rice
   Basil, coriander, dill, oregano, paprika, parsley, poppy seeds, rosemary, thyme
Salads & Dressings
   Basil, caraway, celery seed, fennel, garlic, ginger, lemon peel, mint, mustard, oregano, paprika, parsley, rosemary, thyme
Soups
   Basil, bay, black pepper, chives, chili, cilantro, cumin, dill, fennel, garlic, paprika, parsley, rosemary, thyme
Sweets
   Anise, cardamom, cinnamon, cloves, fennel, ginger, lemon peel, nutmeg, orange peel, rosemary, saffron
Vegetables
   Chili, cumin, mustard, curry powder, garam masala, ginger, dill, cilantro, black pepper, garlic, mint, paprika, thyme, turmeric

Here is a description of some of the more common spices and their typical uses.

Allspice: Pungent, spicy, like a mix of nutmeg, cloves and cinnamon. Virtually anything, from salads to desserts.
Anise: Sweet, similar to licorice. Flavoring in cookies, candies and pastries.
Basil: Pungent, somewhat sweet. Tomato dishes, salads, cooked vegetables.
Bay leaves: Bitter, pungent. Soups, stews, tomato sauces. Remove leaf before serving
Black pepper: Pungent, somewhat hot. Virtually anything.
Borage: Mild. Garnish or in salads or in herbal tea mixtures.
Capers: Pungent. In sauces, as a garnish.
Caraway seeds: Sweet, nutty. Cookies and cakes, apple sauce, vinegars.
Cardamom: Sweet, pungent, fragrant, strong taste. Stews, curries.
Cayenne pepper: Very hot. In anything you want to taste hot.
Celery seed: Pungent celery flavor. Flavoring in tomato juice, sauces and soups.

Chervil: Similar to parsley. Flavoring in soups, casseroles, salads.

Chile powder: Spicy, hot. In chili or other spicy dishes.

Chives: Sharp, onion or garlic flavor. Fresh; frozen if fresh not available Garnish, blended with soft cheeses, added to salads

Cilantro: Spicy, sweet or hot. Common ingredient in Mexican salsas.

Cinnamon: Sweet, fragrant. Sweet dishes, curries and stews.

Cloves: Sweet or bittersweet. Sweet dishes or as a contrast in stews and curries.

Coriander: Warm, aromatic. Cakes, cookies, breads, curries.

Cumin: Peppery, aromatic. Soups, stews, sauces.

Curry powder: Hot. Curries.

Dill: Bittersweet, cool. Potatoes, meats, breads, salads, sauces, curries.

Fennel: Similar to anise, but sweeter, lighter, warm. Salads, soups, stews.

Fenugreek: Sweet, somewhat like burnt sugar. Pastries, beverages, syrups.

Garlic: Pungent, onion-like. Roasted, or flavoring for pasta sauces. Good in any dish meal.

Ginger: Mix of pepper and sweetness. Cakes, breads, cookies, Asian dishes.

Green peppercorns: Mild, slightly sweet. Vinegars, in sauces.

Horseradish: Sharp, similar to mustard. As condiment.

Lovage: Similar to celery, but stronger. Use as you would celery, in soups, stews, salads.

Mace: Similar to nutmeg, but stronger. Custards, spice cakes, fruit desserts.

Marjoram: Delicate taste. Soups, stews, marinades.

Mint: Sweet, aromatic, cooling. Salads, vegetables.

Mustard, brown: Sharp, pungent, hotter than yellow mustard. Use as condiment.

Mustard, yellow: Hot, tangy, less of a bite than brown mustard. Use as a condiment.

Nutmeg: Warm, spicy, sweet. Cakes, cookies, sweet potatoes.

Oregano: Delicate taste. Pasta dishes, chili, vegetables, soups.

Paprika: Sweet, warm. Soups, potato salad.

Parsley: Mildly peppery. Garnish in sauces, soups and salads.

Poppy seed: Nutty, aromatic. Muffins, cakes, salad dressings.

Rosemary: Aromatic. Sauces, vegetables.

Saffron: Pungent, aromatic, fragrant. Rice, stews, curries.

Sage: Musty, slightly bitter. Stews, vegetables.

Sesame seed: Nutty. Breads, salad dressings.

Star Anise: Very similar to anise. Flavoring in cookies, candies and pastries.

Summer savory: Cross between thyme and mint, milder than winter savory. Soups, bean dishes.

Tarragon: Sweet, pungent. Vegetables.

Thyme: Minty, lemony. Soups, salads, cooked vegetables.

Turmeric: Pungent, somewhat bitter, warm. Curries. Primary ingredient in yellow commercial mustard.

Vanilla: Sweet, aromatic, fragrant. Desserts.
White pepper: Similar to black peppercorn, milder. As a condiment.
Winter savory: Combination of thyme and mint. Soups, bean dishes, vegetables.

Sauces

You can, of course, make your own sauces, but there are hundreds of commercial brands that are available and more convenient to use. Experiment and mix your favorite sauces together to create a new sauce just for you. Here are just a few of my favorites:

A1 Steak sauce
Barbeque sauce
Black bean sauce
Chipotle sauce
Cranberry sauce
Dijon Mustard
Hoisin sauce
Hot pepper sauce
Plum sauce
Salsa
Tamari (soy sauce - low-sodium, or Bragg Liquid Aminos if sensitive to soy)
Tabasco sauce
Teriyaki sauce (low-sodium)
Tomato sauce
Tomato ketchup
Vegetarian Worcestershire sauce

Note: Ingredients will vary for a particular sauce, depending on who makes it, so inspect the label closely before purchasing it.

A Better Tomato (Pasta) Sauce

There are very few prepared pasta sauces that do not contain oil and are low in sodium. The best way is to simply make your own – and it's incredibly easy.

All you have to do is purchase cans (or jars) of tomato sauce and canned or fresh cut tomatoes. (Note: there should not be oil or sodium added).

Just chop up some of your favorite vegetables (or throw them in a food processor), mix them into the tomato sauce with the tomatoes and add your favorite herbs or just use Italian seasoning and Voila! You have your own pasta sauce.

You can flavor the sauce however you want. I usually add some Tabasco sauce or horseradish to give it a little zing. Or feel free to add any other spices, herbs or sauces for flavor. Once you get it down, you'll have a pasta sauce that tastes the way you like it. I usually just buy the tomato sauce and add whatever I have on hand at the moment. As you'll discover, the taste is much cleaner than the oily stuff sold on the shelf.

Salad Dressings

Balsamic vinaigrette dressings
Other vinegar-based dressings
Salad dressings (oil-free)

Paula's No Oil Dressings
http://www.sweetadelaide.com/
(Click on Salad Dressings – No Oil, No Fat)

Cuisine Perel makes a wide range of vinegar-based dressings that are fabulous.
http://www.gourmetofoldecity.com/perelvinegars.html

Condiments

Applesauce	Mustards
Banana chips	Mushrooms
Cilantro	Olives
Corn relishes	Pickles
Ginger	Potatoes
Hummus	Salsa
Lemon juice	Sunflower seeds
Lime juice	Tomato sauce

Sweeteners

All of the sweeteners listed below, although healthier than refined sugar, should be used very sparingly, if at all. Ideally, only fresh or dried whole fruits should be used as sweeteners.

Agave nectar
Barley malt syrup
Brown rice syrup
Concentrated fruit juice syrups
Date sugar (ground, dehydrated dates)
Fresh or dried fruits

Maple sugar
Maple syrup
Molasses (black strap)
Organic unrefined cane sugar.
Organic dairy-free chocolate
Sorghum syrup
Turbinado sugar

Fast Food: Meals In Minutes

Most of us come home from work and the last thing we want to do is cook a meal. For myself, I usually open the refrigerator or pantry door and see what I have on-hand, then prepare a quick meal.

If this is you, one of the best ways to eat is to open your freezer door and "pour" out a meal using frozen vegetables. Frozen fruits and vegetables are almost as good as fresh and sometimes better (in terms of nutrients) because they're often picked and processed at their peak of ripeness, using techniques that lock in a slew of nutrients. They're also better than canned because most don't have added sodium. Any grocery store will have bags of frozen vegetables you can use.

Just pour them into a bowl, stir-fry them together or heat them up in the microwave. Add spices or stir in some tomato sauce with spices and Voila! You have a meal in minutes.

Also, baked potatoes cook fast in the micro.

What about work? Again, think frozen. Just pour some vegetables into a container and take it to work. By lunchtime, the vegetables are pretty much thawed. Pop it in the micro and you have lunch. I did this for years.

And, don't forget, you can always visit your local salad bar on the way home from work!

I usually make a big pot of rice every week. Use any "filler" food like rice or potatoes as the base and pour frozen vegetables into it. Add tomato or another sauce, stir it up and you have your lunch in minutes.

If you're on the go and like fast meals, you should set aside some time on the weekend to cook large amounts and then refrigerate or freeze it in serving sizes appropriate for your appetite. The idea is not that you eat the same meal seven days in a row, but you build a supply of various meals. This will work like magic and you'll spend far less time preparing large meals that last through the week than you would preparing separate, individual meals.

Here are a few samples. It's not the foods, as much as the technique because you can substitute any foods for a quick meal, depending on what you have in the refrigerator or pantry.

3-Step Quickie
1) Cut up assorted vegetables (or buy pre-cut) and sauté or stir-fry them in water or a vegetable broth. Cook over medium heat.

2) Stir in your favorite seasonings and sauce (e.g., tomato sauce, black bean sauce, curry, Thai sauce, etc. See *Seasonings* and *Sauces*).

3) Serve on a bed of your favorite "filler" food, like brown rice or potatoes.

Rice, Beans & Vegetables
Brown rice in the bottom of the bowl (rice usually prepared beforehand in large quantities).

When finished, add cut raw or steamed vegetables and beans. (Note: vegetables can be frozen and heated in a pan or micro-waved in the bowl.)

Mix-in any tomato or other sauce for flavoring, along with herbs and spices.

Heat in pan or microwave.

Any and All Vegetable Soup
Cut up your favorite vegetables in large quantities. Put them all in a pot full of water (large enough to handle your vegetables).

Add your favorite herbs, spices and sauces.

Cook until done. (Note that crock-pots or pressure cookers are ideal for this.)

This will last for days or longer and can stored in the refrigerator or freezer.

When ready to eat, just heat it up and serve.

Keeping Brown Rice
I usually prepare a large quantity of brown rice using a rice cooker. This is a great investment because it takes me literally two minutes to prepare the rice and when it's done, the cooker goes into automatic warmer mode so I don't have to watch over it.

Just add the brown rice and twice the amount of water, e.g., 1 cup rice = 2 cups water.

Add seasonings to taste.

Press the appropriate buttons and you're done.

Rice can be stored in the refrigerator. It will cake and stick together, but will be fine once you heat it up again in a small amount of water, either in a pan or microwave.

Substitution Guide

You can continue to enjoy many of your favorite meals by using substitutes, so don't throw away your existing cookbooks. You can adapt your recipes easily or just make the "side dishes" in your traditional cookbook, the main dishes.

There are all kinds of meat and dairy substitutes available at supermarkets, and a much wider selection at health food stores. Don't be shy about asking about a substitute at your grocery or health food store. These substitutes can be used initially as a bridge to a 100 percent, natural plant-based diet – or as an occasional treat. Their biggest benefit is they contain no cholesterol and they are generally lower in fat. But like all packaged goods, they usually have high levels of sodium. Most of these products are made from soy, which is high in fat, so go easy on them. Inspect the fat content and ingredients label closely. (See *Reading Labels & Ingredients*.)

Some people get "hooked" on processed soy products like veggie burgers or dogs and think they're eating a plant-based diet – and wonder why they're not losing weight! Many processed soy products are really "refined" foods and most of the nutrients have been lost in the refining process. Products such as seitan, tempeh, tofu, textured vegetable protein (TVP) and other refined soy products should only be eaten during the transition phase to a natural, 100 percent plant-based RAVE Diet of unrefined plant foods.

Lastly, do not expect substitutes to taste like the original. Some are very close to the original, but others will disappoint you. Our advice: don't attempt to continue your old eating habits with substitutes. The point of the RAVE Diet is to *change* your old eating habits, so use substitutes only as a bridge to a new way of eating.

Meat, Dairy & Other Substitutes

Here's a short list of substitutes for common meat, dairy and other products. If you're not familiar with many of these products, just go to your health food store and ask for help.

Butter: butter substitutes
Buttermilk: clabbered soymilk (mix 2 teaspoons white vinegar or lemon juice per cup of soymilk)
Cheese: soy or nut-based cheeses
Cottage cheese or ricotta: crumbled tofu
Cream Cheese: soy substitute
Eggs: egg replacers, crumbled or pureed tofu
Gelatin: agar-agar, arrowroot, ground nuts and seeds, gums, kudzu
Gravies: soy substitutes

Half & Half: soy substitute

Ice cream: soy/rice ice creams

Mayonnaise: soy mayonnaise

Meat, chicken or seafood stock: apple, cranberry, orange or pomegranate juice, garlic broth, miso (soybean paste) diluted with water, sherry, vegetable bouillon cubes, vegetable stock, wine, beer

Meat: potatoes, rice, beans, corn, cauliflower, seitan (from wheat), tempeh (from soy), textured vegetable protein, tofu. Everything from bacon to burgers to hot dogs, sausages, turkey and shrimp has a commercially available substitute – but go easy on them because they are refined products.

Meats, smoked: chipotle chilies, roasted vegetables, toasted nuts, smoked tofu

Milk: soymilk, nut milk, rice milk, oat milk

Oil for sautéing: apple juice, sherry, vegetable stock, wine; Balsamic vinegar

Oil in baked goods: any pureed fruit, e.g., applesauce, apple butter, pureed bananas, pureed prunes

Salad dressing: non-oil dressings, vinegar-based dressings, citrus juices

Salt: Mrs. Dash, Salt-Free Spike

Sausage: crumbled tofu seasoned with favorite spices

Sour Cream: soy sour cream

Sugar (refined): maple syrup, bananas, barley malt syrup, molasses, brown rice syrup, raw organic sugar, dried fruits, fruit juices

Whipped Cream: soy substitute

White flour (for baking): whole wheat flour, buckwheat flour, brown rice flour, oat flour, soy flour, barley, buckwheat, corn, kamut, oats, rice, rye, spelt

White sauce: pureed white beans

Yogurt: soy substitute

Recipes on the Web

The recipes contained in this book are meant to be only representative samples and a book cannot contain the wealth of possible recipes that can be made with the RAVE Diet. To that end, there are tens of thousands of recipes you can conveniently look up and search for on the Internet. Below are just a few of the web sites containing recipes for every occasion.

Just remember the rules when preparing recipes: substitute whole foods for refined foods (e.g., white pasta with whole wheat pasta) and use oil substitutes. (See *Cooking Without Oil*.)

The best and most extensive recipe archive, in my opinion, is the first one, FatFree.com.

FatFree.com
http://www.fatfree.com/
A Taste of Vitality (complete cookbook download)
http://www.vitalita.com/cookbooks.html
Abbey Levine
http://www.abbeysvegetarianrecipes.com/vegan.html
Asian Recipes
http://asiarecipe.com/
Recipe Source
http://www.recipesource.com/special-diets/vegetarian/
The Vegan Chef
http://www.veganchef.com/
VegWeb Recipes
http://vegweb.com/food/

Sample Recipes

The following presents a wide variety of recipes. Some will include "refined" products, such as non-dairy milk. These recipes are for those of you who are eating a "transition" diet. If you wish to follow the RAVE Diet, simply substitute water or your favorite fruit juice for non-dairy milk.

Breakfast

Suggestions
Avocado slices on whole wheat bread
Baked apple with raisins and cinnamon
Mixed fruits (cantaloupe, banana, peaches, pears, apples, etc.) with whole wheat bread
Oatmeal with berries and whole wheat bread
Whole grain cereal with raisins, bananas, ground flaxseed, almond, soy, rice or oat milk
Whole grain or flaxseed muffins
Whole grain muffins
Fruit smoothie
Sliced bananas with raw carob powder sprinkled on top
Buckwheat, oat flour and flaxseed pancakes

Be your own chef. If you don't particularly like the texture of rolled oats, for example, mix-in Grape-Nuts with them and have your very own designer-breakfast the way you like it. Instead of using jellies and jams, try spreading whole fruits on toast, such as a banana.

Anything "instant," such as instant oatmeal, should be put back on the shelf.

Good Cereals
Here are some of the more popular cereal brands, which contain whole grains. Be sure to inspect the ingredients list. (See *Reading Labels & Ingredients*.)

Whole grains - Cold
Arrowhead Mills Organic Amaranth Flakes
Cheerios
Erewhon Crispy Brown Rice (like Rice Krispies)
Grape-Nuts (not flakes)
Health Valley Organic Fiber 7 Multigrain flakes
Heart-To-Heart (Kashi)
Nature's Path Organic Cereals

Puffed Wheat
Raisin Bran
Quaker Old-Fashioned (rolled) Oats (not instant)
Shredded wheat

Whole grains - Hot
Oat bran
Oatmeal (never buy instant oatmeal)
Quaker Multigrain
Quaker Old-Fashioned (rolled) Oats (not instant)
Ralston High Fiber
Roman Meal
Steel-cut Oats (the best oatmeal)
Wheatena

Fruit Drinks and Other Popular Breakfast Items

Most fruit drinks are bad for you and no more nutritious than carbonated soft drinks. The number one ingredient in most fruit drinks, including Gatorade, V8, Minute Maid, CapriSun, and Sunny Delight, is some form of sugar – sucrose, fructose, glucose, or sorbitol. Most have their fiber removed from them and also contain high levels of sodium.

Look for products that are 100 percent fruit juice, or reconstituted juice, that are *unsweetened*. In most cases, organic juices are the best. If you can't find any, make your own juice or eat an orange or another fruit instead. There's a world of difference from your body's perspective.

If you choose to use soy, rice of another type of plant-based milk, make sure you purchase the fat free or very low-fat variety and that it does not contain oil or carrageenan (some are sensitive to this ingredient and I would recommend avoiding it).

Avoid store bought baked goods because they will likely contain hydrogenated vegetable oils, no matter how healthy they look or are advertised.

Breakfast Recipes

Barley Scones
Makes 12 scones

1 1/8 cup barley flour
1/4 cup non-dairy milk
3 tbsp raisins
2 tbsp maple syrup
1 tbsp applesauce (or oil substitute)
2 tsp vinegar
1 tsp baking powder
1/4 tsp baking soda

Preheat oven to 350. Mix milk, maple syrup, applesauce, and vinegar. Set aside. Combine flour, baking soda and raisins in a food processor. Blend. Add liquid ingredients and process until dough forms. Transfer to flat surface, dusted with barley flour. Flatten into a circle 6 inches in diameter and 3/4 inch thick. Use knife to score dough into 12 wedges (do not separate), then transfer to a baking sheet. Bake for 30 minutes, or until lightly browned.

Black Beans with Salsa on Toast
Serves 2

1 cup dry black beans
1/4 cup diced onions
1 tsp thinly sliced jalapenos
1 large tomato, diced
4 slices of your favorite toast or tortillas
garlic powder, and cumin to taste

Heat and mash beans. For the salsa, mix the jalapenos, tomatoes, and onions, adjusting amounts to taste. Serve the beans and salsa on toast or with tortillas.

Cereal – Rolled Oats Cold

Rolled oats (not cooked)
Banana (or peach, mango, kiwis, melons, apricots, etc.)
Mixed berries
Pineapple slices
Raisins
1 tbsp ground flaxseed or flaxseed meal
Non-dairy milk

Pour rolled oats into bowl. Add fruits and flaxseed. Add milk.

Coffee Cake
Serves 6

2 cups whole wheat flour
1 cup unsweetened apple juice
3/4 cup old-fashioned rolled oats
1/2 cup applesauce
1/2 cup maple syrup
1 tbsp baking powder
2 tsp ground cinnamon
1/2 tsp ground nutmeg
1/4 tsp ground ginger

Preheat the oven to 350. Grease 9-inch square baking pan with an oil substitute and flour. In a large bowl, add flour, 1/2 cup of oats, baking powder, cinnamon, syrup, nutmeg and ginger. Remove 1/2 cup of mixture to a cup or small bowl, add remaining 1/4 cup oats. Cut in 2 tablespoons of applesauce, set the mixture aside. Cut remaining applesauce into the flour mixture in the large bowl. Stir in the apple juice until well combined. Pour the batter into the prepared pan. Top with the reserved oat mixture. Bake about 40 minutes, or until done.

French Toast
Serves 2 to 3

2 medium bananas
2/3 cup non-dairy milk
2 tbsp maple syrup
1/8 tsp ground cinnamon
4 slices bread

Blend bananas, non-dairy milk, maple syrup, and cinnamon until smooth. Pour into a flat, shallow dish and soak bread slices 1 minute on each side. Transfer carefully to a non-stick skillet. Cook first side until lightly browned, about 3 minutes, then turn and cook second side until browned. Serve with fresh fruit, fruit preserves, or maple syrup.

Muffins – Apple Oat
Makes 12 medium muffins

3 cups whole wheat pastry flour
1 12-ounce can apple juice concentrate
2 large apples, finely chopped
1-1/4 cups oat bran
1/2 cup raisins
2-1/2 tsp baking soda
1 tsp ground cinnamon
1/2 tsp grated nutmeg

Preheat oven to 325. In a large bowl, mix flour, oats, spices and baking soda. Add the chopped apple along with the apple juice concentrate and raisins. Stir just enough to mix. Spoon batter into nonstick muffin tins and bake for 25 minutes.

Muffins – Pumpkin Spice
Makes 10 to 12 muffins

2 cups whole wheat pastry flour
1/2 cup maple syrup
1/2 cup raisins
1 tbsp baking powder
1/2 tsp baking soda
1/2 tsp cinnamon
1/4 tsp nutmeg
1 15-ounce can solid-pack pumpkin

Preheat oven to 375. Mix flour, maple syrup, baking powder, baking soda, cinnamon, and nutmeg in a large bowl. Add pumpkin, 1/2 cup water, and raisins. Stir until just mixed. Spoon batter into non-stick muffin cups. Bake 25 to 30 minutes. Remove from oven and let stand 5 minutes. Remove muffins from pan and cool.

Pancakes – Cornmeal
Makes 16 3-inch pancakes

1 cup non-dairy milk
1/2 cup cornmeal
1/2 cup whole wheat pastry flour
2 tbsp maple syrup
1 tbsp cider vinegar
1/2 tsp sodium-free baking powder
1/4 tsp baking soda

In a large bowl mix milk, maple syrup, and vinegar. Set aside. In separate bowl stir together cornmeal, flour, baking powder, baking soda. Add to milk mixture, stirring to remove any lumps and make a batter. Add more milk if batter seems too thick. On non-stick skillet or griddle, pour small amounts of batter onto the heated surface and cook until tops bubble. Turn carefully with a spatula and cook the second sides until browned. Use fruit preserves, fresh fruit, or maple syrup for serving

Pancakes – Old-Fashioned
Makes 16 3-inch pancakes

1 ripe banana, mashed
1 cup non-dairy milk
1/2 cup buckwheat flour
1/2 cup cornmeal
2 tbsp maple syrup
1 tbsp vinegar
1/2 tsp sodium-free baking powder
1/4 tsp baking soda

Mix buckwheat flour, cornmeal, baking powder, baking soda. In a large bowl, combine mashed banana, maple syrup, vinegar, and milk. Add flour mixture, stirring just enough to remove any lumps and make a batter. Add more milk if batter seems too thick. On non-stick skillet or griddle, pour small amounts of batter onto the heated surface and cook until tops bubble. Turn carefully with a spatula and cook the second sides until browned. Use fruit preserves, fresh fruit, or maple syrup for serving

Granola – Maple Walnut
Makes about 6 cups

3 cups rolled oats
1 cup wheat germ
1/2 cup chopped walnuts
1/2 cup raisins
1/2 cup dried cranberries (optional)
1/4 cup sesame seeds
1/4 cup maple syrup
2 tbsp molasses
1 tsp cinnamon

Preheat oven to 300. Combine all ingredients in a large bowl and mix thoroughly. Transfer to a 9 × 13-inch baking dish. Bake, turning often with a spatula, until mixture is golden brown, about 25 minutes.

Muesli
Makes 3 cups

2 cups rolled oats
1/2 cup chopped dried fruit (apples, figs, apricots, etc.)
1/2 cup raisins

Combine all ingredients. They may be left whole or ground in a food processor until they are of a fairly fine, uniform texture. Store in an airtight container in the refrigerator. Serve with non-dairy milk with cut fresh fruit toppings.

Waffles – Oatmeal
Makes 6 waffles

1 banana
2 cups rolled oats
2 cups water
1 tbsp maple syrup
1 tsp vanilla

Preheat non-stick waffle iron to medium-high. Combine oats, water, banana, maple syrup and vanilla in a blender. Blend on high speed until completely smooth. Pour in batter and cook until golden brown (5-10 minutes without lifting lid.) Serve with fresh fruit.

Whole Wheat Pancakes
Makes 24 2-inch pancakes

1 banana
1 1/4 cups non-dairy milk
1 cup whole wheat pastry flour or whole wheat flour
1 tbsp maple syrup
2 tsp sodium-free baking powder

In a large bowl, mash banana, then stir in milk and maple syrup. In a separate bowl mix flour and baking powder. Add to banana mixture and stir until smooth. Pour small amounts of batter onto a preheated non-stick griddle or skillet with a small amount of oil substitute and cook until tops bubble. Flip with a spatula and cook second side until golden brown, about 1 minute. Use fruit preserves, fresh fruit, or maple syrup for serving

Lunch or Dinner Recipes

Suggestions for Lunch/Dinner

The following are simply suggestions that you can whip up on your own without following any recipe.

Acorn squash with rice
Angel hair zucchini with marinara sauce and sweet potato or squash
Avocado, tomato, cucumber and hummus sandwich
Bean enchiladas (frozen)
Bean soup and stir-fried vegetables
Bean, vegetable and barley soup
Beets, raisins and carrots
Brown rice and vegetables
Carrot soup
Corn chowder
Corn stew
Garden salad
Garden salad wrap
Green beans and garlic mashed potatoes (keep the skins)
Lentil, tomato, etc. soup with whole wheat bread
Pasta, tomato sauce and vegetables
Pasta and vegetables
Pasta, tomato sauce and vegetables
Portobello mushroom burgers and beans
Raw vegetables
Rice and vegetables
Roasted eggplant, corn & zucchini wrap
Roasted peppers stuffed with rice and vegetables
Salad stuffed pita
Salad and raw vegetables
Soy chili
Stir-fry vegetables
Vegetable soup
Vegetable pate sandwich
Vegetarian chili

Salads

Salad - Antipasto
Makes about 6 cups

1 large red potato, scrubbed
1 carrot, sliced
1 cup Italian green beans, fresh or frozen
1 cup cauliflower florets
1 small red bell pepper, sliced or diced
2 garlic cloves, pressed
2 tbsp finely chopped parsley
2 tbsp balsamic vinegar
1 tbsp seasoned rice vinegar
1 tbsp vegetable broth
1 tbsp lemon juice
2 tsp apple juice concentrate
1 tsp stone ground or Dijon-style mustard
1/4 tsp black pepper

Dice potatoes and steam with carrots over boiling water until just tender, about 10 minutes. Place in a salad bowl. Steam green beans and cauliflower until just tender. Add to salad. Add bell pepper and parsley. Mix vinegars, vegetable broth, lemon juice, apple juice concentrate, garlic, mustard and pepper in a small bowl. Pour over vegetables, and toss to mix.

Salad – Aztec
Makes about 8 cups

2 15-ounce cans black beans, drained and rinsed
2 tomatoes, diced
2 garlic cloves, pressed or finely minced
1 lemon or lime, juiced
1 15-ounce can corn kernels, drained, or 1 10-ounce bag frozen corn, thawed, or 2 cups fresh corn
3/4 cup chopped fresh cilantro (optional)
1/2 cup finely chopped red onion
1 green bell pepper, seeded and diced
1 red or yellow bell pepper, seeded and diced
2 tbsp seasoned rice vinegar
2 tbsp apple cider or distilled vinegar
2 tsp ground cumin
1 tsp coriander
1/2 tsp red pepper flakes or a pinch of cayenne

In a large bowl, combine beans, onion, bell peppers, corn, tomatoes, and cilantro. In a small bowl, whisk together vinegars, lemon juice, garlic, cumin, coriander, and red pepper flakes. Pour over salad and toss gently to mix.

Salad – Black Bean & Corn

2 cans (15 oz.) black soybeans, drained and rinsed
2 cups frozen corn kernels, thawed
2 tomatoes, chopped
1 red pepper, chopped
1 jalapeno pepper, minced
1 cup chopped green onions
1/2 cup chopped red onion
1/2 cup chopped cilantro
1-2 tbsp Juice from 1 lime
1 tbsp vegetable broth
1 tsp minced garlic

Combine first seven ingredients in a large bowl. Make dressing with lime juice, cilantro, garlic, pepper and vegetable broth. Combine well. Pour over salad ingredients and toss lightly to combine. Chill several hours before serving.

Salad – Black-eyed Peas Salad
Makes about 5 cups

2 cups cooked black-eyed peas
1-1/2 cups cooked brown rice
1 celery stalk, thinly sliced (about 1/2 cup)
1 tomato, diced
1/2 cup finely sliced green onions
2 tbsp finely chopped parsley

Combine the above ingredients in a mixing bowl. Add no-oil salad dressing.

Salad – Broccoli
Makes about 4 cups

1 bunch broccoli
1–2 garlic cloves, minced
1/2 cup finely sliced red onion
1/2 cup seasoned rice vinegar
1 tbsp vegetable broth
1/2 tsp dried red pepper flakes

Cut or break broccoli into small florets. Transfer to a salad bowl. Add remaining ingredients and toss to mix. Chill, tossing once or twice, for 20 minutes or longer before serving.

Salad – Colorful
Serves 4

1 sweet red pepper, cut into chunks
1 orange
1 cup of snap peas, cut in half
1 cucumber, peeled and cut into chunks
8 fresh basil leaves, sliced
1 tbsp seasoned rice vinegar
cracked black pepper, to taste

Remove the peel off the orange and cut the peeled fruit into bite size chunks. In medium bowl, mix together the orange, red pepper, cucumber, and basil. Sprinkle with rice vinegar and season with pepper. Toss and serve.

Salad – Crunchy
Serves 6

1 15-ounce can diced beets, drained
2 medium-size carrots, peeled and cut into thin strips or diced
1 small jicama, peeled and cut into thin strips or diced
3 tbsp of lemon juice
2 tbsp seasoned rice vinegar
2 tsp stone ground mustard
1/2 tsp dried dill weed

Place beet cubes into a large salad bowl, along with jicama and carrot pieces. In a small bowl, mix lemon juice, vinegar, mustard, and dill; pour over the salad. Toss to mix. Serve warm or chilled.

Salad – Cucumber Arame
Serves 4 to 6

1 cucumber
1 cup arame
1 cup water
2 tbsp lemon juice
2 tbsp water
1 tbsp brown rice vinegar
1 tsp low-sodium Tamari (soy sauce)

Peel and halve the cucumber lengthwise. Transfer to a bowl and let stand 15 minutes. Drain thoroughly. Meanwhile, soak the arame in one cup of water until soft, 10 to 15 minutes. Mix together lemon juice, Tamari, vinegar and 2 tablespoons of water to make dressing. Drain any excess water from arame, then combine with cucumber and dressing.

Salad – Cucumber, Mango & Spinach
Serves 10-12

1 bag or bunch of spinach
1 mango, peeled and cut into bite size pieces
1 large English cucumber, peeled and sliced
6 scallions, thinly sliced
1/2 cup fresh, chopped basil leaves
Juice of 1 lime
1/2 cup seasoned rice vinegar
Fresh cracked black pepper to taste

Wash and drain spinach, tear into bite-sized pieces if necessary, and put into a large serving bowl. Toss mango, cucumber, scallions, and basil in a medium bowl. Dress with lime juice and vinegar. Arrange mango mixture on spinach and sprinkle with fresh cracked black pepper.

Salad – Fiesta
Serves 10

3 15-ounce cans black beans
2 cups frozen corn, thawed
2 large tomatoes, diced
1 large green bell pepper, diced
1 large red or yellow bell pepper, diced
3/4 cups chopped cilantro
1/2 cup chopped red onion

Combine beans with the corn, tomatoes, bell peppers, red onion, and cilantro. Toss with no-oil dressing.

Salad – Mediterranean Rice Salad
Serves 6 to 8

3 Roma tomatoes, cut into chunks
3 cups cooked brown rice
1 green pepper, chopped
1 cucumber, peeled and cut into chunks
1 cup green beans, broken into small pieces, blanched or raw
1/2 cup fresh basil leaves, sliced
1/2 cup seasoned rice vinegar
1 tbsp mustard
1 tbsp vegetable broth
1/2 tsp dried parsley flakes
juice of 1 lemon

In medium bowl, mix together rice, pepper, green beans, cucumber, tomato, and basil. Stir together mustard, rice vinegar, lemon juice, vegetable broth, and parsley. Pour over salad and toss to mix. Season with pepper. Toss and serve.

Salad – Mixed Greens With Apples & Walnuts
Makes about 4 cups

6 cups salad mix or washed and torn butter lettuce
1 tart green apple (Granny Smith, pippin, or similar)
1/4 cup chopped walnuts
3-4 tbsp seasoned rice vinegar

Place salad mix or torn leaf lettuce into a bowl. Core and dice apple and add to salad along with walnuts. Sprinkle with seasoned rice vinegar and toss to mix.

Salad – Pasta Salad
Serves 8-10

12 ounces pasta shells (about 2 cups)
1 jar water-packed artichoke hearts, drained and quartered
2-3 cups button mushrooms (about 1/2 pound)
1 garlic clove
1 small red bell pepper, diced
1/2 cup chopped green onions
1/3 cup seasoned rice vinegar
1/4 cup cider vinegar
3 tbsp water
3 tbsp chopped fresh parsley
2 tbsp fresh lemon juice (optional)
2 tsp stone-ground or Dijon-style mustard
1/2 tsp each dried basil and oregano
1/4 tsp black pepper

Cook until pasta is tender. Rinse, drain, place in a large bowl. Add artichoke hearts and mushrooms. In a blender, combine the vinegars, lemon juice, mustard, 1/4 cup green onions, garlic, seasonings, and water. Process until smooth. Pour over pasta, and allow to marinate until pasta is cool. Add the remaining green onions, parsley, and red bell pepper and gently toss to mix.

Salad – Rice Salad

3 cups cooked brown rice
3 Roma tomatoes, cut into chunks
1 green, yellow or red pepper, chopped
1 cucumber, peeled and cut into chunks
1 cup raw green beans, cut into small pieces
1/2 cup basil leaves, sliced
1/2 cup seasoned rice vinegar
1 tbsp mustard
1/2 tsp dried parsley flakes
1/2 tsp Italian seasoning
juice of 1 lemon

In bowl, mix together rice, pepper, green beans, cucumber, tomato, and basil. Stir together mustard, rice vinegar, lemon juice and parsley. Pour over salad and toss to mix. Season with pepper and Tabasco (optional) to taste. Toss and serve.

Salad – Spanish Wild Rice

2 cups wild rice
Dried apricots, diced
Walnuts, chopped
Orange zest from one orange
Spring onions, chopped
1 cup of orange juice
Balsamic vinegar

Cover the rice with water and orange juice. Cook until done, but still a little firm. Toss in some dried apricots, walnuts and spring onions. Pour Balsamic vinegar to taste over the rice and chill.

Salad – Spinach
Serves 2

2 cups spinach
1/2 cup sliced mushrooms
1/4 cup chopped green onions
Tamari (optional)
Sesame seeds, for garnish

Thoroughly wash the spinach, tearing the larger leaves. Drain well. Add the mushrooms and green onions, and toss well. Sprinkle with Tamari, if desired, then sprinkle each serving with sesame seeds.

Salad – Spinach with Fruit
Serves 4

4 cups cleaned spinach leaves
2 oranges, peeled, sliced, and quartered
1 cucumber, peeled, sliced and quartered
1 sweet red pepper, seeded and chopped
2 tbsp raw or roasted sunflower seeds

Toss spinach with cucumber, orange, and red pepper chunks in medium sized bowl. Sprinkle with sunflower seeds. Serve with no-oil dressing on the side.

Salad – Squash, Corn & Bean Salad
Makes about 8 cups

1 15-ounce can corn, drained
1 15-ounce can black beans, drained and rinsed
1 red bell pepper, diced
2 cups butternut or kabocha squash, julienne or cut into 1/4-inch cubes (available frozen in health food stores)
1 cup jicama, julienne or cut into 1/4-inch cubes
1/2 cup red onion
1/2 cup chopped cilantro
1/4 cup pumpkin seeds
1/4 cup seasoned rice vinegar
2 tbsp lemon or lime juice
1 tsp each: cumin, coriander, chili powder
1 garlic clove, pressed or minced

Combine squash, jicama, bell pepper, corn, beans, onion, cilantro and pumpkin seeds in a large bowl.
Mix vinegar, lemon juice, cumin, coriander, chili powder and garlic. Pour over salad and toss to mix.

Salad – Stuffed Tomato
Serves 5

5 large ripe tomatoes
1 can garbanzo beans
1 stalk celery, chopped (optional)

Scoop out tomatoes, saving pulp for a sauce. Fill tomatoes with beans and celery. Season with pepper. Garnish with sauce and lettuce or sprouts.

Salad – Three Bean
Serves 4

1 cup cooked kidney beans
1 cup cooked garbanzo beans
1 cup cooked lima beans
1 cup onion, chopped
1/2 cup green pepper, chopped
4 tsp vegetable broth

Toss ingredients together. Serve hot or cold with a grain or bread. To serve cold for a salad, add a few drops of lemon juice or vinegar.

Salad – Tomato, Cucumber & Basil
Serves 6

4 fresh tomatoes, quartered and sliced
1/2 large English cucumber, peeled, quartered and sliced
1/2 cup fresh basil leaves,
3-4 tbsp balsamic vinegar

Arrange cucumber and tomato in a flat bowl. Add basil leaves, dress with balsamic vinegar, and sprinkle with fresh cracked black pepper.

Salad – White Bean
Makes about 2 1/2 cups

1 15-ounce can white beans, drained and rinsed
1 small red bell pepper, diced
1/2 cup finely chopped fresh parsley
1 lemon, juiced
2 tsp balsamic vinegar
1/4 tsp garlic granules or powder
1/4 tsp black pepper

Combine all ingredients in a large bowl and toss to mix. Let stand 10 to 15 minutes before serving.

Soups & Stews

Chowder – Corn
Serves 5

2 17-ounce cans no-dairy creamed corn
2 stalks celery and 2 carrots, chopped
1 potato, chopped
2 cups water
1 cup non-dairy milk
1 onion, chopped
1 tbsp vegetable broth
1-1/2 tsp garlic powder
1/4 tsp nutmeg

Sauté onion in vegetable broth over medium-high heat until soft. Add water, chopped celery and carrots. Cook 10 minutes. Add creamed corn, non-dairy milk, chopped potato, and spices. Continue cooking for another 10 minutes.

Chowder – Kale and Rice
Serves 6

1 14 ounce can seasoned, diced stewed tomatoes
2 cups vegetable broth
2 cups chopped kale
1 cup cooked brown rice
1 cup drained canned garbanzo beans
1 cup chopped onion
1 cup chopped red bell pepper
1 1/2 cups water
1/2 cup chopped leeks
1/3 cup sliced almonds
1 tbsp paprika
2 tsp vegetable broth for sautéing
2 bay leaves

Heat the broth over medium-high heat. Add the onion, pepper, leeks, and almonds. Sauté for 2 minutes. Add the almonds, paprika, bay leaves, water, tomatoes, and broth. Bring to boil. Add the kale, rice, and garbanzo beans. Reduce heat and simmer 10 minutes, or until thoroughly heated.

Soup – Black Bean Creamy
Serves 4 to 6

3 cloves garlic, crushed
6-7 cups water
2-1/2 cups (1 pound) dried black beans
1 cup non-dairy milk
1 tbsp vegetable broth
tortillas for garnish (whole wheat)
lettuce for garnish

Soak beans overnight. Drain and cover with water. Add the garlic and cook until soft, about 2 hours, or five minutes in a pressure cooker. Blend beans with the cooking water and return to pot. Reheat with vegetable broth and non-dairy milk. Garnish with thinly sliced fried tortillas and strips of lettuce.

Soup – Carrot and Red Pepper
Serves 4

6 carrots, thinly sliced
2 red bell peppers, roasted
1 onion, chopped
2 cups non-dairy milk
2 cups water or vegetable stock
2 tsp lemon juice
2 tsp balsamic vinegar
1/4 tsp freshly ground black pepper

Place the chopped onion and carrots into a pot with the water and simmer, covered, over medium heat until the carrots can be easily pierced with a fork, about 20 minutes. Roast the peppers by placing them over an open gas flame or directly under the broiler. Place in a bowl, cover, and let stand about 15 minutes. Cut the peppers in half and remove the seeds. Blend the carrot mixture along with the peppers in several small batches. Add some of the non-dairy milk to each batch to facilitate blending. Return to the pot and add the lemon juice, vinegar and pepper. Heat until steamy.

Soup – Chilled Cucumber-Dill
Makes 1 serving

1-1/2 cups non-dairy milk
1/2 cucumber
1 tbsp fresh dill weed or 1 tsp dried dill weed

Chill the non-dairy milk in the freezer for 15 minutes. Put the cucumber through a juicer. Combine the cucumber juice and non-dairy milk in a blender. Pour into a bowl and top with the dill weed.

Soup – Cream of Asparagus
Makes about 7 cups

2 medium-size white potatoes, diced
1 medium-size bunch asparagus (about 4 cups chopped)
2 cups water
2 cups shredded cabbage
1-2 cups non-dairy milk
1 cup (loosely packed) chopped fresh parsley
1/4 cup chopped fresh basil

Dice potatoes (do not peel them). Place them into a large pot with the water. Bring to a simmer, cover and cook until tender. Remove the tough ends from the asparagus, then break stalks into 1- to 2-inch lengths. When potatoes are tender, add asparagus along with cabbage, parsley, and basil. Cover and simmer for about 5 minutes, or until asparagus is just tender when pierced with a fork. In a blender purée the vegetables with cooking liquid, in 2 or 3 batches. Add enough of the non-dairy milk to each batch to facilitate blending. After puréeing all vegetables, pour soup into the pan, then heat gently until steamy.

Soup – Creamy Beet
Makes about 3 cups

1 15-ounce can diced beets
1 cup non-dairy milk
2 tbsp apple juice concentrate
1 tsp balsamic vinegar
1/2 tsp dried dill weed

Place diced beets, non-dairy milk, apple juice concentrate, vinegar, and dill weed into blender. Blend on high speed until completely smooth. Transfer to a medium saucepan and heat gently until steamy. Serve hot or cold.

Soup – Curried Potato and Onion
Serves 6

2 medium onions, chopped
2 large garlic cloves, pressed or minced
4-1/2 cups vegetable broth or bouillon
2 to 3 cups peeled and diced potatoes
3/4 cup non-dairy milk
2 tsp vegetable broth
1-1/2 tsp ground cumin
1-1/2 tsp curry powder, or to taste
1 tsp ground tumeric
chopped fresh chives or cilantro for garnish

In a large soup pot, sauté the garlic and onion in the broth until transparent. Add spices and 1/4 cup broth; stir well and cook for 5 minutes. Add the potatoes and remaining broth. Simmer gently for 20 minutes, or until potatoes are soft. Purée in batches in a food processor or use a hand held blender and blend until smooth. If serving cold, refrigerate for at least 6 hours.

Soup – Curried Sweet Potato
Serves 6

5 cups cubed, peeled sweet potato
4 cups vegetable broth
1 cup chopped onion
1 cup water
1/8 cup vegetable broth
2 tsp curry powder
minced cilantro (optional)

Heat broth in a large saucepan over medium heat. Add the onion and curry
powder and sauté for 2 minutes. Add the water, broth, and sweet potatoes. Cook
for 30 minutes, or until the sweet potatoes are tender. Place one-third of the sweet
potato mixture in a blender and process until smooth. Repeat the procedure with
the remaining sweet potato mixture in batches. Return the puréed mixture to the
saucepan. Bring the soup to a boil and remove from heat. Garnish with cilantro,
if desired.

Soup – Gazpacho
Serves 4

1 plum tomato, seeded and finely diced
2 garlic cloves, chopped
2 cups tomato juice
1/4 cup seeded and diced cucumber
1/4 cup finely diced green bell pepper
1/4 cup red onion, finely diced
1/4 cup zucchini, finely diced (optional)
4 tbs. vegetable broth
2 tbs. bread crumbs
1 tbs. white wine vinegar

Place the tomato juice, garlic and broth in a blender and process until the garlic is
puréed. Add the bread crumbs and vinegar, and blend to combine. Add favorite
seasonings. Pour into a covered container and chill well, from 2 hours to
overnight. When ready to serve, check the seasoning and adjust if necessary.
Divide the soup among 4 serving bowls. Add 1 Tbs. each of the diced cucumber,
pepper, tomato and onion, plus the zucchini if desired.

Soup – Lentil
Serves 8

2 onions, halved and sliced
4 cloves garlic, minced
3 parsnips, peeled and sliced
10 cups water
5 cups packed chopped dandelion greens or kale
2 cups red lentils, rinsed and drained
1/8 cup vegetable broth
1 5 ounce can tomato paste
3 tbsp chopped parsley, divided
1 tsp dried oregano
1 tsp dried basil
1 tsp black pepper

In a large pot, heat vegetable broth over medium-high heat. Add onions and sauté for 3 minutes. Add garlic and sauté 1 minute more. Add water, lentils, tomato paste, parsnips, 1 tablespoon parsley, oregano, basil, and pepper. Bring to a boil. Reduce heat to low, cover and simmer for 30 minutes. Add dandelion greens and simmer an additional 15 minutes or until greens are soft. Garnish with remaining parsley.

Soup – Minestrone
Makes about 2 1/2 quarts

1 15-ounce can kidney beans, drained
1 small onion, chopped
1 carrot, cut into chunks
1 celery stalk, sliced including top
1 potato, scrubbed and cut into chunks
1 small zucchini, diced
4 garlic cloves, minced
2 cups tomato juice
2 cups water or vegetable broth
1 cup finely chopped kale, collard greens, or spinach
2 tbsp chopped parsley
1/4 tsp black pepper
1/4 cup pasta shells
1 tbsp chopped fresh basil or 1 tsp dried basil
1 tsp mixed Italian herbs

Combine onion, garlic, carrot, celery, potato, and parsley in a large pot. Add tomato juice, water or broth, Italian herbs, and black pepper. Bring to a simmer, then cover and cook 20 minutes. Add zucchini, pasta, kidney beans, chopped greens, and basil.

Cover and simmer until pasta is tender, about 20 minutes. Add extra tomato juice or water for a thinner soup.

Soup – Mushroom and Barley
Makes about 3 cups

2 cups non-dairy milk
1 cup cooked barley
1 4-ounce can mushrooms, including the liquid
2 tbsp barley flour
1/4 tsp garlic powder
pinch each of dried marjoram, sage, thyme, and dill weed

Place non-dairy milk and barley flour into blender. Blend on high speed for a few seconds. Add barley and blend until barley is chopped coarse. Add mushrooms with their liquid. Blend just enough to coarse-chop mushrooms. Transfer the blended mixture to a medium-sized saucepan and add all the remaining ingredients. Cook over medium heat until soup is hot and somewhat thickened.

Soup – Split Pea & Barley
Makes 8-9 cups

2 quarts water
1 carrot, chopped
3 stalks celery, diced
1 potato, diced
1 onion, diced
1 cup green split peas
1/4 cup barley
1 tsp celery seed
1/2 tsp basil
1/2 tsp thyme

Sauté onion until soft in a little water, along with the celery seed. Stir in peas and barley. Add water and bring to a boil. Cook on low heat, partially covered, for about an hour and a half. Add pepper, vegetable and herbs. Simmer another 30 to 45 minutes.

Soup – Vegetable Soup with Hominy
Serves 4

1 15-ounce can of white hominy
1 15-ounce can of stewed tomatoes with garlic, green pepper, and celery
4 carrots, sliced
3 cloves garlic, minced
1 large onion, chopped
1 red pepper, chopped
3 cups of water or low-sodium vegetable stock
1 cup green beans, broken into bite-sized lengths
3/4 tsp chili powder
1/2 tsp cumin
1/4 tsp pepper

In medium stock pot, braise garlic and onion in 1/2 cup water until soft. Add carrots and water or stock, and simmer 5 to 10 minutes. Drain and rinse hominy and add to the pot. Stir in the tomatoes, red pepper, green beans, and spices. Simmer for 15 minutes. Serve piping hot with little bowls of the toppings. Use salsa or chopped lettuce as toppings.

Stew – Green Split Pea and Barley

3 garlic cloves
2 large white potatoes, coarsely chopped
2 stalks celery, diced
2 large carrots, diced
6 cups water
2 cups chopped fresh spinach
1 medium yellow onion -- diced
1 cup green split peas -- rinsed
1/2 cup pearl barley
2 tbsp dried parsley
2 tbsp vegetable broth
2 tsp dried oregano or thyme leaves
1/2 tsp black pepper

In a large saucepan, heat the broth over medium heat. Add the onion, celery, carrots, and garlic and cook, stirring, for about 7 minutes. Add the water, split peas, barley, potatoes, parsley, oregano, and pepper and bring to a simmer over medium-high heat. Reduce the heat to medium and cook until peas are tender, about 1 hour. Stir in the spinach and cook over low heat for 10 to 15 minutes.

Ladle into bowls and serve with warm whole wheat bread. (Note: To speed up the cooking time, soak the split peas in water for 1 hour before cooking.)

Stew – Lentil and Barley Stew
Makes about 1 1/2 quarts

1 small onion, chopped
1 garlic clove, pressed or minced
1 carrot, diced
1 celery stalk, sliced
1 quart vegetable broth or water
1/2 cup lentils, rinsed
1/4 cup hulled or pearled barley
1/2 tsp oregano
1/2 tsp ground cumin
1/4 tsp red pepper flakes
1/4 tsp black pepper

Place all ingredients into a large pot and bring to a simmer. Cover and cook, stirring occasionally, until lentils and barley are tender, about 1 hour.

Stew – Spicy Pumpkin
Serves 6

1 15-ounce can red kidney or pinto beans
1 16-ounce can corn kernels, drained
1 medium onion, thinly sliced
3 4 cups of small chunk (1/2-inch) raw pumpkin or butternut squash
1 cup vegetable stock
1 cup tomato sauce
1/2 cup salsa
1 tsp minced garlic
1 tsp chili powder
1/2 tsp hot red pepper flakes
1/2 tsp cumin
3-4 drops of Tabasco

Simmer pumpkin or squash in vegetable stock until tender. Add remaining ingredients and simmer uncovered over low heat for 30 minutes. Season to taste.

Stew – Summer
Makes about 2 1/2 quarts

1 15-ounce can cannelini beans or navy beans
1 12-ounce jar water-packed roasted red peppers, including liquid
5 large garlic cloves, minced
2 onions, chopped
4 cups eggplant, cut into 1/4-inch thick slices
3 cups zucchini, sliced
2 cups chopped fresh basil
1 green bell pepper, diced
1 cup water or vegetable broth
2 tbsp vegetable broth
1/4 tsp black pepper

Heat broth in a large pot, add onions. Cook over medium heat until onions are lightly browned. Add a small amounts of water if onions begin to stick. Add eggplant, bell pepper, and garlic, then cover and cook five minutes.. Coarsely chop red peppers and add, with their liquid. Add zucchini, basil, and water. Cover and cook over medium heat, stirring occasionally, for 3 minutes. Stir in cannelini beans, including liquid, and black pepper. Cover and cook until zucchini is just tender, about 3 minutes.

Mix-Ins/Side Dishes

Asparagus With Garlic & Pecans
Serves 4

1 pound asparagus, broken into bite-sized pieces
3 cloves garlic, minced
1/2 cup pecans, halved
1 tbsp low-sodium Tamari (soy sauce)
2 tsp vegetable broth

Sauté garlic in broth in medium skillet. Add asparagus and Tamari. Cook 4-6 minutes stirring often until asparagus is tender. Add pecans, continue heating for 1-2 minutes and serve.

Asparagus With Raspberry Sauce
Serves 4

1 pound of asparagus
1 cup frozen raspberries
1/2 fresh orange or 1 tsp frozen orange juice concentrate
1 tsp orange zest (optional)

Put frozen raspberries in saucepot with orange juice or juice concentrate. Simmer until raspberries have fallen apart and mixture looks like a sauce. Remove from heat and set aside. Steam asparagus over hot water until just tender.. Pour sauce over asparagus. Serve hot or at room temperature. Garnish with orange zest, if desired.

Beans – Baked Beans
Makes about 8 cups

1 15-ounce can tomato sauce
1 onion, chopped
2-1/2 cups dried navy beans (or other small white beans)
1/2 cup molasses
2 tbsp vinegar
2 tsp stone ground or Dijon mustard
1 tsp Bakkon yeast (optional – found at health food stores)
1/2 tsp garlic granules or powder

Rinse beans and soak in 6 cups of water for 6 to 8 hours or overnight. Drain and rinse. Place beans in a large pot with onion. Cover and simmer until beans are tender, about 2 hours. Add tomato sauce, molasses, mustard, vinegar, garlic granules and Bakkon yeast if using. Cook, loosely covered, over very low heat for 1 to 2 hours. Or, transfer to an ovenproof dish and bake at 350 for 2 to 3 hours.

Beans – Barbecued
Makes 6 cups

1 16-ounce can vegetarian baked beans
1 15-ounce can kidney beans
1 10-ounce package frozen baby lima beans
1 6-ounce can crushed tomatoes
1 cup finely chopped onion
1 tbsp cider vinegar
1 tbsp molasses
2 tsp stone-ground mustard
1 tsp chili powder

Combine all ingredients in a saucepan and cook at a slow simmer for 25 to 30 minutes.

Beans – Black Beans and Tomatoes
Makes 4 cups

2 15-ounce cans black beans, rinsed and drained
2 14-ounce cans diced tomatoes, drained
2 garlic cloves, minced
1/2 cup chopped onion
1/4 cup vegetable broth
2 tbsp canned, chopped green chilies
1 tbsp chopped cilantro or parsley
1/2 tsp cumin
1/2 tsp ground red pepper
1/4 tsp chili powder

Heat 1/4-cup vegetable broth in non-stick cooking skillet and heat over medium-high heat. Add chopped onion and garlic. Sauté in broth until tender. Add tomatoes and chilies. Reduce heat and cook uncovered 6 to 8 minutes or until mixture is slightly thickened, stirring occasionally. Stir in beans and remaining ingredients. Cover and cook five minutes or until thoroughly heated.

Beans – Refried Beans (spicy)
Makes about 5 cups

1 4-ounce can diced green chilies
4 garlic cloves, minced or pressed
1 onion, chopped
1 cup crushed or finely chopped tomatoes
1 1/2 cups dry pinto beans
1 1/2 tsp cumin
1/4 tsp cayenne

Clean and rinse beans, then soak in about 6 cups of water for 6 to 8 hours. Discard soaking water, rinse beans and place in a large pot with 4 cups fresh water, minced garlic, cumin, and cayenne. Simmer until tender, about 1 hour. Heat 1/2 cup of water in a large skillet. Add onion and cook until soft, about 5 minutes. Stir in tomatoes and diced chilies. Cook, uncovered, over medium heat for 10 minutes, stirring occasionally. Add cooked beans, including some cooking liquid, a cup at a time to tomato mixture. Mash some of the beans as you add them. When all the beans have been added, stir to mix, then cook over low heat, stirring frequently, until thickened.

Beets In Dill Sauce
Makes about 4 cups

4 medium-sized beets
2 tbsp lemon juice
1 tbsp stone-ground mustard
1 tbsp cider vinegar
1 tbsp apple juice concentrate
1 tsp dried dill weed, or 1 tbsp fresh dill, chopped

Wash and peel the beets, then slice them into 1/4-inch thick rounds. Steam over boiling water until tender when pierced with a fork, about 20 minutes. Mix the remaining ingredients in a serving bowl. Add the beets and toss to mix. Serve immediately, or chill before serving.

Barley Cakes – Spinach
Makes 10 barley cakes

1 10-ounce package frozen spinach
1 small onion
2 medium garlic cloves
1 small carrot
2 cups fresh mushrooms
2 cups cooked barley
4 tbsp vegetable broth
2 tbsp shelled sunflower seeds

Grind the sunflower seeds in a food processor. Add the onion, garlic, carrot, and mushrooms. Grind thoroughly and then add the remaining ingredients and process for about 1 minute, or until well mixed. Preheat a large, non-stick skillet. Form the barley mixture into patties. Cook each side over medium-high heat for about 3 minutes, or until golden brown.

Broccoli and Ginger (sautéed)
Serves 4

1 clove garlic, minced
1 medium leek, sliced thin (white part only)
1/2-inch piece fresh ginger root, peeled and grated
1 pound broccoli, cut into florets
2 tbsp vegetable stock
4 tsp vegetable broth
1 tsp low-sodium Tamari

Sauté the garlic and ginger in the broth in a large skillet for 1 minute. Add the broccoli, leek, and stock. Toss together all the ingredients to mix well. Cover the pan and cook for 3 minutes. Remove the cover and continue to sauté, stirring frequently, until the vegetables are just tender, about 10 minutes.

Bruschetta
Makes 1-1/2 cups

1 cup diced tomatoes, hearts discarded
2 garlic cloves, minced
1/4 cup diced red onion
1/4 cup minced fresh parsley
1/4 cup fresh basil, minced

Combine ingredients in glass or ceramic pan. Refrigerate until ready to serve. To serve, spoon onto thin slices of toasted whole wheat bread.

Buckwheat and Cabbage
Makes about 2½ cups

2 cups finely chopped cabbage
1 cup vegetable broth or water
1/2 cup buckwheat groats
4 tsp vegetable broth for sautéing

Heat broth in a large saucepan. Add kasha and shredded cabbage and cook over medium-high heat, stirring constantly, for 1 minute. Stir in 1 cup vegetable broth. Cover and simmer until buckwheat is tender and all the liquid is absorbed, about 10 minutes.

Collards or Kale – Braised
Makes 3 cups

1 bunch collard greens or kale (6 to 8 cups chopped)
2-3 garlic cloves, minced
1/4 cup water
2 tsp vegetable broth
2 tsp low-sodium Tamari (soy sauce)
1 tsp balsamic vinegar

Wash greens, remove stems, then chop leaves into 1/2-inch wide strips. Combine broth, Tamari, vinegar, garlic, and water in a large pot or skillet. Cook over high heat about 30 seconds. Reduce heat to medium-high, add chopped greens, and toss to mix. Cover and cook, stirring often, until greens are tender, about 5 minutes.

Cornbread
Serves 8

1-1/2 cups non-dairy milk
1 cup cornmeal
1 cup whole wheat pastry flour
4 tbsp vegetable broth
1-1/2 tbsp vinegar
2 tbsp maple syrup
1 tsp baking powder
1/2 tsp baking soda

Preheat oven to 425. Combine non-dairy milk and vinegar and let stand. Mix dry ingredients and maple syrup in a large bowl. Add the non-dairy milk mixture and the broth and stir until blended. Spread the batter into a nonstick 9-inch square baking dish and bake for 25 to 30 minutes or until done. Serve hot.

Crostini (herbed bread) with Roasted Red Peppers
Makes 1 baguette (about 20 slices)

10 sun-dried tomato halves
1 garlic clove, pressed
1 small whole wheat baguette, cut into 1/2-inch thick slices
1 cup boiling water
2/3 cup roasted red peppers (about 2 peppers)
2 tbsp fresh basil, finely chopped OR
1 tsp dried basil
1/8 tsp black pepper

Pour boiling water over tomatoes and set aside until softened, about 10 minutes. Drain and chop coarsely. Chop roasted red peppers and add to tomatoes, along with garlic, basil, and black pepper. Let stand 30 minutes. Preheat oven to 350. Slice baguette and arrange slices in a single layer on one or two baking sheets. Toast in preheated oven until outsides are crisp, 10 to 15 minutes. Remove from oven and cool slightly, then spread each piece with 1 to 2 tablespoons of tomato mixture.

Curried – Cauliflower with Peas (spicy)
Makes about 6 cups

1 10-ounce bag frozen peas
1 large onion, chopped
1 cauliflower, cut or broken into florets (about 4 cups)
1/2 cup vegetable broth or water
1-2 tbsp low-sodium Tamari (soy sauce)
1 tsp coriander
1 tsp whole mustard seed
1/2 tsp each: turmeric, cumin
1/4 tsp each: cinnamon, ginger, cardamom, cayenne pepper

Combine coriander, mustard seed, turmeric, cumin, cinnamon, ginger, cardamom, and cayenne in a large skillet. Heat, stirring constantly, until spices darken slightly and just begin to smoke: about one minute. Remove from heat and cool slightly. Add vegetable broth, Tamari, and onion. Cook until onion is soft, stirring occasionally, about five minutes. Stir in cauliflower, then cover and cook over medium heat until tender when pierced with a fork, about five minutes. Stir in peas and cook until hot, another minute or two. For a less spicy taste, cut back on the cayenne pepper. Carrots and potatoes are optional.

Curried – Chickpea
Makes 8 to 10 servings

1 can tomato sauce
4 cans of chickpeas, drained
8 cloves garlic, minced
2 1/2 medium onions, thinly sliced
2 green peppers, cut into small pieces
1/8 cup vegetable broth
2 tsp turmeric
1 tsp cumin
1 tsp allspice
1 1/2 tsp cayenne pepper
1/2 tsp ginger

Sauté the onions in the broth. When brown, add the tomato sauce, garlic and the spices and sauté for a few minutes. Add the chickpeas and the green peppers and sauté over fairly high heat until everything is browned, about 15 minutes. Add water, if needed, turn down the heat and cover. Simmer for about 1 hour, stirring frequently. Serve over rice.

Curried – Vegetables

1 8 oz can tomatoes
4 cardamoms, bruised
2 medium zucchinis, cut into 1 inch chunks
2 bay leaves
1 small onion, peeled and finely chopped
1 large potato, peeled and diced
1 small cauliflower, stalks removed and florets divided up
1/2 cup green beans
1/4 pint hot water
1 tbsp vegetable broth
1 tbsp turmeric
1 tsp fenugreek seeds
1 tsp coriander seeds
1/2 tsp mustard seeds
1/4 tsp freshly milled black pepper

Put onion into a very large bowl with broth and place in the microwave. Cook on full power for 4 minutes until the onions start to brown. Add the cardamoms, fenugreek, mustard, coriander seeds and turmeric. Cook on full power for 1 minute, stirring halfway through cooking. Add the diced potato to the mixture and cook on full power for 3 minutes, stirring twice. Add the zucchinis, cauliflower florets, beans, tomatoes and bay leaves, cover and cook on full power for 5 minutes. Add about half the water. Cover and cook for 10 minutes. Reduce the setting to defrost/low and cook for 15 minutes, stirring occasionally, until the vegetables are tender, adding the remaining water if necessary. Adjust seasoning to taste.

Garlic Bread
Makes about 20 slices

2 roasted garlic heads
1 loaf whole wheat French (or other) bread, sliced
1–2 tsp mixed Italian herbs

Preheat oven to 350. Peel roasted cloves or squeeze flesh from skin and place in a bowl. Mash with a fork, then mix in Italian herbs. Spread on sliced bread. Wrap tightly in foil and bake for 20 minutes.

Green Beans – Italian Style
Makes about 6 cups

1 pound fresh green beans
2 cups chopped tomatoes, fresh or canned
2 large garlic cloves, minced
1 tbsp vegetable broth
2 tbsp chopped fresh basil or 1 tsp dried basil

Trim ends off beans and cut or break into bite-sized lengths. Steam until just tender, about 10 minutes, then set aside. Heat vegetable broth in a large skillet, then add tomatoes and garlic. Simmer 10 minutes. Add green beans and basil. Cook until beans are very tender, about 5 minutes, stirring occasionally. Season to taste.

Green Beans with Basil
Serves 4

1 lb. fresh or frozen green beans
1 tbsp minced onion
1 tsp vegetable broth
1 tsp dried basil leaves
1 tsp garlic powder
Dash pepper

Trim and snap green beans into thirds. Mince the onion. Put water on to boil to steam beans for 12-17 minutes or until tender. Sauté the onions in vegetable broth until tender. Add steamed beans, basil, garlic powder and pepper. Toss beans with basil sauce to coat evenly and serve.

Lentil–Bulgur Pilaf
6 servings

1 medium onion, minced
2 1/2 cups water
1 cup lentils
1 cup uncooked bulgur
1/2 cup minced fresh parsley
3 tbsp vegetable broth
1/2 tsp ground cumin
1/8 tsp cayenne pepper

Place lentils in a large saucepan. Add water and bring to a boil. Reduce heat, cover, and simmer for 15 minutes. Remove from heat. Stir in bulgur, cover, and set aside for 20 minutes, until bulgur is tender. Drain excess liquid. Heat broth in a skillet over medium heat. Add onion and sauté until lightly golden. Combine lentil-bulgur mixture, onion, parsley, cayenne pepper, and cumin in a large bowl and mix well.

Lentils – French Green
Makes about 6 cups

1 large onion, chopped
4 cups vegetable broth
1 cup French green lentils
1/2 cup chopped cilantro
1 tsp black mustard seeds
1 tsp turmeric
1 tsp cumin
1 tsp coriander
1/2 tsp ginger
1/4 tsp cayenne

Rinse lentils and place in a large pot with vegetable broth, onion and cilantro. Combine mustard seeds, turmeric, cumin, coriander, ginger, and cayenne in a small skillet. Toast over medium-high heat, stirring constantly, until spices are fragrant and just begin to smoke, about 2 minutes. Add to lentils. Cover and simmer until lentils are tender, about 30 minutes.

Mushrooms – In Barbeque Sauce
Serves 4

1 12-ounce package button or cremini mushrooms, sliced
1 small yellow onion, finely chopped
1/2 cup barbeque sauce

Braise onions in 1/4-cup water for 3-4 minutes. Add mushrooms and continue cooking for 4-5 more minutes. Add barbeque sauce and cook until sauce is desired thickness. Serve over veggie burgers, potatoes, or rice.

Polenta (cornmeal)
Makes 4 cups

4 cups water
1 cup polenta or stone-ground yellow cornmeal
1/2 tsp crushed dried rosemary (optional)

Bring water to a boil, then slowly pour in the polenta, stirring constantly with a whisk to prevent it from lumping. Lower heat and simmer, stirring fairly constantly until thick, about 10 minutes. (Note: polenta can be purchased at health food stores already prepared.)

Succotash

2 cups whole-kernel corn
2 cups cooked shell beans, lima or kidney
1 1/2 cups non-dairy milk
1/2 cup combination of red and green peppers, chopped

Combine all the ingredients in a large saucepan in water or a vegetable broth. Cook over low to medium heat, stirring the vegetables. Add the optional chopped sweet red and green pepper. Serves 4 to 6.

Sweet Potato Fries

4 large sweet potatoes, cut like fries
2 tbsp maple syrup
1 tsp vegetable broth
1 tsp ground cinnamon

Toss cut vegetables, broth, cinnamon in a bowl. Transfer to non-stick baking sheet. Bake in a 450 oven for about 50 minutes, or until the vegetables are tender. During the last 30 minutes of roasting, toss vegetables occasionally. At the end of baking, toss with maple syrup.

Vegetable Korma

14 fl oz can coconut milk
2 oz flaked almonds
1 lb mixed vegetables cut into bite size chunks (e.g., carrot, potato, broccoli, cauliflower, peas)
1 onion, finely chopped
1 tbsp vegetable broth
1 tbsp curry paste

Heat the broth in a large saucepan and cook the onion over a fairly high heat for 5 minutes until golden brown. Stir in the curry paste and cook for 1 minute. Add the vegetables and coconut milk, cover and simmer for 15 minutes until the vegetables are tender. Place the almonds in a non-stick frying pan and dry fry for 2-3 minutes, tossing the almonds until golden brown. Season curry to taste with pepper and sprinkle over the toasted almonds. Serve immediately with rice, naan or bread.

Vegetables with Thai Peanut Sauce
Serves 5 to 8

Thai Peanut Sauce
4 cups vegetables, fruits, and nuts
2 tbsp vegetable broth
1 tbsp water
1 tbsp minced garlic

Use any combination of broccoli, carrots, cauliflower, red cabbage, green peppers, scallions, tomatoes, mushrooms, unsalted cashew halves, cilantro, raisins, and pineapple chunks totaling 4 cups. Sauté the vegetable/fruit/nut mixture with the water, garlic, and vegetable broth. Serve over rice topped with Peanut Sauce.

Main Dishes

Basmati, Vegetables & Fruit
Serves 4

1 19-ounce can pineapple chunks, drained
2 unripe bananas
1 medium onion, cubed
1 medium carrot, grated
2 cups broccoli florets
1 cup basmati rice
2 tbsp vegetable broth
1 tbsp chopped parsley
1 tbsp chopped chives
1 tbsp chopped fresh basil
1/2 tsp curry powder

Cook the rice in 2 cups of water for 20 minutes, or until done. Cut the broccoli florets into small flowers. Cut the pineapple into bite-sized pieces and the banana into large slices. Heat the broth in a pan, and add the onion. Add the broccoli and carrot. Lower the heat, cover the pan and let it simmer for a few minutes. Add the curry, pineapple, banana and pepper, and fry for a few more minutes. The vegetables should be just tender. Add the herbs shortly before serving. Serve on rice.

Basmati and Wild Rice Pilaf
Makes about 6 cups

2 garlic cloves, minced
2 stalks celery, thinly sliced
1 onion, finely chopped
2-1/2 cups vegetable broth
2 cups thinly sliced mushrooms
1/2 cup wild rice, rinsed
1/2 cup brown basmati rice, rinsed
1/3 cup chopped pecans
1/3 cup finely chopped parsley
1/2 tsp thyme
1/2 tsp marjoram
1/4 tsp black pepper

Combine wild rice and vegetable broth in a saucepan. Cover and simmer 20 minutes. Add basmati rice, then cover and continue cooking over very low heat until tender, about 50 minutes. Preheat oven to 375. Place pecans in a small oven-proof dish and bake until fragrant, about 8 minutes. Set aside. Heat 1/2 cup of water in a large non-stick skillet and cook onion and garlic until all the water has evaporated. Add 1/4 cup of water and cook until the water has evaporated. Repeat until onions are browned, about 20 minutes. Lower heat slightly and add mushrooms, celery, parsley, thyme, marjoram and black pepper. Cook, stirring frequently, for 5 minutes. Add cooked rice and toasted pecans. Stir to mix, then transfer to a baking dish and bake 20 minutes.

Broccoli with Buckwheat and Black Bean Sauce
Makes about 8 cups

1 15-ounce can black beans, drained
1 large bunch broccoli
4 cups boiling water
2 cups buckwheat groats (or kasha for stronger flavor)
1/2 cup roasted red pepper
2 tbsp lemon juice
2 tbsp vegetable broth
1/2 tsp chili powder
1/4 tsp ground cumin
1/4 tsp ground coriander
1/4 cup chopped fresh cilantro

Cut off broccoli stems. Cut or break the tops into bite-sized florets. Peel the stem with a sharp knife, then slice into 1/2-inch thick rounds. Set aside. Into the water in a large saucepan, place buckwheat groats. Cover and simmer for about 10 minutes, or until all the liquid has been absorbed. While buckwheat (kasha) is cooking, combine and purée all the remaining ingredients in a food processor or blender. Just before you are ready to eat, steam broccoli over boiling water for about 5 minutes, or until it is bright green and just tender. Place a generous about of buckwheat on each serving plate, then top with steamed broccoli and black-bean sauce.

Buckwheat (roasted) Pilaf
Serves 4

1 small carrot, sliced
1 small onion, cut in 8 pieces
1/2 celery rib, sliced
2 cups vegetable broth
1/2 cup whole buckwheat groats (aka kasha)

In a food processor, pulse the carrot, onion and celery until they are finely chopped. In a large, heavy saucepan or small Dutch oven, heat the 2 tablespoons of broth over medium-high heat. Stir in the chopped vegetables. Sauté until they are soft, 4 minutes, stirring occasionally. Mix the buckwheat into the sautéed vegetables. Stir until it is fragrant and looks slightly darker in color, 1-2 minutes. Pour in the broth. Cover the pot tightly. When the liquid boils, reduce the heat and simmer 10 minutes. Turn off the heat and let the pilaf sit 5 minutes. Fluff the pilaf with a fork.

Bulgur Pilaf (spicy)
Makes about 4 cups

1 medium onion, chopped
2 garlic cloves, minced
1/2 red bell pepper, finely diced
1-3/4 cups boiling water or vegetable stock
1 cup bulgur wheat
2 tbsp vegetable broth
2 tsp chili powder
3/4 tsp cumin
1/8 tsp celery seed

Heat broth in a large skillet or pot and cook onion for 3 minutes. Stir in garlic, bulgur, chili powder, cumin, and celery seed. Continue cooking, stirring often, until onion is soft, about 5 minutes. Add bell pepper and boiling water. Stir to mix, then cover and simmer until bulgur is tender and all liquid is absorbed, about 20 minutes. Oven method: Preheat oven to 350. Prepare as above, except before adding boiling water, transfer bulgur mixture to an ovenproof dish. Add boiling water, cover with foil and bake until bulgur is tender and all liquid is absorbed, about 30 minutes.

Bulgur – Spanish
Serves 8

3-1/2 cups boiling water
2 cups bulgur
2 garlic cloves, minced
4-6 tsp chili powder
2 tsp vegetable broth
1 tsp ground cumin

Place the bulgur in a large bowl and pour the boiling water over it. Cover the bowl and let stand 20 minutes, until the bulgur is tender. Drain off any excess water. In a large skillet, sauté the garlic in vegetable broth (or water). Do not let it brown. With the pan still on the heat, stir in the soaked bulgur and add the chili powder and cumin. Turn with a spatula to mix in the spices and continue cooking until the mixture is very hot.

Burger – Beet
Serves 6

1 cup uncooked oats
1/2 cup cooked oats
1/2 cup coarsely ground walnuts
1/4 cup coarsely ground almonds
1/4 cup minced green pepper
1/4 cup minced onion
2 tbsp low-sodium Tamari (soy sauce)
2 tbsp sesame seeds
1 tbsp instant dry vegetable broth
1 tbsp nutritional yeast flakes (optional)
1 tbsp finely grated raw beet
1 tsp dried basil
1/4 tsp dried thyme
1/4 tsp ground sage
1/4 tsp mustard powder
tomato slices, for garnish

Mix all ingredients together well. Form into 6 patties and grill until cooked through. Serve on whole wheat rolls with tomato slices and your favorite condiments.

Burger – Lentil
Makes 8 burgers

1 small onion, chopped
1/2 cup short-grain brown rice
1/2 cup lentils
2 cups water
1 small carrot
1 medium-sized celery stalk
2 tsp stone-ground mustard
1 tsp garlic powder
vegetable-oil spray, for skillet

In a medium-sized saucepan, combine onion, rice, lentils, and water. Bring to a slow simmer, then cover and cook for about 50 minutes, or until rice and lentils are tender and all the water has been absorbed. Chop carrot and celery until fine (a food processor makes this easy). Add them to the hot lentil mixture, along with the remaining ingredients. Stir to mix, then chill completely. (You can make the patties while the mixture is still warm, but forming is much easier once it is chilled.) Form mixture into 2- to 3-inch patties. Lightly coat a large, nonstick skillet with vegetable-oil spray. Cook patties over medium heat for about 4 minutes per side, or until lightly browned.

Burger – Nut and Seed
Makes 4 burgers

1 carrot, grated
1 stalk celery, finely chopped
1/2 cup ground almonds
1/2 cup ground raw sunflower seeds
1/2 cup finely chopped onion
egg replacer equivalent to 1 egg
1 tbsp vegetable broth
1 tsp dill weed
1 tsp marjoram
garlic powder to taste
black pepper to taste

Preheat oven to 350. Grind the nuts in a coffee grinder or food processor, and chop vegetables into small pieces. Mix all the ingredients together, and shape into burgers. Bake for 15 minutes on each side on a non-stick cookie sheet.

Burritos – Black Bean
Makes 4 burritos

Black bean burritos make a quick meal when time is short or they can be made ahead and refrigerated for lunches and easy instant snacks. Instant black bean flakes are sold in natural food stores and some supermarkets.

4 flour tortillas
2 tomatoes, sliced
2 green onions, sliced
1/2 avocado, sliced (optional)
2 cups shredded romaine lettuce
1 cup instant black bean flakes (sold in health food stores)
        or 1 15-ounce can fat-free, low-sodium refried black beans
1/2 cup salsa

Mix bean flakes with boiling water in a small pan or bowl. Let stand until completely softened, 3 to 5 minutes. If using canned beans, heat on the stove or in a microwave if desired. Warm tortillas in a large dry skillet. Spread warm tortilla with approximately 1/2 cup of bean mixture. Top with lettuce, tomatoes, onions, avocado if using, and salsa. Roll tortilla around filling. Serve or wrap in plastic and refrigerate.

Chili – Black Bean
Makes 6 cups

2 15-ounce cans black beans, including liquid
1 4-ounce can diced chilies
2 medium-sized cloves garlic, minced
1 medium-sized onion, chopped
1 small bell pepper, diced fine
1/2 cup water
1/2 cup crushed tomatoes or tomato sauce
1 tsp ground cumin

In a large skillet or pot, heat the water. Add onion, garlic, and pepper. Cook over high heat until onion is translucent. Add remaining ingredients and simmer for about 15 minutes or until flavors are blended.

Chili – Three Bean

2 cans (14 oz.) diced tomatoes
1 can (15 oz.) white soybeans
1 can (15 oz.) black soybeans
1 can (15 oz.) red beans
1 can (15 oz.) tomato sauce
1 1/2 cups chopped onion
2 tbsp maple syrup
2 tbsp minced garlic
1 tbsp chili powder
2 tsp ground cumin
2 tsp vegetable broth
1 tsp black pepper

Heat broth in large pot over medium-high heat. Cook onions until soft. Drain and rinse three beans and add to onions. Stir in all remaining ingredients. Bring to a boil and then reduce heat to low and simmer for 30 to 45 minutes.

Chili – Vegetarian
Serves 4

2 15-oz. cans pinto beans, rinsed and drained
1-3 jalapeno peppers, seeded and minced
1 medium yellow onion, chopped
1 medium green bell pepper, cut in ½-inch pieces
1 cup coarsely chopped canned tomatoes, drained
2 cups vegetable broth, divided
1/4 cup chopped cilantro leaves
2 tsp ground ancho chile, or 1 Tbs. chili powder
1 tbsp finely chopped garlic
1 tsp ground cumin
1 tsp dried oregano
2 tsp masa or corn meal
Freshly ground black pepper, optional

In a medium Dutch oven, sauté the onion, bell pepper and garlic in a small amount of vegetable broth until the onion is translucent.. Add the jalapeno pepper, cumin, ancho chile or chili powder and oregano. Stir until the spices are fragrant. Add the beans, chopped tomatoes, all but 3 tablespoons of the vegetable broth and the cilantro. Set the remaining vegetable broth aside. Bring the chili to a boil. Reduce the heat and simmer, uncovered, for 10 minutes. Place the masa or corn meal in a small bowl. Mix in the reserved vegetable broth, stirring to make a smooth mixture. While stirring the chili, blend in the corn mixture, blending it in well. Add pepper, if desired. Continue simmering the chili 10 minutes longer. For the best flavor, let the chili sit 1-2 hours in the refrigerator. Reheat and serve.

Couscous – Moroccan
Serves 4

1 15-oz. can chick peas
1 sweet potato or small winter squash, cubed
1 zucchini, cubed
1 red bell pepper, diced
1 yellow bell pepper, diced
1 clove garlic, minced or pressed
2 cups uncooked couscous
1/2 cup raisins
1/4 cup water
2 tbsp vegetable broth
1 tsp ground cumin
1/2 tsp allspice
1/2 tsp ground ginger
1/2 tsp turmeric
1/2 tsp paprika
1/4 tsp cayenne
1/4 tsp cinnamon

Sauté the zucchini, sweet potato or squash, and garlic in the broth until partially cooked, about 5 minutes. Use water as necessary to keep the vegetables from sticking. Drain and rinse the chick peas. Add the spices, chick peas, and pepper to the pan. Cover and cook for about 5 minutes. Meanwhile, place the couscous and raisins in another saucepan. Add enough water so that the couscous is covered by about 1/2 inch. Bring the mixture to a boil, then cover tightly, remove from the heat, and let set for at least 10 minutes. Remove the cover from the pepper/chick pea mixture, stir, and cook a few minutes longer to heat thoroughly and thicken. Serve the bean pepper stew over the couscous.

Curried – Mushrooms, Avocados & Rice

Cooked rice
4 avocadoes
2 tomatoes
1 lb mushrooms
1 large onion
2 tbsp vegetable broth
2 tsp (or more to taste) curry powder
4 tsp lemon juice

Chop the onion. Sauté in the broth along with the mushrooms until tender. Stir in the curry powder and cook for a few moments longer. Chop the tomato and add to the saucepan. Heat through. Add the lemon juice. Stir well and heat until just below boiling point. Peel and halve the avocados. Place on the rice and fill with the mushroom mixture.

Eggplant "Steaks"
Makes 4 servings

2 small eggplants
1 clove garlic, minced
1 tbsp balsamic vinegar
6 tbsp vegetable broth
1 tsp minced fresh parsley
1/2 tsp hot sauce
1/3 tsp dried rosemary

Remove the stem ends from the eggplants and cut off enough of the skin to square the sides. Slice each eggplant lengthwise into two pieces, each approximately 1/2-inch thick. Heat the oven to 350. In a small bowl, stir together 2 tablespoons of broth and the hot sauce. Brush evenly over both sides of the eggplant slices. Bake on a baking sheet for 15 minutes, turning over once. Then broil for 1 minute per side or until the slices are well browned and tender. In a small bowl, stir together the remaining broth, garlic, vinegar, parsley, and rosemary. Brush on the cooked eggplant. Let stand for 5 minutes before serving.

Falafel

2 15oz cans chickpeas
6 scallions, minced
4 cloves garlic, minced
1/3 cup whole wheat flour (or brown rice flour, quinoa flour)
1/4 cup minced fresh parsley
1/4 cup water or reserved bean liquid
1 tbsp lemon juice
1 tsp turmeric
cayenne to taste

Mix everything but flour in food processor (or mash it). Add flour and stir till well mixed. Form into small patties.
Bake at 375, turn, until both sides are crispy. Wrap in spinach leaves. Dip in favorite dressing.

Falafel – Quick
Makes 12 falafels

1 package falafel mix
2 green onions, sliced
6 pieces whole wheat pita bread
4 cups shredded lettuce
1 cup sliced cucumber
1 medium tomato, diced

Prepare falafel patties according to package directions. Warm pocket bread until it is soft. Cut warm pita bread in half and carefully open the pocket. Fill it with two falafel patties. Garnish with lettuce, cucumber, tomato, green onions, and mustard. Repeat with remaining pita bread.

Ginger Noodles
Serves 6 to 8

1 package whole wheat soba noodles (approximately 8 ounces)
2 garlic cloves, minced
2 green onions, finely chopped, including tops
1/4 cup fresh cilantro (optional)
1 jalapeno pepper, finely chopped
3 tbsp seasoned rice vinegar
3 tbsp low-sodium Tamari (soy sauce)
2 tsp finely chopped fresh ginger

Cook the noodles in boiling water according to the package directions. When tender, drain, and rinse. Mix all the remaining ingredients, then pour over the noodles and toss to mix.

Greens and Beans With Garlic
Serves 4

12 oz. can of cannellini beans
2 large cloves garlic, minced
3 cups chopped kale
3 cups chopped broccoli rabe
2 cups collards, cut in 1/2-inch ribbons
3 cups fresh spinach or a 10 oz. frozen package, defrosted
1 cup vegetable broth
3/4 cup small leek, white part only, sliced
1/2 cup scallions, green and white parts, chopped
Season to taste.

In a large, heavy skillet over medium heat, sauté the leeks, scallions and garlic in a few tbsp of vegetable broth. Add the kale, broccoli rabe and collards, stirring until they are wilted. Mix in spinach and beans. Add the vegetable broth and simmer until the greens are tender, stirring occasionally. Season to taste. Serve over pasta or polenta.

Mushrooms – Portabello Grilled
Serves 4

4 large portabello mushrooms
2 medium-size cloves garlic, minced
4 tsp of vegetable broth
2 tbsp of red wine
2 tbsp low-sodium Tamari (soy sauce)
1 tbsp of balsamic vinegar

Clean mushrooms and trim stems flush with the bottom of the caps. In a large skillet, mix the remaining ingredients. Heat until the mixture begins to bubble; add mushrooms, tops down. Reduce to medium heat. Cover and cook for about 3 minutes, or until tops are browned. (If pan becomes dry, add 2 to 3 tbsp of water.) Turn the mushrooms and cook for about 5 minutes more, or until tender when pierced with a sharp knife.

Pasta – Artichoke
Makes 4 servings

1 (14-oz.) can artichoke hearts, quartered
1 (12-oz.) can diced tomatoes
1 (8-oz.) can tomato sauce
1/2 pound tri-colored whole wheat pasta
2 cloves garlic, minced
1/2 medium onion, chopped
2 tbsp vegetable broth

Cook the pasta according to the package directions. While the pasta is cooking, sauté the onion and garlic in the broth for 1 to 2 minutes. Add the artichokes, tomatoes, and tomato sauce. Drain the pasta and combine all the ingredients.

Pasta – Asparagus
Serves 4

2 pounds fresh asparagus
1 28-ounce can tomatoes, chopped
8 ounces spaghetti
1 medium onion, chopped
2 tbsp water or vegetable stock
1 tbsp chopped fresh basil
1/4 tsp ground sage

Heat water or vegetable stock in a large, non-stick pan. Add onion and sauté over medium heat for 3 minutes, until translucent. Add tomatoes, asparagus, basil, and sage. Bring to a boil, cover, and simmer for 7 minutes. Remove from heat and keep warm. Cook pasta in water only without salt. Drain pasta and place in a serving bowl. Add the asparagus mixture and toss.

Pasta – Buckwheat Pasta
Serves 6

12 ounces whole wheat soba noodles
1 medium onion, chopped
3 cups sliced fresh mushrooms
1-1/2 cups cold water
4 tbsp vegetable broth
2 tbsp whole wheat flour
2 tsp low-sodium Tamari (soy sauce)
1/2 tsp garlic powder
1/4 tsp black pepper

Sauté the onion in a large skillet with the broth until transparent, then add the mushrooms. Cover and continue cooking until mushrooms are brown. Whisk flour and water together until smooth, then add to the skillet along with the Tamari, garlic powder, and pepper. Cook, uncovered, over medium-low heat until thickened. Bring water to boil in a large kettle. Add the noodles and boil until al dente, about 8 minutes.

Pasta – Cold Linguine & Asparagus
Makes 4 servings

3/4 lb. asparagus, cut diagonally into 1 1/2-inch pieces
8 oz. linguine whole wheat pasta
1/2 cup orange juice (unsweetened)
1/2 cup sliced green onions (green part only)
2 tbsp low-sodium Tamari (soy sauce)
3 tsp vegetable broth
1 tsp minced roasted garlic
1 tsp grated, fresh ginger root
1 tsp grated orange peel
1/4 tsp brown sugar
Dash hot pepper sauce, or to taste

Cook the noodles according to the package directions. Place the asparagus in a colander. Pour the noodles into the colander, on top of the asparagus, and drain—the hot water and noodles will lightly steam the asparagus. Leave in the colander for 10 minutes. Combine the remaining ingredients in a large bowl and mix well. Add the noodles and asparagus and stir gently until well blended. Refrigerate for several hours or overnight, stirring occasionally. Stir again before serving and serve cold.

Pasta – Lentils and Artichoke Hearts

1 pound farfalle, rotini or other whole wheat pasta
1 1/2 cups artichoke hearts
2 large garlic cloves, pressed or minced
1 bay leaf
1 cup dry red lentils
3 cups water
2 cups canned tomatoes
2 cups diced onions
2 tbsp lemon juice
2 tsp ground cumin
1 tsp ground coriander
1/4 tsp crushed red pepper

Combine the water, lentils, and bay leaf, bring to a boil, lower the heat and simmer for 15-20 min. Sauté onions until golden, add the garlic, cumin, and coriander, stir frequently. Add the lemon juice, tomatoes, artichoke hearts and crushed red pepper and simmer for 10 minutes. Drain the cooked lentils, save some of the cooking liquid (in case sauce is dry). Then add lentils to the tomato mixture, simmer for 10 minutes, adding 1/2 cup of the cooking liquid from lentils if sauce is dry. Boil water for pasta, and then top the pasta with the sauce.

Pasta – Mediterranean

12 or more kalamata olives
4 spring onions, sliced
2 sweet red peppers, sliced thinly
2 cloves of garlic, minced
3 tbsp vegetable broth
Fettuccini, linguini or angel hair

Over a medium flame, sauté the garlic in the broth for a minute. Add the green onions and sauté 2 more minutes. Add the olives and peppers and sauté a few more minutes then take it off heat and serve it over the pasta.

Pasta – Penne with Fresh Spinach, Tomatoes, and Olives
Serves 4

2 14.5-ounce cans tomatoes, diced
8 ounces whole wheat penne pasta
1 pound fresh spinach, coarsely chopped
1 medium onion, chopped
1/2 cup kalamata olives, pitted, sliced
2 tbsp vegetable broth
1 tbsp chopped fresh parsley

Heat broth in a large, nonstick skillet. Add onion and sauté over medium heat for 3 minutes. Add chopped tomatoes. Bring to a boil and then reduce heat, cover, and simmer for 20 minutes. Add sliced olives, chopped spinach, and parsley. Cook an additional 5 minutes. Meanwhile, cook pasta. Drain and transfer to a serving bowl. Add spinach mixture and toss.

Pasta – Roasted Vegetables
Serves 6

16-ounces penne or other bite-sized pasta
10-12 baby bella or cremini mushrooms, quartered
2 Roma tomatoes, chopped
1 medium zucchini, quartered and sliced
1 sweet red pepper, cut into bite-sized chunks
1 small onion, cut into bite-sized chunks
1/2 large eggplant, cut into bite-sized chunks
1/2 head garlic (about 6 cloves)
2 tbsp vegetable broth
2 tsp fresh thyme
crushed red pepper, to taste (optional)

Heat oven to 400. Peel garlic cloves and cut in half. Spread eggplant, zucchini, red pepper, onion, mushrooms, and garlic cloves on a flat nonstick pan (baking dish or cookie sheet). Sprinkle with 1 tablespoon of vegetable broth and toss. Roast for 25 to 35 minutes, turning vegetables once during cooking, until vegetables are soft and have crispy edges. Cook pasta according to package directions, drain, and rinse. Toss pasta with vegetables, tomatoes, fresh thyme, and the remaining tablespoon of broth. Serve warm or at room temperature.

Pasta Supper
Makes about 6 cups

1 15-ounce can red kidney beans, including liquid
8 ounces whole wheat pasta spirals
1 onion chopped
2 cups finely chopped fresh kale
1 cup tomato juice
1/2 cup chopped fresh basil
1/4 cup chopped garlic
1 tbsp vegetable broth

Cook the pasta until just tender. Transfer to a colander. Rinse and drain. Set aside. Heat the broth in a large skillet or pot. Add the onion and garlic and cook over medium heat, stirring often. Stir in 1/4 cup of water. Add the tomato juice, kidney beans with their liquid, kale and basil. Stir to mix, then cover and simmer until the kale is tender. Stir in the cooked pasta.

Pie – Tamale

1 can kidney beans, rinsed and drained
1 can corn
1 can sliced or whole black olives
1 chopped onion
1 chopped bell pepper
1 1/2 pints home-canned tomatoes
1 cup cornmeal
1/2 cup water
1 tbsp chili powder
Garlic powder

Mix all together and pour into casserole. Bake at 350, covered, for 30 min. Uncover to brown top.

Pie – Tamale 2
Serves 8

6 cups Chili Beans, with juice
2 cups non-dairy milk
2 tbsp vinegar
2 cups cornmeal
4 tbsp vegetable broth
2 tsp baking soda

Preheat oven to 400. Combine the non-dairy milk and vinegar and let stand 5 minutes or more. Heat the beans until very hot, then pour into a 9- x 12-inch baking dish. Mix the dry ingredients in a large bowl, and add the non-dairy milk mixture and broth. Stir just to mix, then pour over the hot beans, and bake until the bread is set and golden brown, about 30 minutes.

Pizza
Makes 4 servings.

4 individual whole wheat pizza shells
1 small eggplant, sliced
1 medium zucchini, sliced
1 red onion, cut into small wedges
1 red bell pepper, thinly sliced
1 yellow bell pepper, thinly sliced
2 tbsp vegetable broth
1 tbsp balsamic vinegar
1/2 tsp dried thyme
1/2 tsp black pepper
1/2 cup tomato sauce

Preheat the oven to 425. Combine the eggplant, zucchini, onion, bell peppers, broth, vinegar, thyme, and pepper in a large baking dish and toss to mix well. Bake, stirring occasionally, for 20 minutes, or until the vegetables are tender. Set aside. Place the pizza shells on baking sheets. Spread about 2 tablespoons of the tomato sauce on each pizza shell, then top with the roasted vegetables. Bake for 10 to 12 minutes or until the pizza shells and vegetables are heated through.

Pizza – Pita Pizzas
Makes 6 pizzas

6 pieces of whole wheat pita bread
1 15-ounce can tomato sauce
1 6-ounce can tomato paste
2 green onions, thinly sliced
1 red bell pepper, diced
1 cup chopped mushrooms
1 tsp garlic granules or powder
1/2 tsp basil
1/2 tsp oregano
1/2 tsp thyme

Preheat oven to 375. Combine tomato sauce, tomato paste, garlic granules and herbs. Prepare vegetables as directed. Turn a piece of pita bread upside down and spread with 2 to 3 tablespoons of sauce. Top with chopped vegetables. Repeat with remaining pita breads. Arrange on a baking sheet and bake until edges are lightly browned, about 10 minutes. (Note: Refrigerate or freeze the remaining sauce for use at another time or use with another meal.)

Polenta – Grilled with Portabella Mushrooms
Serves 4

4 large portabella mushrooms
1 roasted red pepper, cut into thin strips for garnish (optional)
2 cups vegetable broth
1/2 cup polenta (coarsely ground cornmeal)
1/2 cup water
2 tbsp vegetable broth
2 tbsp low-sodium Tamari (soy sauce)
2 tbsp balsamic vinegar
2 tbsp red wine
2 garlic cloves, crushed

Combine the polenta, 2 cups vegetable broth, and the 1/2 cup of water in a saucepan. Bring to a simmer and cook, stirring frequently, until very thick, 15 to 20 minutes. Pour into a 9- x 9-inch non-stick baking dish and chill completely. To grill, cut into wedges and cook over medium heat until nicely browned. Clean the mushrooms, remove stems. Prepare the marinade by stirring the remaining ingredients together in a large bowl. Place the mushrooms upside down in the marinade and let stand 10 to 15 minutes. Turn right side up and grill over medium-hot coals about 5 minutes. Turn and pour some of the marinade into each of the cavities. Grill until mushrooms can be pierced with a skewer, about 5 minutes longer. Serve with grilled polenta. Garnish with roasted red pepper strips, if desired.

Polenta – Stuffed Peppers
Makes 4 servings.

1 (1-lb.) package cooked polenta
2 medium tomatoes, diced
1 green, 1 red, 1 yellow, and 1 orange bell pepper (or any combination you choose)
2 tbsp vegetable broth
1/2 tsp minced fresh garlic
1/4 tsp pepper
Paprika

Preheat the oven to 375. Cut the tops off the peppers and scoop out the insides. Place peppers on a baking tray. Sauté the garlic in the broth over low heat. Add the tomatoes and pepper. Heat briefly and stir into the polenta.
Fill the peppers with the polenta mixture and sprinkle with paprika. Cook for 30 to 40 minutes.

Potato Pancakes
Serves 4

4 large potatoes, grated
2 carrots, grated
1 medium onion, grated
1/4 cup chopped cilantro
2 tbsp whole wheat flour (optional)

Mix ingredients, press firmly into patties, and cook in nonstick pan, pressing down occasionally while cooking. Turn and cook on other side. Serve two pancakes per person, with apple sauce.

Potatoes – Cottage Fries
Serves 6

4 medium red potatoes
1 medium onion, chopped
1 green bell pepper, diced
2 tbsp vegetable broth
1 tsp paprika
1/4 tsp black pepper

Dice potatoes into generous bite-size pieces. Steam over boiling water until they are just tender when pierced with a fork, about 15 minutes. In a large skillet, sauté the onion and bell pepper in 1 teaspoon vegetable broth until the onion is soft, about 5 minutes. Transfer to a bowl and set aside. Add 1 tablespoon broth to the skillet and sauté the potatoes over medium-heat until hot and lightly browned, about 5 minutes. Return the onion mixture to the pan, add remaining ingredients, toss to mix, and serve. Add more broth as needed.

Potatoes – Golden
Serves 6

4 large red potatoes
2 tsp whole mustard seed
1 onion, chopped
1 cup water
1/2 tsp turmeric
1/2 tsp cumin
1/4 tsp ginger
1/8 tsp cayenne
1/8 black pepper
1-1/2 tsp low-sodium Tamari (soy sauce)

Steam potatoes over boiling water until tender when pierced with a fork, 40 to 50 minutes. Cool completely, then cut them into 1/2-inch cubes. Toast the spices in a large nonstick skillet for 1 to 2 minutes, then carefully pour in 1/2 cup of the water. Add the chopped onion and cook, stirring frequently, until the onion is soft and most of the liquid has evaporated, about 5 minutes. Add the potatoes along with the remaining water and the Tamari. Stir to mix, then cover and cook over medium heat for 5 minutes. Stir before serving.

Quesadillas
Makes 8 quesadillas

1 15-ounce can garbanzo beans
8 corn tortillas
1 garlic clove, peeled
1/2 cup chopped green onions
1/2 cup salsa
1/2 cup water-packed, roasted red pepper
3 tbsp lemon juice
1 tbsp vegetable broth
1/4 tsp cumin

Drain garbanzo beans and place in a food processor or blender with roasted peppers, lemon juice, broth, garlic, and cumin. Process until very smooth, 1 to 2 minutes. Spread a tortilla with 2 to 3 tablespoons of garbanzo mixture and place in a large non-stick skillet over medium heat. Sprinkle with chopped green onions, and salsa. Top with a second tortilla and cook until the bottom tortilla is warm and soft, 2-3 minutes. Turn and cook the second side for another minute. Remove from pan and cut in half. Repeat with remaining tortillas.

Ratatouille
Makes 4 to 5 servings.

4-5 cloves garlic, crushed
2 large tomatoes, cut into medium wedges
1 medium zucchini, sliced
1 green bell pepper, chopped
1 red bell pepper, chopped
1 small eggplant, cut into small cubes
1 large onion, diced
1 bay leaf
1/2 cup tomato juice
5 tbsp tomato paste
4 tbsp dry red wine
1 tbsp vegetable broth
1 tbsp dried basil
1/2 tbsp dried marjoram
1/2 tbsp dried oregano
1/2 tsp black pepper
Dash of ground rosemary

Sauté the onion in the broth until translucent. Add the bay leaf and tomato juice and stir well. Then add the garlic, herbs and pepper and mix until well blended. Cover the saucepan and simmer for 10 minutes over low heat. Add the zucchini and peppers, stir well, cover, and simmer for another 5 minutes. Add the eggplant, tomatoes, and tomato paste and stir again. Cover and continue to simmer until the vegetables are tender, about 8 minutes more. Serve over rice or with crusty French bread.

Rotini with Ginger Peanut Sauce
Serves 6

8 ounces rotini
2 tbsp peanut butter
1 to 2 tbsp chopped fresh ginger root
1 tbsp low-sodium Tamari (soy sauce)
1-1/2 tbsp vinegar
1 tsp Dijon mustard
1 cup steamed carrots
1 cup steamed broccoli
3 scallions, finely chopped

Boil the rotini until tender. Drain, saving 1/2 cup of the water. In a blender, whir the 1/2-cup pasta water and the ginger, peanut butter, Tamari, vinegar, and mustard. Toss pasta with sauce. Top with carrots, broccoli, and chopped scallions. (Note: you can use prepared peanut sauce instead of making it.)

Sandwich – Chickpea Pita Pockets

4 whole wheat pitas
1 x 16 oz / 450 g can chick peas, rinsed, drained and mashed
1/3 cup chopped celery
1 t minced onion
2 t pickle relish (or piccalilly)
2 t mustard
Dash of garlic powder
Lettuce, tomato slices, grated carrot, etc for toppings

Place the chickpeas, celery, onion, relish, mustard and garlic powder in a bowl and mix well. Cut the pitas in half and open up into pockets. Fill each pita pocket with 1/4 of the chickpea spread, top with lettuce, tomato or other vegetables and serve.

Sandwich – Garbanzo Salad
Makes 4 sandwiches

1 15-ounce can garbanzo beans, drained
8 slices whole wheat bread
4 lettuce leaves
4 tomato slices
1 stalk celery, finely sliced
1 green onion, finely chopped
1 tbsp sweet pickle relish

Mash garbanzo beans with a fork or potato masher, leaving some chunks. Add sliced celery, chopped onion and pickle relish. Spread on whole wheat bread and top with lettuce and sliced tomatoes.

Sandwich – Grilled Portobello
Serves 4

4 large Portobello mushrooms
4 whole wheat buns
1 cup red wine vinegar
1 cup vegetable broth
1 cup low-sodium Tamari (soy sauce)
Grilled onion

Take equal parts of red wine vinegar, vegetable broth and Tamari and place in a blender to mix then pour over the mushrooms. Let them sit overnight then grill. Add onion and other toppings and a bun.

Sandwich – Toasted Wheat Roll

Whole wheat sandwich roll
Lettuce
Tomato
Onions
Pickles
Pepperoncini (Tuscan peppers)
Basil
Pepper
Dijon Mustard
Slice ingredients so they all fit onto a sandwich roll. Toast bun. Add mustard and any other seasoning or sauce.

Sloppy Joes
Serves 8

1 16-ounce can tomato sauce
1-1/2 cups boiling water
1-1/2 cups dry texturized vegetable protein (TVP)
1 cup coarsely chopped onions
2 tbsp vegetable broth
2 medium green bell peppers, coarsely chopped
1 tbsp chili powder (more to taste)
1 tsp dried mustard

Heat the broth and sauté the onions and pepper for 5 minutes. Add the remaining ingredients and simmer for 20 minutes. Serve over hamburger rolls.

Spinach with Garlic
Serves 4

1 large bunch of fresh spinach
3 cloves of garlic
1 tsp vegetarian Worcestershire sauce

Wash and de-stem spinach. Peel and mince garlic. Braise garlic in Worcestershire sauce over medium heat, stirring, until lightly browned. Add spinach to hot skillet. Use tongs to turn spinach until it is just wilted. Serve hot or at room temperature.

Squash – Pinto Beans
Makes 4 servings

1 16-ounce can pinto beans, drained
1 14.5-ounce can diced tomatoes, undrained
2 garlic cloves, minced
3 thyme sprigs
2 cups hot cooked brown rice
1 cup (1/2-inch-thick) sliced yellow squash
1 cup (1/2-inch-thick) sliced zucchini
1/2 cup fresh corn kernels
1/2 cup chopped onion
1/4 cup vegetable broth (or more, as needed, to sauté in)
2 tsp minced seeded jalapeno pepper

Heat broth in a large skillet over medium-high heat. Add the onion, jalapeno, and garlic, and sauté 2 minutes. Stir in squash and zucchini, and sauté 2 minutes. Add corn, beans, tomatoes, and thyme; cover, reduce heat, and simmer 10 minutes. Discard thyme. Serve over rice.

Squash – Spanish
Serves 4

1 8-ounce package of button mushrooms, sliced
2 small zucchini, quartered lengthwise and sliced
1 small yellow onion, finely chopped
1-1/2 cups frozen corn
2 tbsp water
1/2 tsp cumin
1/2 tsp chili powder

Braise onion in 1 tablespoon of water, stirring until liquid has evaporated. Add sliced zucchini, mushrooms, and the remaining water. Stir in spices and simmer for 5 minutes, covered, until mushrooms are soft. Stir in corn and cook for 2 more minutes to heat through. Add black pepper to taste.

Squash – Winter
Makes 4 cups

1 medium winter squash (e.g., butternut)
1/2 cup water
2 tsp low-sodium Tamari (soy sauce)
2 tbsp maple syrup

Slice the squash in half and then peel and remove the seeds. Cut the squash into 1-inch cubes. Place cubes into a large pot with the water. Add the Tamari and syrup. Cover and simmer over medium heat for 15 to 20 minutes, or until squash is tender when pierced with a fork.

Split Pea – Indian Dahl
Serves 6

1 large onion, chopped
1 small green pepper, chopped
1-1/2 cups yellow split peas
3 cups water
1/2 cup water
1-1/2 tsp black mustard seeds
1 tsp turmeric
1/2 tsp curry powder
juice of 1 lemon

Simmer split peas in 3 cups water for 30 minutes or until tender. Add more water, if needed. In another saucepan, simmer chopped onions, green peppers, turmeric, curry powder, mustard seeds and 1/2 cup water for 15 minutes or until onions and peppers are tender. Mix with peas and add lemon juice. Serve over a generous portion of brown rice.

Stir Fry – Sesame Bok Choy & Carrot
Serves 2

5 cups bok choy, cut into 1/2-inch pieces
4 cloves garlic, minced
3 carrots, cut diagonally into 1/4-inch slices
3 cups cooked quinoa
1/2 cup chopped green onions
1/4 cup vegetable broth
2 tsp minced ginger root
2 tbsp toasted sesame seeds

In a large nonstick skillet or wok, stir-fry garlic, carrots and green onions in 3 tbsp vegetable broth for 3 minutes. Add bok choy and stir-fry another 2 minutes. Stir in vegetable broth and ginger. Reduce heat and simmer 5 minutes. Sprinkle sesame seeds over stir-fry. Spoon over quinoa.

Stir Fry – Vegetables
Makes 4 to 6 servings.

3 carrots, cut into 2-inch strips
2 green onions, chopped
1 medium onion, sliced
1 green pepper, sliced
2 cups cooked rice
1 cup cauliflower florets
1 cup broccoli florets
1 cup snow peas
1 cup sliced mushrooms
1/4 cup low-sodium Tamari (soy sauce)
1/4 cup lemon juice
1/3 cup vegetable broth
1-2 tsp grated fresh ginger root

Mix together the Tamari, lemon juice, and ginger. Heat the broth in a large pan and add the cauliflower, broccoli, carrots, onion, green pepper, and tofu. Stir frequently, cooking evenly. Add the snow peas, mushrooms, and green onions. Continue to stir frequently until the vegetables are cooked but still crunchy. Serve over rice, topped with the marinade.

Tabouli
Serves 6

4 green onions, chopped
1 cucumber, chopped
1 tomato, chopped
1 red pepper, chopped
1 cup boiling water
1 cup bulgur
1/2 cup parsley, minced

Let soak for 30 minutes bulgur and boiling water or until water is absorbed: Stir in remaining ingredients. Toss well and chill. Add favorite dressing.

Tabouli – Quinoa
Serves 4 to 6

2 small tomatoes
3 green onions, chopped
2-1/2 cups cooked quinoa (1 cup dry)
2 cups finely chopped parsley
3/4 cup chopped mint
1/2 cup diced seedless cucumbers
3 tbsp lemon juice
1 tbsp vegetable broth
1/4 tsp black pepper

Rinse quinoa thoroughly. Bring 1 cup quinoa and 1-3/4 cup water to a full boil over medium heat, cover, and reduce to simmer. Continue simmering for 15 minutes. Remove from heat and uncover. Allow to cool. In a bowl, combine quinoa, mint, cucumbers, parsley, tomatoes, and onions. In a small bowl, whisk together the lemon juice, broth and pepper. Pour over salad; toss. Serve at room temperature or refrigerate and serve cold.

Tacos and More

Brown rice
Black beans from a can juice and all
Chopped tomatoes
Chopped videlia, green or any onion
Frozen corn thawed in hot water
Chopped red, yellow or green peppers
Grated or julienned carrots
Water chestnuts
Chopped cilantro
Chopped arugala
Low-sodium Tamari (soy sauce)
Salsa
Taco shells (whole wheat)

Cook rice. Heat beans. Put all chopped vegetables in individual dishes. Start on your plate with rice and just pile it up high and top it all with low-sodium Tamari and/or salsa. Put all leftovers in a bowl and use for salad the next day adding balsamic vinegar.

Vegetables – Grilled
Makes about 4 servings

2 ears fresh corn
1 red onion
1 red bell pepper
1 medium zucchini or other summer squash
2 cups button mushrooms
2 tsp vegetable broth
2 tsp garlic granules or powder
2 tsp mixed Italian herbs
2 tsp chili powder

Preheat grill. Cut onion, bell pepper, and zucchini into generous chunks. Place in a large mixing bowl. Clean mushrooms and add. Husk corn, cut it into 1-inch lengths, and add. Sprinkle vegetables with broth and toss to coat. Sprinkle with garlic granules, Italian herbs and chili powder. Toss to mix. Spread vegetables in a single layer on a grilling rack and place over medium-hot coals. Cover and cook 5 minutes. Turn with a spatula and cook until tender when pierced with a sharp knife, about 5 more minutes. Repeat with remaining vegetables.

Wraps – Thai Wraps
Serves 6

6 large flour tortillas
1 small onion, chopped
1 carrot, thinly sliced
1 celery stalk, thinly sliced
1/2 red bell pepper, diced
2 cups sliced mushrooms
2 cups finely chopped kale
2 cups cooked brown rice
1/2 cup chopped cilantro
6 tbsp Plum Sauce
1 tbsp peanut butter
2 tbsp low-sodium Tamari (soy sauce)
1-1/2 tsp curry powder

Mix the peanut butter with 3 tablespoons of water. Set aside. Heat 1/2 cup of water and the Tamari in a large, nonstick skillet. Add the onion, carrot, celery, and mushrooms and cook until the vegetables are tender. Stir in the curry powder, red bell pepper, cilantro, kale, and peanut butter mixture. Cover and cook until the kale is tender. Heat the tortillas in a dry skillet until soft. Place about 1/2 cup of the vegetable mixture along the center of the tortilla. Top with 1/4 cup of brown rice and 2 tsp of Plum Sauce. Roll the tortilla around the filling.

Wraps – Veggie Wrap
Makes 4 wraps

4 whole wheat tortillas
1 carrot, shredded
1 cup bean sprouts
1–2 cups hummus
1–2 cups mixed salad greens or torn leaf lettuce
1/4 cup sunflower seeds

Preheat oven or toaster oven to 375. Place sunflower seeds in a small ovenproof dish and roast until lightly browned and fragrant. Set aside. Warm tortillas, one at a time, in a large dry skillet, flipping to warm both sides until soft and pliable. Spread each tortilla evenly with about 1/2 cup of hummus, leaving edges uncovered. Divide remaining ingredients evenly among tortillas. Wrap tortillas around filling.

Yams and Bok Choy
Serves 4

2 large cloves of garlic, minced
2 small bok choy, finely sliced
2 small yams, cut into bite-sized chunks
1 onion, sliced and quartered
1 tbsp vegetarian Worcestershire sauce
1/2 tsp Thai chili paste
1/2 lemon

Put yams in a deep skillet and just cover them with water. Cover skillet and boil yams 5 to 10 minutes until soft when pierced with a fork. Add onions and garlic and continue to simmer until about half of the water has boiled away. Add Worcestershire sauce, chili paste, and bok choy. Simmer until the bok choy is soft. Squeeze lemon over the mixture and serve.

Yams With Cranberries and Apples
Serves 8

4 yams, peeled
1 large, green apple, peeled and diced
1 cup raw cranberries
1/2 cup raisins
1/2 cup organic orange juice
2 tbsp maple syrup
Maple syrup

Preheat oven to 350. Cut peeled yams into 1-inch chunks and place in a large baking dish. Top with diced apple, cranberries, and raisins. Sprinkle with maple syrup or other sweetener, then pour orange juice over all. Cover and bake for 1 hour and 15 minutes, or until yams are tender when pierced with a fork.

Dips, Spreads and Sauces

Apple Chutney
Makes 3 cups

1-1/2 pounds tart apples (about 3 large apples)
1 medium garlic clove, minced
1 cup raw, maple syrup
1 cup cider vinegar
1/2 cup orange juice
1 tbsp chopped fresh ginger or 1/2 tsp ground ginger
1 tsp each ground cinnamon and cloves
1/4 tsp cayenne, or more to taste

Coarsely chop the apples, then combine them with all the remaining ingredients in a heavy saucepan. Bring to a boil, then lower heat and simmer uncovered, stirring occasionally, for 1 hour, until most of the liquid is absorbed.

Balsamic Vinaigrette
Makes 1 cup

1 garlic clove, pressed
2 tbsp balsamic vinegar
2 tbsp seasoned rice vinegar
1 tbsp ketchup
1 tsp stone ground mustard

Whisk all ingredients together.

Bread Dressing
Makes about 4 cups

3 cups sliced mushrooms (about 1/2 pound)
2 celery stalks, thinly sliced
1 onion, chopped
4 cups cubed whole wheat bread
1 cup vegetable broth
1/3 cup finely chopped parsley
1 tbsp vegetable broth
1/2 tsp thyme
1/2 tsp marjoram
1/2 tsp sage
1/8 tsp black pepper

Sauté onion in broth until translucent. Add sliced mushrooms and celery. Cover and cook over medium heat, stirring occasionally, for 5 minutes. Preheat oven to 350. Stir bread into onion mixture, along with parsley, thyme, marjoram, sage, and black pepper. Lower heat and continue cooking 3 minutes, stirring often. Stir in vegetable broth, a little at a time, until dressing obtains desired moistness. Spread in a nonstick baking dish, cover and bake 20 minutes. Remove cover and bake 10 minutes longer.

Brown Gravy
Makes 2 cups

2 cups water or vegetable broth
3 tbsp low-sodium Tamari (soy sauce)
2 tbsp cornstarch
1 tbsp cashews
1 tbsp onion powder
1/2 tsp garlic granules or powder

Pour water or broth into a blender. Add cashews, onion powder, garlic granules, cornstarch, and Tamari. Blend until completely smooth, 2 to 3 minutes. Transfer to a saucepan and cook over medium heat, stirring constantly, until thickened.

"Cheese" Sauce

2 cups water
1/2 cup nutritional yeast flakes
1/2 cup whole wheat flour
1/2 tsp garlic powder
1/4 cup vegetable broth
1 tsp wet mustard

In a 2-quart saucepan, mix together nutritional yeast flakes, flour and garlic powder, then 2 cups water. Cook over medium heat, whisking until it thickens and bubbles. Cook 30 seconds more, then remove from head and whisk in vegetable broth and mustard. Sauce will thicken as it cools but will thin when heated. Good for a macaroni and cheese casserole, as a topping for lasagna, or a pan of enchiladas.

"Cheesy" Garbanzo Spread
Makes about 2 cups

1 15-ounce can garbanzo beans
1/2 cup roasted red peppers
3 tbsp vegetable broth
3 tbsp lemon juice

Drain the garbanzo beans, reserving the liquid, and place them in a food processor or blender with the remaining ingredients. Process until very smooth. If using a blender, you will have to stop it occasionally and push everything down into the blades with a rubber spatula. The mixture should be quite thick, but to thin add a tablespoon or two of the reserved bean liquid.

Chunky Ratatouille Sauce
Serves 6

1 15-ounce can fire-roasted tomatoes
8 ounces of cremini mushrooms (also called baby bellas)
6 cloves garlic, minced
2 stalks celery, chopped
2 small onions, chopped
1 large eggplant, cut into 1-inch chunks
1/2 cup vegetable broth
1/4 to 1/2 cup water
1 tsp Italian herbs
1/2 tsp thyme
1/2 tsp black pepper (add more to taste)

Soak eggplant chunks in water for 10 minutes. Drain, rinse, and drain again.
Braise onion, celery, and garlic in 1/4 cup of broth. When the vegetables are soft,
add the eggplant chunks and 1/4 cup of water. Simmer, stirring occasionally,
until the eggplant is soft. Add more water, if necessary, to keep mixture from
drying out. Add mushrooms, spices, remaining wine, and can of tomatoes.
Simmer for 5 minutes. Serve over whole wheat pasta shells, brown rice, or your
favorite grain.

Corn Butter
Makes about 2 cups

1 cup boiling water
1/4 cup cornmeal
2 tbsp raw cashews
1-1/2 tsp agar powder
1 tbsp finely grated carrot
1 tsp nutritional yeast (optional)
2 tsp lemon juice

Combine the cornmeal with 1 cup of water in a small saucepan. Simmer, stirring
frequently, until very thick, about 10 minutes. Set aside. Combine the agar
powder with 1/4 cup of cold water in a blender. Let stand at least 3 minutes. Add
1 cup boiling water and blend to mix. Add the cooked cornmeal, cashews, lemon
juice, grated carrot, and yeast if using. Cover and blend until totally smooth.
Transfer to a covered container and chill until thickened, 2-3 hours.

Cranberry Persimmon Relish
Makes about 2 cups

2 fuyu persimmons
1 cup cranberries, fresh or frozen
2 tbsp orange juice concentrate
1 tbsp maple syrup
1/2 tsp ginger

Remove stems, then coarsely chop persimmons in a food processor. Add cranberries, orange juice concentrate, syrup and ginger. Process using quick pulses until coarsely and uniformly chopped. Let stand 20 minutes before serving.

Creamy Spinach Dip
Serves 10 to 12

1 package frozen spinach, thawed and drained
1 package vegetable soup mix
1 container Tofutti (non-dairy) sour cream
1 tbsp lemon juice
1/2 cup salsa

Combine ingredients and refrigerate for 1 hour before serving. Serve with raw vegetable pieces or chunks of crusty bread.

Garlic Bean Dip
Serves 2

2 cloves garlic, minced
1-1/2 tbsp vegetable broth
1/3 pound green beans
1 tsp low-sodium Tamari (soy sauce)
1/2 tsp onion powder

Steam green beans for 10 minutes in about a cup of water until tender. Rinse beans under cold water when done. Place remaining ingredients in a blender or food processor. Add cooked beans. Blend 2 minutes or until creamy. Serve with whole wheat crackers.

Guacamole
Serves 6

1 avocado
2 cups cooked peas or 1 cup cooked green beans
2 tbsp chopped onion
1/4 cup salsa (or more to taste)
2 tbsp fresh lime juice

Blend the avocado and peas or green beans together in a blender, until smooth. Stir in the onion and salsa. Just before serving, stir in the fresh lime juice.

Hummus Dip
Makes 2 cups

1 15 oz jar of garbanzo beans
1 garlic clove (or more to taste)
2 (or more) tbsp of vegetable broth (add more if needed for consistency)
2 tbsp of lemon juice
1/4 tsp ground cumin.

Put everything in a food processor and let it rip until smooth.

Maple Sweet Potato Spread
Makes about 2 cups

3 dried figs, finely chopped
1 large sweet potato, peeled and quartered
1 small onion, peeled and quartered
1 tbsp vegetable broth
1 tbsp maple syrup

Steam sweet potato and onion pieces until soft. Transfer to a food processor with remaining ingredients. Blend until thick and smooth. Pour into a small container. Keep covered and refrigerate until ready to serve.

Mint Chutney
Makes 1/4 cup

2/3 cup fresh mint leaves
1/4 cup ground walnuts
1 tsp soy sour cream
1/2 tsp tumeric

Wash, dry, and mince the mint leaves. Mix them with the walnuts. In a small cup, stir the soy sour cream and tumeric together, then blend with the mint and walnuts. Cover and allow to set for 30 minutes before serving.

Mustard and Vinegar Dressing
Makes 3/4 cups

2-3 medium cloves
1/2 cup mustard
3 tbsp lemon juice or rice or cider vinegar
3 tbsp water
1 tsp light miso
1 tsp low-sodium Tamari (soy sauce)
1/2 tsp maple syrup
1/2 tsp curry powder

Purée all the ingredients in a blender

Peanut Sauce
Serves 5 to 8

1 cup low-sodium Tamari (soy sauce)
1 cup peanut butter
1/4 cup water
1/4 cup cooking sherry
1 cup lemon or lime juice
2 tbsp minced fresh garlic
1 tbsp red curry paste
1/2 tbsp onion powder
1/2 tbsp basil
1/2 tsp cayenne
1/4 tsp paprika
2 to 3 dashes of Tabasco

Mix all ingredients using a whisk or blender, until creamy.

Plum Sauce

1 17-ounce can purple plums in heavy syrup
2 garlic cloves
2 tbsp seasoned rice vinegar
1 tbsp cornstarch
1 tbsp low-sodium Tamari (soy sauce)
1/8 tsp cayenne (more or less to taste)

Remove pits from the plums, then purée plums in a blender or food processor along with their liquid and the remaining ingredients. Heat in a saucepan, stirring constantly, until thickened.

Refried Beans
Makes about 5 cups

1 4-ounce can diced green chilies
4 garlic cloves, minced or pressed
1 onion, chopped
1 1/2 cups dry pinto beans
1 cup crushed or finely chopped tomatoes
1 1/2 tsp cumin
1/4 tsp cayenne

Clean and rinse beans, then soak in about 6 cups of water for 6 to 8 hours. Discard soaking water, rinse beans and place in a large pot with 4 cups of fresh water, minced garlic, cumin, and cayenne. Simmer until tender, about 1 hour. Heat 1/2 cup of water in a large skillet. Add onion and cook until soft, about 5 minutes. Stir in tomatoes and diced chilies. Cook, uncovered, over medium heat for 10 minutes, stirring occasionally. Add cooked beans, including some cooking liquid, a cup at a time to tomato mixture. Mash some of the beans as you add them. When all the beans have been added, stir to mix, then cook over low heat, stirring frequently, until thickened.

Salsa Fresca
Makes about 6 cups

1 15-ounce can tomato sauce
4 ripe tomatoes, chopped (about 4 cups)
4 garlic cloves, minced
1 small onion, finely chopped
1 bell pepper, finely chopped
1 jalapeño pepper, seeded and finely chopped or 1 teaspoon red pepper flakes
(more or less to taste)
1 cup chopped cilantro leaves
2 tbsp cider vinegar
1-1/2 tsp cumin

Combine all ingredients in a mixing bowl. Stir to mix. Let stand 1 hour before
serving.

Desserts

Apple Crisp
Serves 10

4 large tart apples
1-1/2 cups rolled oats
3/4 cup natural sweetener
1/2 cup flour
1/3 cup soy or rice margarine
1 tsp cinnamon

Preheat the oven to 350. Peel the apples, if desired, then core and slice them thinly. Toss with 1/2-cup sweetener, 1 tablespoon flour, and cinnamon. Spread evenly in a 9- x 13-inch baking dish. Mix the rolled oats with the remaining flour and sweetener. Add the margarine and work the mixture until it is uniformly crumbly. Sprinkle evenly over the fruit. Bake for 45 minutes, until lightly browned. Let stand 10 minutes before serving.

Applesauce - Strawberry
Makes 2 cups

2 cups peeled, cored, and coarse-chopped apples
2 cups hulled strawberries, fresh or frozen
1/2 cup frozen apple juice concentrate

In a medium-sized saucepan combine all ingredients. Bring to a simmer, then cover and cook over very low heat for about 25 minutes, or until apples are tender. Mash lightly or purée in a food processor, if desired.

Banana Cake
Serves 8

4 ripe bananas
2 cups whole wheat pastry flour
1-1/2 tsp baking soda
1 cup chopped walnuts
1 cup maple syrup
1/3 cup applesauce
1/4 cup water
1 tsp vanilla extract

Preheat oven to 350. Mix flour, baking soda in a bowl. In a large bowl, beat maple syrup, applesauce together. Add bananas and mash them. Stir in water and vanilla, mix thoroughly. Add flour mixture, chopped walnuts and stir to mix. Spread in a non-stick 9-inch square baking pan. Bake for 45 to 50 minutes, or until a toothpick inserted into the center comes out clean.

Berry Cobbler
One 9 x 9-inch cobbler

Berry mixture:
5-6 cups fresh or frozen berries (blueberries, blackberries, raspberries, or a mixture)
1/4 cup whole wheat pastry flour
1/2 cup natural sweetener

Topping:
1 cup whole wheat pastry flour
2/3 cup non-dairy milk
2 tbsp natural sweetener
1-1/2 tsp baking powder

Preheat oven to 375. Spread berries in a 9 x 9-inch baking dish. Mix in flour and sugar. Place in oven until hot or about 15 minutes. To prepare topping, mix flour, sugar, baking powder in a bowl. Add non-dairy milk and stir until batter is smooth. Spread evenly over hot berries, then bake until golden brown, 25 to 30 minutes.

Berry Sauce
Serves 6 (as dessert topping)

1-1/2 cup frozen raspberries
1 cup fresh or frozen blueberries
1/4 cup orange juice

Combine raspberries and orange juice in a small saucepan. Simmer until raspberries become sauce like, about 5 minutes. Add blueberries and cook for 2 more minutes. Serve warm over fruit sorbet, poached pears, or vanilla non-dairy ice cream.

Fresh Peach Cobbler
Serves 8

4 cups fresh peaches, sliced
1 1/2 cup water
1 cup whole wheat pastry flour
1/2 cup natural sweetener
2 tbsp cornstarch or arrowroot powder
1-1/2 tsp baking powder
ground cinnamon, to taste

Combine 2 tablespoons of natural sweetener and cornstarch in a saucepan, then stir in the peaches and water. Bring to a boil, then boil 1 minute, stirring constantly. Pour into a 9-inch square baking dish, and sprinkle with cinnamon. Preheat oven to 400. Combine flour, 1/2 cup natural sweetener and baking powder. Blend until mixture resembles cornmeal (add water if necessary). Stir in water until mixed, then drop by spoonfuls onto the hot fruit. Bake until golden brown, about 25 minutes.

Gingerbread Cookies
Makes about 48 cookies

2-1/4 cups whole wheat pastry flour
1/3 cup molasses
1/3 cup water
1/2 cup maple syrup
1-1/2 tsp baking soda
1 tsp powdered ginger
1 tsp cinnamon

Mix the maple syrup, ginger, cinnamon and baking soda in a large bowl. Add the molasses and water and mix well. Add 1 cup of flour and mix well. Mix in enough of the remaining flour to make a very stiff dough. Preheat oven to 275. Dust 2-3 non-stick baking sheets with flour. On a floured surface, roll a portion of the dough with a flour-dusted rolling pin to a very fine thickness, about 1/16-inch thickness. Cut the dough into shapes with a flour-dusted cookie cutters or a flour-dusted knife. Transfer cookies to the baking sheets. Bake until the edges are dry and the centers give just slightly when pressed, about 20 minutes. Allow to cool on a baking sheet for 5 minutes, then transfer with a spatula to a wire rack to cool. Once cooled, store in an airtight container.

Gingered Melon Wedges
Serves 6

1 large cantaloupe
1 tbsp natural sweetener
1 tbsp candied ginger (optional)
1/2 tsp ground ginger

Cut melon in half and seed. Then cut each half into chunks. Stir together sweetener and ground ginger. Sprinkle over melon chunks and chill.

Fruit Compote
Makes 2 cups

2 cups sliced fresh peaches
2 cups hulled fresh strawberries
1/2 cup white grape juice concentrate or apple juice concentrate

In a large saucepan combine all ingredients. Bring to a simmer and cook for about 5 minutes, or until fruit just becomes soft. Serve warm or cold.

Fruit Gel
Makes about 4 cups

2 cups blueberries, fresh or frozen
1-1/2 cups strawberries, fresh or frozen
3/4 cups apple juice concentrate
1/2 cup water
1/2 tsp agar powder
1 tbsp kudzu powder

Chop strawberries by hand or in a food processor. Transfer to a pan. Add apple juice concentrate, water, agar, and kudzu. Stir to mix. Bring to a simmer and cook 3 minutes, stirring often. Remove from heat and chill completely. Fold in blueberries and transfer to serving dishes.

Monkey Bars
Makes 24 small bars

4 small firm ripe bananas (about 1 pound)
1/2 cup crispy brown rice cereal
1 tbsp natural peanut butter
1 tbsp maple syrup
1 tsp unsweetened cocoa

Cut the bananas in half lengthwise and set aside. Combine all other ingredients in small bowl, blending well. Spread 1 tablespoon of the brown rice/peanut butter mixture over the cut sides of 4 banana halves and then top with the remaining halves. Cut each crosswise into 6 pieces.

Nutty Fruit Balls
Makes about 30 pieces

2/3 cup raisins
2/3 cup golden raisins
2/3 cup dried apricots
2/3 cup dried figs
2/3 cup cashews
1/2 cup peanut butter
1/2 cup carob powder
1/3 cup pitted dates

Grind the dried fruits and nuts into small pieces in a food grinder or heavy-duty food processor. Add the peanut butter and carob powder, mixing thoroughly. Roll into balls the size of walnuts.

Peaches (flambé) with Berries

Fresh or frozen raspberries or blueberries
1 ripe peach
2 tsp natural sweetener
1 tsp lemon juice

Wash and halve peach. Remove pit. Place peach half, flat side up, in center of a square piece of doubled aluminum foil. Fill cavity of peach half with fresh or frozen raspberries or blueberries. Sprinkle the sweetener and lemon juice on the top. Wrap in foil. Grill approximately 15-20 minutes over hot flame, turning once.

Peanut Butter Balls
Makes 20 balls

3/4 cup peanut butter
1/4 cup low-fat granola
1/4 cup sunflower seeds
1/4 cup raisins
1/4 cup finely shredded carrots
2 tbsp natural sweetener

Mix together the granola, sweetener, sunflower seeds, raisins, and carrots. Blend in the peanut butter a little at a time to form a smooth mixture. Store the mixture in the refrigerator overnight. Form into balls.

Pudding – Brown Rice
Makes about 3 cups

2 cups cooked brown rice
1 1/2 cups water
1/3 cup raisins
1/4 cup maple syrup
1 tbsp cornstarch
1/4 tsp cinnamon
1 tsp vanilla

Whisk milk and cornstarch together in a medium saucepan. Add cooked rice, maple syrup, raisins, and cinnamon. Simmer over medium heat 3 minutes, stirring constantly. Remove from heat and stir in vanilla. Serve warm or cold.

Pudding – Chocolate
Makes about 2 cups

2 cups water
1/2 cup natural sweetener
5 tbsp cornstarch
3 tbsp cocoa
1 tsp vanilla

Combine milk, cocoa, cornstarch, sugar, and vanilla in a saucepan. Whisk smooth. Cook over medium heat, stirring constantly until pudding is very thick. Pour into individual serving dishes and chill.

Pudding – Fruit
Serves 4

8 to 10 dried apricot halves
2 to 3 medium dried figs
1 medium apple
3 cups water
1 cup quick rolled oats
1/4 cup raisins
1/4 tsp cinnamon

Chop the apricot halves, figs, and raisins in a food processor. Cut and core the apple and then add to fruit in food processor. Chop fine. Transfer the mixture to a medium-sized saucepan and add remaining ingredients. Simmer slowly for about 5 minutes, or until thickened.

Pudding – Sweet Potato
Makes about 1 1/2 cups

1 cup cooked sweet potato or yam
1/2 cup water
1/3 cup rolled oats
1 tbsp maple syrup
1/4 tsp cinnamon

Combine all ingredients in a blender and blend until smooth.

Pudding – Rice
Makes 6 1/2-cup servings

2 cups cooked brown rice
1-1/2 cups water
3 tbsp raisins
2 tbsp maple syrup
1 tsp vanilla extract
1/4 tsp cinnamon
1/4 tsp vanilla extract

In a medium-size saucepan, combine all ingredients and bring to a slow simmer. Cook uncovered for about 20 minutes, or until thick. Serve hot or cold.

Pudding – Vanilla
Makes about 3 cups

2 cups water
1 cup cooked, peeled yam
5 tbsp maple syrup
2 tbsp cornstarch
1 tbsp potato flour
1/2 tsp vanilla extract

Combine milk, cooked yam, and maple syrup in a blender and process until completely smooth. With blender running, add cornstarch, potato flour and vanilla extract. Transfer to a saucepan and heat, stirring constantly, until mixture bubbles and thickens. Remove from heat and transfer to individual serving dishes if desired. Cool before serving.

Pumpkin Raisin Cookies
Makes 24 3-inch cookies

2 cups whole wheat pastry flour
1 cup pumpkin
1/2 cup water
1/2 cup raisins
1/2 cup natural sweetener
1/2 cup chopped pecans or walnuts (optional)
2 tsp baking powder
1/2 tsp baking soda
1/2 tsp cinnamon
1/4 tsp nutmeg

Preheat oven to 350. Mix flour, sugar, baking powder, baking soda, cinnamon, and nutmeg together in a large bowl.
Add pumpkin, water, raisins, and nuts. Mix completely. Drop by tbspfuls onto a non-stick baking sheet. Bake 15 minutes, until bottoms are lightly browned. Remove from oven and let stand 2 minutes. Carefully remove from baking sheet with a spatula and place on a rack to cool.

Rainbow Delight
Serves 6

2 apples, grated
2 carrots, grated
2/3 cup shredded coconut
1/2 cup raisins
1/2 cup chopped walnuts

Toss all ingredients together in a bowl and serve.

Food Lists

The following are lists of foods to provide you with suggestions and to also show you the wide variety of foods that available with the RAVE Diet.

Breads
(whole wheat only)

Bagel
Bread - Italian
Bread - French
Bread - pumpernickel
Bread - whole wheat
Bread - rye - American - light
Bread - mixed whole grain
Bread - pita

Bread - oatmeal and bran
Corn taco shells - organic
Muffin - English
Roll - homemade
Spelt and sprouted grain breads
Sprouted whole wheat

Fruits

Apple
Apricot
Avocado
Bananas
Blackberries
Blueberries
Boysenberries
Breadfruit
Carambola
Carissa
Cherimoya
Cherries
Cranberry sauce
Dates
Elderberries
Figs
Gooseberries
Grapefruit
Grapes
Guavas

Kiwifruit
Lemons
Limes
Loganberries
Longans
Loquats
Lychees
Mangos
Melons - cantaloupe
Melons - casaba
Melons - honeydew
Mulberries
Nectarines
Oranges
Papayas
Passion fruit
Peaches
Pears
Persimmons
Pineapple

Pitanga
Plantains
Plums
Pomegranates
Pricklypears
Prunes
Pummelo
Quinces
Raisins
Raspberries
Roselle
Sapodilla
Sapotes
Soursop
Strawberries
Tamarinds
Tangerines
Watermelon

Whole Grains

Amaranth
Pearled barley
Barley flakes
Basmati rice (brown)
Buckwheat
Bulgur
Couscous
Cornmeal
Cracked wheat
Kamut – whole grain

Kamut flakes
Matzos
Matzo meal
Millet
Popcorn – air popped
Quinoa
Rice - brown
Rolled oats
Rye
Spelt

Spelt flakes
Steel cut oats
Teff
Wehani rice
Wheat, cracked
Wheat flakes
Wheat germ
Wild rice

Nuts and Seeds

For nuts, get the unsalted and roasted or raw

Almonds
Beech
Brazil
Breadfruit
Cashews
Chestnuts
Coconut
Filbert/hazel
Hickory
Macadamia
Peanut butter – (oil separated)

Peanuts
Pecans
Pine nuts
Pistachio
Pumpkin/squash seeds
Sesame seeds
Soybean kernels
Sunflower seeds
Walnut
Walnuts

Pasta

Organic soy pasta
Brown rice pasta
Spaghetti – whole wheat
Spelt pasta
Lentil pasta
Quinoa pasta
Whole wheat pasta

Vegetables

Alfalfa seeds - sprouted
Amaranth
Artichokes
Asparagus
Balsam pear
Bamboo shoots
Beans - Great Northern
Beans - green
Beans - snap - yellow/wax
Beans - black
Beans - French
Beans - adzuki
Beans - garbanzo
Beans - green
Beans - lima
Beans - mung
Beans - navy
Beans - red kidney beans
Beans - small white
Beets
Beet greens
Broccoli
Brussels sprouts
Burdock root
Cabbage - savoy
Cabbage - celery
Cabbage - common
Cabbage - red
Cabbage - white mustard
Carrot
Cauliflower
Celery - pascal
Chard - Swiss
Chicory greens
Chickpeas
Chinese vegetables mixed
Chives
Collards
Corn
Cress
Cucumber
Dandelion greens

Eggplant
Endive
Escarole
Fennel
Garlic
Ginger root
Gourd - white flowered
Hummus
Jerusalem artichokes
Kale
Kohlrabi
Leeks
Lentils
Lettuce - iceberg
Lettuce - red leaf
Lettuce - romaine
Lettuce – butter head
Lotus root
Miso - fermented soybeans
Mung bean sprouts
Mushrooms
Mustard greens
Natto - fermented soybeans
Chestchinese
Okra
Onions - mature
Onions - young green
Parsley
Parsnips
Peas - edible podded
Peas - blackeye/cowpeas
Peas - snow pea pods
Peas – split green
Peppers - sweet
Peppers - hot chili
Poi - taro root product
Potato - baked - whole
Potato skin - baked
Pumpkin
Radishes
Rutabaga
Seaweed - spirulina

Seaweed - kelp (kombu)
Shallots
Soybeans - sprouted
Soybeans - green
Spinach
Squash - acorn
Squash - zucchini
Squash - butternut
Squash - summer
Sweet potato - baked
Taro leaf

Taro root
Tempeh - soybean product
Tofu
Tomatoes
Turnip greens
Turnips
Waterchestchinese
Water chestnuts
Watercress
Yam - mountain - Hawaii
Zucchini

Notes

Protein

When you ask the typical American, "Where does protein come from?" they'll stammer for a moment, and then say something like, "From meat, dairy and eggs." And they'll be dead wrong. Protein doesn't come from any of these sources. All protein on the planet comes from plants. In fact, protein is the result of the interaction of sunlight on plants. Although many people don't think plants have protein at all, plants are the mothers of *all* the protein we eat.

Most people think only animal products have protein, but the lawn in your front yard is full of protein. You may not recognize it, but a cow would. Herbivores, such as cows, eat plants to get their protein. When carnivores eat herbivores, they are actually eating the protein that originally came from the plants eaten by herbivores. The problem with eating protein from animals is that it comes in a package of saturated fat and cholesterol, the two most deadly ingredients in the American diet.

For most Americans, getting enough protein simply means eating animal foods. You'll have doctors and dieticians flatly state that you won't get enough protein by just eating plant foods. Unfortunately, they are following the protein requirements of our government, which have been set by the meat, dairy and egg industry through lobbying efforts – and they are not only ridiculously high, but also potentially dangerous. Because this standard has the flag wrapped around it, nutritionists and health professionals have taken it as "science" and preach this gospel to the public. They are, in fact, mindlessly acting as sales persons for industries selling high-protein foods, which have paid off politicians.

A friend recently went to her nutritionist who said that in order to get the protein her body requires purely from vegetables, she would need to consume more vegetables than she could possibly eat. This is not only scientifically false, but an affront to common sense because if that were true, the human race would not have made it to the 20th century.

It's extremely easy to meet protein needs on virtually any diet. In fact, you'd have to be starving not to get enough protein eating anything other than a junk food diet.

Here's a simple quiz for you. Which has more protein? Steak, broccoli or spinach? Spinach has the most protein, then broccoli and steak comes in last place.

The USDA dietary guidelines call for protein levels above 10 percent of total calories. Ten percent is four times what the average adult actually needs (see below). This exaggeration is, unfortunately, not based on human needs, but the needs of food lobbies selling high-protein foods.

The protein in human mother's milk is only five percent of total calories. Mother's milk is providing protein during the fastest growth period humans will ever experience. At no other time in our lives will we need a greater amount of protein. In fact, the average adult needs only half that amount, or two and one-half percent of calories from protein.[1]

Since 1974, the World Health Organization (WHO) has recognized this, but they doubled their recommendation to 5 percent of total calories in order to account for infants and people who are sick. Guess what? The WHO recommendation is exactly what mother's milk provides.

Now, why would the U.S. Government – or anyone else for that matter – recommend anything greater than five percent? Unfortunately, any protein standard higher than five percent is due to money and lobbying, not science.

Most of us would say, well, there's no harm in getting too much protein. But, in fact, there is potentially great harm because high protein diets can result in kidney disease, osteoporosis, cardiovascular disease and cancers.

If you're eating more protein than your body needs to repair tissue, it's burned as a fuel. Unfortunately, protein is both an inefficient fuel and a dirty fuel. It's inefficient because you have to expend more energy to take protein molecules apart than you do to break down carbohydrates and fats, due to the complicated structure of protein. It's dirty because protein contains nitrogen. Instead of producing clean carbon dioxide and water, burning protein produces nitrogenous residues that not only are irritating to the immune system and toxic to the liver, but also put a big workload on the kidneys. High-protein diets can also cause fatigue, digestive strain and aggravation of allergies and autoimmune diseases.

Given all this, why are our protein requirements so high? There is some dubious "science" behind the political efforts of food industries to raise our protein requirements. This science hinges on studies involving rats. In fact, the USDA protein requirements for Americans are based on the nutritional needs of *rats*. The very first study was done back in 1914, but subsequent studies with rats have continued since then and have formed the basis, i.e., the "science," behind our protein requirements. Needless to say, the high-protein food industries embraced these studies as if they were manna from heaven.

In the excitement over these studies, it apparently never occurred to anyone there might be just a slight problem: rats, in fact, are not humans. Rats do not eat like humans, digest food like humans, metabolize food like humans, grow like humans and their protein requirements are not at all like humans. In addition, mother's milk from rats is a whopping 49 percent of calories (vs. five percent for human mother's milk), and the amino acid profiles for rats are not at all like human amino acid profiles. This shouldn't come as a big surprise to most of you because, among other things, just comparing a rat and a human should tell you right off there are monumental differences between the two species. But this incidental fact did not deter the "scientists" from their work and making our protein requirements "rat-like" to this day.

In every study conducted with humans, protein from plant foods exceeded human nutritional requirements. Studies in which humans were fed wheat bread alone - or potatoes alone - or corn alone - or rice alone - have all shown that humans were able to meet their protein needs and get all the essential amino acids they needed.[2] And vegetables have an average protein content of 25 percent of calories, far in excess of what we need.[3]

But the rat standard for protein has led us into even more difficulties because people have embraced the notion of a "complete" protein and pointed to eggs as the gold standard. This gold standard is, however, based on the nutritional needs of *rats*. In fact, the human body does quite well on foods containing "incomplete" proteins because the body is smart enough to mix and match amino acids in order to meet the body's needs. In fact, the first thing the body does when it encounters a "complete" protein is break it apart into an incomplete protein, so it can mix and match amino acids according to the body's current needs. The whole notion of a "complete" protein is outdated, based on worthless "science," and should be discarded because it does not apply to human beings. Nor does the current U.S. government standard for protein.

Problems With the Glycemic Index

One of the latest trends in nutrition is a simple-minded, single-variable analysis called the Glycemic Index (GI), which almost every major authority in the country has embraced, despite it's serious flaws. Why have they embraced such a flawed tool? Because it has the air of "science" behind it – the GI categorizes foods by simple numbers. Hence, a food can be categorized by a number and placed on a scale. Unfortunately, the GI is of little practical value, despite the fact that there are a number of diets out there based solely on this dubious tool.

The Glycemic Index was designed to measure the effect of a *single food* on blood sugar levels. And that is a big problem. If we were to eat a single food for a meal, the GI might be of limited value. Unfortunately, few people eat a single food for a meal. Factors which throw off the GI in the real world are the mix of fiber, fat and protein in foods comprising a meal, how refined the ingredients are, whether the food was cooked, fried, how ripe a fruit is, etc.

Another problem is that the GI may predict the effect of a single food on blood sugar levels, but it does not accurately predict how much insulin the body will release in response to a rise in blood sugar – and *this is far more important than blood sugar levels*. As a result, the GI produces very strange results. Lentils, which are good according to the index, actually provoke *higher insulin levels* than potatoes, which are bad, according to the index. A fried potato, containing artery-clogging trans fats, is better than a baked potato. Adding vinegar to a meal can lower the GI of any food and – believe it or not – adding sugar to a food has *no effect* on the index. Ice cream, according to the index, is better for you than whole wheat bread. Sugar-sweetened chocolate is better for you than carrots and a Mars candy bar is better for you than a potato.

Advocates of high-fat diets, such as the Atkins diet, say that eating carbohydrates raises insulin levels and therefore causes weight gain, while eating animal proteins and fats does not. They are dead wrong. Beef raises insulin levels more than *refined,* white pasta and *27 times* more than brown rice. And fish raises insulin levels more than whole grain bread.[1]

In fact, most of the foods with low GI's are fruits, vegetables, grains, beans and whole grains, the very foods such high-fat (low-carb) diets say you should avoid.

This is just a small sampling of the incoherent contradictions involved with the Glycemic Index that defy common sense. The GI is so unreliable that the American Diabetes Association does not recommend using the index in the prevention or treatment of diabetes. Because of all these contradictions, the GI is of little practical value in determining what you should be eating and boils down to little more than a red herring that some Diet Doctors are using to distract people from good nutrition.

Forget the Glycemic Index. There is a better, simpler and more reliable measure. Instead of focusing on numbers, choose whole, natural plant foods and you will always be eating the best foods you can buy.

Osteoporosis and Acidic Diets

"In fact, the scientific literature states clearly that a "calcium deficiency disease" due to a low calcium intake from natural diets simply does not exist. In other words, all diets provide adequate calcium to meet our health needs...." - John A. McDougall, McDougall's Medicine

Your entire body chemistry changes according to the type of food you eat and that has consequences to your health. Because of our change in diet during the last century, American bodies have become very acidic and virtually all degenerative diseases ranging from cancers to tooth decay – are associated with excess acidity in our bodies.

Blood acid levels are measured on a pH scale from 1 to 14. Ideally, your blood should be slightly alkaline at 7.4. A soda, for example, has a pH of 2 and is highly acidic, whereas tap water has a pH of 8.4, which is very alkaline.

There are three ways to make your blood less acidic: first, eat more plant foods because plant foods are alkaline and have a higher percentage of water than other foods. Second, drink more water. Not water containing anything else, just plain, simple water. Third, eliminate foods from your diet that make the blood acidic.

The major acid forming foods in our diets include animal proteins, soft drinks, sugar, salt, caffeine and alcohol. Americans consume too much of all these products. In the case of sodium, we get most of it not from table salt, but indirectly in packaged and processed foods. In fact, dairy products and processed meat are the biggest sources of sodium in the American diet.

High acidity is bad for a number of reasons. First, high acid levels make our bodies more cancer friendly by reducing the delivery of oxygen to cells. Also, cancer cells love highly acidic environments and do not do well in healthy, alkaline environments. Second, a highly acidic environment disrupts the function of enzymes and the digestion of food. Undigested food gets passed into the colon and sits there, rotting, and this can lead to toxic buildups and a number of health problems. The average American stores 10 to 20 pounds of old (sometimes decades old!) fecal matter in their colons. Crayons people have swallowed as children have even been discovered in 60-year old colons! Third, when blood becomes too acidic, our bodies pull calcium from our bones and teeth to neutralize the acid and this contributes to bone loss, or osteoporosis. The body also pulls water from cells to neutralize high acid levels and this leads to cell dehydration, which many experts believe is the number one cause of premature aging.

The way Americans consume antacids is a reflection of just how acidic our diet has become. But taking a calcium pill to neutralize high acid levels is treating a symptom. If you want to eliminate the problem, you'll have to radically cut back on acidic foods, including protein from animals.

By continually eating foods which cause high blood acid levels, we put our bodies in a state of constantly having to neutralize this acid by using the calcium stored up in our bones. Animal proteins are one of the most acid forming foods in existence and because of our high-protein diets, the biggest cause of high acid levels. One reason dairy products are poor choices for calcium is because they contain excessively high amounts of protein. Cow's milk has over three times more protein than human mother's milk. It was, after all, designed for a calf that will weigh over 300 pounds within a year of its birth.

When you consume dairy products, the calcium simply passes through your body and ends up in the toilet — and your blood is even more acidic because of the protein. Low-fat dairy products are highest in protein, so you may lower your fat intake, but you will raise your blood acid level and this will contribute to bone loss. Skim milk, for example, contains almost twice the amount of protein as whole milk. And because of the high sodium content of dairy products, they provide a double-boost to your acid levels.

In short, consuming dairy products turns out to be the worst possible way to build strong bones. You don't need the sodium, the fat, the acidic proteins, the cholesterol – and you don't need the excess calcium, which can result in painful kidney stones.

The cause of osteoporosis is _not_ a lack of calcium in the diet, regardless of the advertising from the dairy industry. Populations that consume the highest amount of calcium have the highest rates of osteoporosis. In fact, the more calcium they consume, the higher their rates of osteoporosis. Obviously, something else is going on because it's not a lack of calcium that's causing osteoporosis.

What gives? Although Americans are swimming in calcium, the World Health Organization has yet to document a single case of calcium deficiency.[1] In fact, there has not been a single recorded case of calcium deficiency of a dietary origin in the history of the entire planet.[2] Yet, the dairy industry tells Americans they have a calcium deficiency.

The problem, of course, is that the dairy industry has set US standards for calcium consumption through lobbying efforts. The calcium scare that has been going on in this country is, without question, the biggest nutritional scam ever conceived. If you think this is an outrageous statement, then show me a single case of calcium deficiency of a dietary origin. (If you're thinking of rickets, that disease is caused by a lack of vitamin D, not a lack of calcium.)

You'll hear health authorities say that women should get between 1,000 and 1,500 mg of calcium per day, while men should get 1,000 mg per day. What would these health authorities say to men and women throughout the world who get only 200 mg a day – and have bones much stronger than Americans? In fact, 70-year-old women in Third World countries who have nursed multiple children have bones stronger than most 40-year-old women in this country. And they get their calcium from plant foods, not dairy products.

Osteoporosis is not genetic and you don't have to suffer bone loss if you change your exercise and eating habits. When people say it runs in the family, it simply means the family has led a sedentary lifestyle over generations. Many women, including Dr. Ruth Heidrich (interviewed in the film *Eating*), increased their bone mass during and after menopause without dairy products or hormone replacement therapy.

Bones are just like muscles. The single best thing you can do to prevent (and reverse) osteoporosis is to start exercising your bones, because *a lack of physical activity is the primary cause of osteoporosis*.

Acidic diets will cause bone loss, but not as rapidly as a lack of exercise. People who argue that acidic diets are the primary cause of bone loss have a big flaw in their argument: there are lots of meat-eaters with strong bones. This is because their activity levels strengthen their bones, despite a bad diet. Also, obese women and men never get osteoporosis because they get lots of weight bearing exercise just carrying their bodies around, regardless of their diet and calcium intake. Lighter woman and men have increased chances of osteoporosis simply because their bodies don't have enough weight – unless they run or jog to add stress to their bones. In other words, lighter men and women need to engage in more weight-bearing activity in order to strengthen their bones. Swimming is a good illustration of how a lack of stress on bones plays out – because runners have higher femur bone densities than swimmers.

It's never been proven that a plant-based diet alone can reverse osteoporosis. It has been proven that exercise reverses osteoporosis. In fact, NASA regularly reverses osteoporosis in astronauts when they return to earth with an exercise program, not a change in diet. In fact, on that basis alone, exercise is the most proven way to reverse bone loss. (Osteoporosis is a potentially huge problem for long-term space flight because, due to the lack of gravity, NASA is afraid they'd end up with boneless astronauts!)

There are no studies, that I am aware of, which factor both exercise and diet into the equation to determine which is most important. There are, however, hundreds – if not thousands of studies – which show far more dramatic differences in bone density between those who get regular exercise and those who do not.[3] And those differences are gigantic compared to studies that show differences in bone density between people eating different diets. On that basis alone, one has to conclude that exercise is the most important factor affecting bone density. The effect of weight-bearing activity on bone density are extraordinarily well-documented and have consistently shown the same results over decades – regardless of diet.

A recent study showed that varying levels of calcium intake, ranging from 500 mg a day to 1800 mg a day, had *absolutely no effect on bone strength*. It was the *exercise* women got that was the key determinant in building strong bones.[4]

We're worrying about vitamin A and vitamin D and getting enough calcium – all these worries – but no one is worrying about getting enough exercise. Our worries are solely the result of advertising by the dairy industry and the government, which sponsors the dairy industry. To think you can just eat your way out of osteoporosis or take calcium supplements is ridiculous.

Don't worry about calcium. Do worry about exercise. We have this crazy idea that somehow cows produce calcium. They're simply storage systems for the calcium they get from the plants they eat. Calcium comes from the earth – like all other minerals – and plant foods are the best place not only to get calcium, but all the other minerals the body needs. Get your calcium from inexpensive plant foods like the rest of the world does. Plant foods will keep your blood acid level in balance because they're alkaline, not acidic. Like protein, calcium is found in all plant foods and the amounts will easily supply the requirements of growing children and mature adults.

Calcium from plant foods is more easily absorbed by bone than calcium from dairy products and unlike dairy, calcium from plants comes in a disease-fighting low-fat, high fiber package. Cut back or eliminate all foods that contribute to high acid levels. Diet and exercise are the keys to preventing and reversing osteoporosis. A change in diet will prevent bone loss and exercise is the *only* way to build strong bones.

To demonstrate just how much calcium is in plant foods, here's a quick comparison of the calcium content of dairy products versus plant foods.

Calcium in Milligrams per 100 Calories

Arugula	1,300	Milk (2-percent)	245
Bok choy	1,055	Green onions	240
Turnip greens	921	Okra	213
Watercress	800	Cabbage	196
Collard greens	559	Whole milk	190
Mustard greens	490	Sesame seeds	170
Spinach	450	Cheddar cheese	179
Broccoli	387	American cheese	160
Romaine lettuce	257	Soybeans	134
Swiss cheese	250	Cucumber	108

Surprised to see all those plant foods have more calcium than two percent milk? Of course, you're probably saying, "but I would have to eat so much more spinach or kale to get adequate calcium." This is not true because individuals on plant-based diets generally eat as many calories as people eating the standard American diet. In other words, you can get all the calcium you need from the original source of calcium, without getting it second-hand in a package of saturated fat and cholesterol.

Another way to look at it is to compare the calcium content of plant foods to mother's milk:

Calcium content of foods (per 100-gram portion)

Human Breast Milk - 33

Almonds - 234	Swiss Chard (raw) - 88
Amaranth - 267	Chickpeas (garbanzos) - 150
Apricots (dried) - 67	Collards (raw leaves) - 250
Artichokes - 51	Cress (raw) - 81
Beans (can: pinto, black) - 135	Dandelion greens - 187
Beet greens (cooked) - 99	Endive - 81
Blackeye peas - 55	Escarole - 81
Bran - 70	Figs (dried) - 126
Broccoli (raw) - 48	Filberts (Hazelnuts) - 209
Brussel Sprouts - 36	Kale (raw leaves) - 249
Buckwheat - 114	Kale (cooked leaves) - 187
Cabbage (raw) - 49	Leeks - 52
Carrot (raw) - 37	Lettuce (lt. green) - 35
Cashew nuts - 38	Lettuce (dark green) - 68
Cauliflower (cooked) - 42	Molasses (dark-213 cal.) - 684

Mustard Green (raw) - 183
Mustard Green (cooked) - 138
Okra (raw or cooked) - 92
Olives - 61
Orange (Florida) - 43
Parsley - 203
Peanuts (roasted & salted) - 74
Peas (boiled) - 56
Pistachio nuts - 131
Potato Chips - 40
Raisins - 62
Rhubarb (cooked) - 78
Sauerkraut - 36

Sesame Seeds - 1160
Squash (Butternut) - 40
Soybeans - 60
Sugar (Brown) - 85
Tofu - 85
Spinach (raw) - 93
Sunflower seeds - 120
Sweet Potatoes (baked) - 40
Turnips (cooked) - 35
Turnip Greens (raw) - 246
Turnip Greens (boiled) - 184
Water Cress – 151

Genetics

Back in the 1940's, there was a dentist named Francis Pottenger who was curious about the role of genetics in health. To satisfy his curiosity, he set up a controlled study of hundreds of cats in order to determine the effects of processed food on their bodies. Half were fed unrefined, natural foods, while the other half were fed refined foods.

What Pottenger's study revealed was how the poor eating habits of parents created increasing health problems *in subsequent generations*. The cats who ate unrefined, natural foods remained healthy, but the first generation of cats who were fed refined foods developed a host of degenerative diseases (e.g., cancers, arthritis, diabetes, etc.) *during the later part of their lives*. What is most interesting is that their offspring, the second generation, acquired these diseases *during the middle of their lives*. And the next (third) generation developed diseases at the *beginning of their lives* and were either unable to conceive or their offspring were spontaneously aborted. (If you read the news at all, this may sound familiar with the current generation of children in America suffering from increasing rates of disease.)

Pottenger next took the sick cats and changed them to a healthy diet. The good news was that the cats recovered – but it took three generations! As the sick cats began eating healthy foods, their genetically weak tissue improved generation after generation. Just as their forebears had suffered the effects of poor nutrition, they were benefiting from good nutrition.

What might we learn from this illustration? Genetics plays an important role, but good nutrition can trump the genetic card. Studies of the dietary habits of twins are also good illustrations that explain why one twin will get a disease as a result of poor dietary habits, whereas the other will not, despite being genetically identical.

People like to blame diseases on their genes, but only a very small percentage of our major diseases are caused by genetics. If genes were important, we would simply not have the explosion of diseases that characterizes the American health landscape today.

Many people are genetically susceptible to adult-onset diabetes, for examle. If they eat a diet full of animal and refined foods, it is a virtual certainty they will get diabetes. If they do not eat these foods, they simply will not get diabetes. In fact, all populations have people who are genetically predisposed to certain diseases. But some populations never get these diseases due to their diet and lifestyle. So despite these genetic predispositions, you can overcome genetic weaknesses through diet. And if you never ate these harmful foods, you would never even know about your genetic predispositions. Heart disease and our common cancers were unknown in many countries throughout the world – until the American diet was introduced to them.

A typical response by cardiologists to the question, "How can I prevent heart disease?" is to answer, "Pick the right parents." Unfortunately, most cardiologists know more about bypass surgeries than they know about the cause of heart disease. In fact, it's almost 100 percent caused by diet.

Genes are important, but often they give us a false sense of security. For example, a small percentage of the population has the ability to get rid of cholesterol very efficiently. Thus, they can eat all the meat they want and keep their total cholesterol levels below 150. (And those people pushing high-fat diets will point to these people and argue that meat has nothing to do with cardiovascular disease.) This is true for only for a very tiny part of the population, who are genetically blessed this way. On the other hand, heart disease is only one of many diseases that have been linked to animal and refined foods and the ability to jettison large quantities of cholesterol from their bodies certainly does not keep them safe from these other diseases.

Genes do matter, but people gamble on them, hoping their good genes will save them from a lifetime of nutritional abuse. At the other end of the spectrum, some people think they're doomed because they have a family history of a disease. Neither case is accurate and to bet your life on your genes will be the biggest gamble you'll ever take.

Don't count on grandpa's genes to save you from a self-destructive lifestyle. Most of us have nutritional time bombs ticking inside of us. If you're smart, you'll play the odds and change your diet to improve the quality of your life so you can, in fact, grow old gracefully and with dignity.

References

Books
A Race for Life, Ruth Heidrich, Ph.D.
Anatomy of an Illness, Norman Cousins
Antioxidants Against Cancer, R.W. Moss, Ph.D.
Baby and Child Care, Benjamin Spock, M.D. (7th edition)
Beating Cancer With Nutrition, Patrick Quillin, Ph.D.
Biological Basis of Cancer, M.V. McKinnell
Crazy Makers: How the Food Industry Is Destroying Our Brains and Harming Our Children, Carol Simontacchi
Diet for a New America, John Robbins
Diet, Genes, Early Heart Attacks, and High Blood Pressure, Nutrition in the '90s: Current Controversies and Analysis, ed. Frank N. Kotsonis & Maureen Mackey
Diet, Nutrition and Cancer, National Academy of Sciences
Dr. Dean Ornish's Program for Reversing Heart Disease, Dean Ornish, M.D.
Dying For a Hamburger: How Modern Meat-Packing Led To An Epidemic of Alzheimer's Disease, Murray Waldman and Marjorie Lamb
Eat More, Weigh Less, Dean Ornish, M.D.
Eat Right, Live Longer, Neal Barnard, M.D.
Eat to Beat Cancer, J. Robert Hatherhill, Ph.D.
Eat To Live, Joel Fuhrman, M.D.
Eat, Drink & Be Healthy, Walter C. Willett, M.D.
Eating In America: A History, Waverly Root & Richard de Rochemont
Ecological Integrity: Integrating Environment, Conservation and Health, David Pimentel, et al.
Fasting and Eating for Health, Joel Fuhrman, M.D.
Fat History, Peter N. Stearns
Fat Land - How Americans Became the Fattest People in the World, Greg Critser
Food In History, Reay Tannahill
Food Politics, Marion Nestle, Ph.D.
Foods That Fight Pain, Neal Barnard, M.D.
Guns, Germs, and Steel, Jared Diamond
Mad Cows and Milk Gate, Virgil Hulse, M.D.
Mirage Of Health, Rene Dubos
McDougall's Medicine: A Challenging Second Opinion, John A. McDougall, M.D.
Modern nutrition in health and disease, Shils ME, Olson JA., Shike M, ed. Lea & Febiger Malvern
Nutritional Biochemistry and Metabolism, Lindner, M.
Nutritional Influences on Illness, M.R. Werbach, M.D.
Obesity: Theory and Therapy, ed. Stunkard AJ, Wadden TA
Reclaiming Our Health, John Robbins
Reversing Coronary Heart Disease, Western Diseases: Their Dietary Prevention and Reversibility, ed. NJ Temple & David Burkitt
Save Yourself from Breast Cancer, Dr. Robert Kradjian, M.D.
Six Modern Plagues and How We Are Causing Them, Mark Jerome Walters

The Cancer Industry, Ralph W. Moss, Ph.D.
The China Project, T. Colin Campbell, Ph.D. (New Century Nutrition)
The Food Factor, Barbara Griggs
The Food Revolution, John Robbins
The Hidden Truth of Cancer, K. Morishita, M.D.
The Macrobiotic Approach to Cancer, Michio Kushi
The Macrobiotic Way, Michio Kushi
The McDougall Program, John A. McDougall, M.D.
The McDougall Program for Women, John A. McDougall, M.D.
The Pleasure Trap, Douglas Lisle, Ph.D. & Alan Goldhamer, D.C.
The Scientific Basis of Vegetarianism, William Harris, M.D.
The Truth About Breast Cancer, Joseph Keon, Ph.D.
The Volumetrics Weight-Control Plan: Feel Full on Fewer Calories, Barbara Rolls, Ph.D.
& Robert Barnett
What Color Is Your Diet, David Heber, M.D., Ph.D.
What to Eat If You Have Cancer, Maureen Keane, M.S. & Daniella Chace, M.S.

Articles

A bovine albumin peptide as a possible trigger of insulin-dependent diabetes mellitus, Karjalainen J, Martin JM, Knip M, et al., N Engl J Med 1992;327:302-7

A case-control study of milk-drinking and ovarian cancer risk, Mettlin CJ, Piver MS, American Journal of Epidemiology 132(5): 871-876, 1990

A fasting and vegetarian diet treatment trial on chronic inflammatory disorders, Lithell H, Bruce A, Gustafsson IB, et al, Acta dermatovererol (Stockh) 1983;63:397-403

A High Ratio of Dietary Animal to Vegetable Protein Increases the Rate of Bone Loss and the Risk of Fracture in Postmenopausal Women, Sellmeyer DE, Stone KL, Sebastian A, et al., Am J Clin Nutr. 2001;73:118-122

A low-nitrogen, low-phosphorus vegan diet for patients with chronic renal failure, Barsotti G, Morelli E, Cupisti A, Meola M, Dani L, Giovannetti S, Nephron. 1996;74:390-394

A proportionate study of cancer mortality among members of a vegetarian society, Kinlen LJ, Hermon C, Smith PG, Br J Cancer

A prospective study of dietary fat and risk of prostate cancer, Giovannucci E, J Natl Cancer Inst. 1993 Oct 6;85(19):1571-9

A prospective study on intake of animal products and risk of prostate cancer, Michaud DS, Cancer Causes Control. 2001 Aug;12(6):557-67

A Soy Sauce Surprise, J. Raloff, Science News, 139:357, 1991

Age dependent growth rate of primary breast cancer, P.G. Peer, J.A. van Dijck, J.H. Henricks, et al, 1993, Cancer 71 (11):3547-51.

Airlines Told to Increase Weight Estimates for Passengers, LA Times, 5/13/03

Alzheimer's Studies Look at Role of Fats, AP, 2/17/03

American Journal of Medical Science, 1995, Volume 310, page 22

An ecologic study of dietary links to prostate cancer, Grant WB, Altern Med Rev. 1999 Jun;4(3):162-9

Animal-Based Nutrients Linked With Higher Risk Of Stomach And Esophageal Cancers, Science Daily Magazine, 10/31/01

Animal fat consumption and prostate cancer: a prospective study in Hawaii, Le Marchand L; Kolonel LN; Wilkens LR; Myers BC; Hirohata T, Epidemiology May 1994, 5 (3) p 276-82

Animal product consumption and mortality because of all causes combined, coronary heart disease, stroke, diabetes, and cancer in Seventh-day Adventists, DA Snowdon, American Journal of Clinical Nutrition, Vol 48, 739-748

Antitumor Effect of Seaweeds, I. Yamamoto et al., Japanese Journal of Experimental Medicine 44:543-46, 1974

Arguing till the cows come home, Coghlan, Andy, New Scientist, October 29, 1994, pp. 14-15

Association of Dietary Fat and Lung Cancer, Ernst L. Wynder, James R. Hebert, and Geoffrey Kabat, Journal of the National Cancer Institute 79:631-37, 1987

Autopsy Study and Cancer, NY Times, 11/8/94

Average Annual Per Capita Consumption of Meat, USDA, 2000.

Axial and peripheral bone density and nutrient intakes of postmenopausal vegetarian and omnivorous women, Tesar R, Notelovitz M, Shim E, Dauwell G, Brown J, Am J Clin Nutr. 1992;56:699-704

Beta-carotene and animal fats and their relationship to prostate cancer risk: a case-control study, Mettlin C, Selenskas S, Natarajan N, Huben R, Cancer 1989;64:605-12

Blood pressure and blood lipids among vegetarian, semivegetarian and nonvegetarian African Americans, Melby CL, Toohey ML, Cedrick J, Am J Clin Nutr. 1994;59:103-109

Bovine growth hormone: human food safety evaluation, Juskevich JC, Science. 1990 Aug 24;249(4971):875-84

Bovine growth hormone: human food safety evaluation, Juskevich, Judith C. and Guyer, C. Greg.,Science, Vol. 249, August 24, 1990

Bovine somatotropin supplementation of dairy cows - Is the milk safe?, Daughaday, William H. and Barbano, David M., Journal of the American Medical Association, Vol. 264, August 22/29, 1990, pp 1003-05

Breast cancer in Argentina: case-control study with special reference to meat eating habits, Matos EL, Thomas DB, Sobel N, Vuoto D, Neoplasma 1991;38(3):357-66

Breast cancer: further metabolic-endocrine risk markers?, Stoll, B.A., British Journal of Cancer, Vol. 76, No. 12, 1997, pp. 1652-54

Brief Case Reports of Medically Supervised, Water-Only Fasting Associated with Remission of Autoimmune Disease, Joel Fuhrman, MD, Barbara Sarter, PhD, RN, FNP, and David J. Calabro, DC, Alternative Therapies, Sept/Oct 2001, VOL. 8, No. 4

Broccoli Chemical Blocks Cancer Cell Growth, AP, 5/15/03

Calcium absorption from kale, Heaney RP, Weaver CM., Am J Clin Nutr 1990;51:656-7

Calcium and osteoporosis, Nordin CBE, Nutrition 1997;3(7/8):664-86

Calcium in evolutionary perspective, S Boyd Eaton and Dorothy A Nelson, American Journal of Clinical Nutrition, 1991, 54; 281S-7S

Calcium, dairy products and osteoporosis, Robert P Heaney, Journal of the American College of Nutrition, 2000; 19: 83S-99S

Calcium, protein, and fruit and vegetables as dietary determinants of bone health, New SA, Am J Clin Nutr. 2003 May;77(5):1340-1

California urges study of alarming breast cancer rates, Reuters, 10/24/02

Can Fungi Join Menu of Cancer Fighters?, LA Times, 12/9/01

Can lifestyle changes reverse coronary heart disease?, Ornish D, Brown SE, Scherwitz LW, Billings JH, Armstrong WT, Ports TA., Lancet 1990;336:129-33

Can Lifestyle Modification Increase Survival in Women Diagnosed with Breast Cancer?, Rock, CL, Demark-Wahnefried, W, J. Nutr. 132: 3504S-3509

Cancer incidence among California Seventh-day Adventists, 1976-1982, Mills PK, Beeson WL, Phillips RL, Fraser GE, Am J Clin Nutr. 1994;59(suppl):1136S-1142S

Cancer Prevention & Early Detection: Facts and Figures 2001, American Cancer Society, 2001

Cancer preventive properties of varieties of Brassica oleracea: a review, Beecher CWW, Am J Clin Nutr 1994;59(suppl):1166S–70S

Cancer Rates and Risks: Cancer Death Rates Among 50 Countries, Edition, National Institutes of Health. National Cancer Institute, Source: WHO, as adapted by the American Cancer Society 1996. U.S. Department of Health and Human Services

Cancer undefeated, Bailar JC, N Engl J Med. 1997 May 29;336(22):1569-74

Cardiovascular Disease Risks in Adolescent Males, Elizabeth Lipp, Donna Deane & Nancy Trimble, Applied Nursing Research 9, No. 3, August 1996: 102-107

Cardiovascular Medicine, Preventative Cardiology, ed. James Willerson & Jay Cohn, 1995, 1809-1827.

Case-control study of diet and prostate cancer in China. Cancer Causes Control, Lee MM, 1998 Dec;9(6):545-52

Case-control study of risk factors for hip fractures in the elderly, Cumming RG, Klineberg RJ, Am J Epidemiol 1994;139:493-505

Dairy products, calcium, and prostate cancer risk in the Physicians' Health Study, Chan J., Am J Clin Nutr. 2001 Oct;74(4):549-54.

Changing dietary patterns, Lands WEM, Hamazaki T, Yamazaki K, et al., Am J Clin Nutr 1990;51:991-3

Changing patterns of cancer in Japan, Hirayama T, In: Hiatt HH, Watson JD, Winsten JA, eds. Origins of Human Cancer. Book A, Incidence of Cancer in Humans. Cold Spring Harbor, NY: Cold Spring Harbor Laboratory, 1977. pp 55-75

Childhood cancer in relation to cured meat intake: review of the epidemiological evidence, Blot WJ, Henderson BE, Boice JD Jr, Nutr Cancer 1999;34:111–8

Childhood Obesity and Self-Esteem, Richard Strauss, Pediatrics, 105, No. 1 (2000): 111.

Chinese folk remedy fights cancer: Plant compound sparks chain reaction that kills tumor cells, MSNBC, 12/4/02

Cholesterol in foods rich in omega-3 fatty acids, Weiner, N Engl J Med 315:833, 1986

Cohort studies of fat intake and the risk of breast cancer--a pooled analysis, Hunter DJ, Spiegelman D, Adami HO, Beeson L, van den Brandt PA, Folsom AR, Fraser GE, Goldbohm RA, Graham S, Howe GR, et al., N Engl J Med 1996 Feb 8;334(6):356-61

Combined Intense Lifestyle and Pharmacologic Lipid Treatment Further Reduce Coronary Events and Myocardial Perfusion Abnormalities Compared With Usual-Care Cholesterol-Lowering Drugs in Coronary Artery Disease, Stefano Sdringola, MD, FACC, Keiichi Nakagawa, MD, Yuko Nakagawa, MD, S. Wamique Yusuf, MBBS, MRCP, Fernando Boccalandro, MD, Nizar Mullani, BS, Mary Haynie, RN, MBA, Mary Jane Hess, RN, K. Lance Gould, MD, FACC, Journal of the American College of Cardiology, JACC Vol. 41, No. 2, 2003, 263–72

Combined-Modality Therapy of Cancer, Steven A. Rosenberg, New England Journal of Medicine 312:1512-14

Comparison of the Effects of Lean Red meat vs. Lean White Meat on Serum Lipid Levels Among Free-Living Person with Hypercholesterolemia, M.H. Davidson, D. Hunninghake, K.C. Maki, et al., 1999, Arch. Intern. Med. 159 (12): 1331-38.

Coronary Disease Among United States Soldiers Killed in Action in Korea, Journal of the American Medical Assn 152, 1953, 1090-1993

Coronary heart disease mortality among Seventh-Day Adventists with differing dietary habits: a preliminary report, RL Phillips, FR Lemon, WL Beeson and JW Kuzma, American Journal of Clinical Nutrition, Vol 31, S191-S198

Correcting calcium nutritional deficiency prevents spine fractures in elderly women, Robert R Recker et al., Journal of Bone and Mineral Research, 1996; 11: 1961-1966

Cow milk and insulin-dependent diabetes mellitus: is there a relationship?, Scott FW, Am J Clin Nutr 1990;51:489-91.

Cross-cultural association between dietary animal protein and hip fracture: a hypothesis, Abelow BJ, Holford TR, Insogna KL., Calif Tissue Int 1992;50:14-8

Diet and the prevention of cancer, Cummings, JH, Bingham,SA.. BMJ 1998;317:1636-1640.

Cured and broiled meat consumption in relation to childhood cancer: Denver, Colorado, Sarasua S, Savitz DA, Cancer Causes Control 1994;5:141-8

Dairy foods and bone health: examination of the evidence, Weinsier R, Am J Clin Nutr. 2000 Sep;72(3):681-9

Dairy Products and 10 False Promises, John McDougall, M.D., The McDougall Newsletter, April 2003

Dairy products and breast cancer: the IGF-1, estrogen, and bGH hypothesis, Outwater JL, Nicholson A, Barnard N., Medical Hypothesis 1997;48:453-61

Dairy products, calcium, and prostate cancer risk in the Physicians' Health Study, American Journal of Clinical Nutrition, Vol. 74, No. 4, 549-554, October 2001

Dairy products, calcium, and prostate cancer risk in the Physicians' Health Study, Chan J, Am J Clin Nutr. 2001 Oct;74(4):549-54

Dairy products, calcium, and prostate cancer risk in the Physicians' Health Study, Chan JM, Stampfer MJ, Ma J, Ajani U, Gaziano JM, Giovannucci E.. Presentation, American Association for Cancer Research, San Francisco, April 2000.

Decreased chemotactic and random migration of leukocytes during intralipid infusion, Nordenstrom J, Jarstrand C, Wiernik A., Am J Clin Nutr 1979;32:2416-22

Delayed reactions to foods: Food allergy and rheumatic disease, Panush RS, Annals of Allergy 1986;56:500-503

Did fat intake in the United States really decline between 1989-1991 and 1994-1996?, Chanmugam P, Guthrie JF, Cecilio S, Morton JF, Basiotis PP, Anand R., J Am Diet Assoc. 2003 Jul;103(7):867-72.

Diet and Coronary Heart Disease, Hans Kloer, Archives of Internal Medicine 65 (1989): S13-S21.

Diet and female sex hormone concentrations: an intervention study for the type of fat consumed, Bennett FC; Ingram DM, Am J Clin Nutr Nov 1990, 52 (5) p 808-12

Diet and Health: What Should We Eat?, Science 264 (April 22, 1994): 532-537.

Diet and reproductive hormones: a study of vegetarian and nonvegetarian postmenopausal women, Armstrong BK, Brown JB, Clarke HT, et al, J Natl Cancer Inst 1981:67:761-7

Diet for a New Century, EVU News, Issue 4 /1997
Diet in Adolescence Linked to Ovarian Cancer Risk, Reuters Health, 11/5/01
Diet May Prevent Alzheimer's Disease, AP, 7/18/02
Diet that prevents cancer: recommendations from the American Institute for Cancer Research, Munoz de Chavez M, Chavez A, Int J Cancer Suppl 1998;11:85-9
Diet, androgens, oxidative stress and prostate cancer susceptibility, Fleshner NE, Cancer Metastasis Rev. 1998-99;17(4):325-30
Diet, body size, and breast cancer, Hunter DJ, Willett W, Epidemiol Rev 1993;15:110–32
Diet, Genes, Early Heart Attacks and High Blood Pressure, roger Williams in Nutrition in the 90's: Current Controversies and Analysis, ed. Frank Kotsonis and Maureen Mackey, 1994.
Diet, life-style and mortality in China: a Study of the Characteristics of 65 Chinese counties, J. Chen, T.C. Campbell, J. Li & R. Peto, 1990.
Diet, nutrition, and cancer: the role of fiber, Kritchevsky D, Cancer 1986;58:1830-6
Dietary alpha-linoleic acid and immunocompetence in humans, Kelley DS, Branch LB, Love JE, Taylor PC, Rivera YM, Iacono JM, Am J Clin Nutr 1991;53:40-6
Dietary and hormonal interrelationships among vegetarian Seventh-Day Adventists and nonvegetarian men, Howie BJ, Am J Clin Nutr. 1985 Jul;42(1):127-34
Dietary animal and plant protein and human bone health: a whole foods approach, Massey LK, J Nutr. 2003 Mar;133(3):862S-865S
Dietary animal fat in relation to ovarian cancer risk, Cramer DW, Welch WR, Hutchison GE, et al., Obstet Gynecol 1984;63:833–5
Dietary calcium, protein, and phosphorus are related to bone mineral density and content in young women, Teegarden D, Am J Clin Nutr. 1998 Sep;68(3):749-54
Dietary calcium: adequacy of a vegetarian diet, Weaver CM, Plawecki KL, Am J Clin Nutr. 1994;59(suppl):1238S-1241S
Dietary calcium: adequacy of a vegetarian diet, Weaver CM, Plawecki KL., Am J Clin Nutr 1994;59 (suppl):1238S-41S.
Dietary carcinogens linked to breast cancer, Medical World News, May 1993, p. 13.
Dietary changes favorably affect bone remodeling in older adults, Heaney RP, McCarron DA, Dawson-Hughes B, et al., J Am Dietetic Assn, 1999;99:1228-33
Dietary Cholesterol and Incidence of Lung Cancer, R. B. Shekelle et al.,American Journal of Epidemiology 134:48084, 1992
Dietary correlates of plasma insulin-like growth factor I and insulin-like growth factor binding protein 3 concentrations, Holmes MD, Cancer Epidemiol Biomarkers Prev. 2002 Sep;11(9):852-61
Dietary determinants of ischaemic heart disease in health conscious individuals, Jim I Mann, Paul N Appleby, Timothy J Key, Margaret Thorogood, Heart 1997;78:450-455
Dietary factors and risk of breast cancer: combined analysis of 12 case-control studies, Howe GR, Hirohata T, Hislop T, et al., J Natl Cancer Inst 1990;82:561-9
Dietary Factors in Cancer of the Lower Urinary Tract, A.M.Y. Nomura et al., International Journal of Cancer 48:199205
Dietary fat and advanced prostate cancer, Bairati I, J Urol. 1998 Apr;159(4):1271-5
Dietary Fat and Health: The Epidemiological Evidence, Acta Cardiologica 44, No. 6, 1989, pp. 446-448.
Dietary Fat and Health: The Epidemiological Evidence, H. Kesteloot, Acta

Cardiologica 44, No. 6 (1989): 446-448

Dietary fat and mammary carcinogenesis, Carroll KK, Braden LM, Nutrition and Cancer 1985;6:254-9

Dietary fat and natural-killer cell activity, Barone J, Hebert JR, Reddy MM, Am J Clin Nutr 1989;50:861-7

Dietary fat and prostate cancer progression and survival, Fradet Y, Eur Urol. 1999;35(5-6):388-9

Dietary Fat and Prostate Cancer: Current Status, Kolonel, LN, Nomura, AMY, Cooney, RV, J Natl Cancer Inst 91: 414-428

Dietary fat and risk of breast cancer, Willet WC, N Engl J Med 1987a;316:22-8

Dietary fat consumption and survival among women with breast cancer, Gregorio DI, Emrich LJ, Graham S, Marshall JR, Nemoto T, J Natl Cancer Inst 1985;75:37-41

Dietary fat, calories, and the risk of breast cancer in postmenopausal women: a prospective population-based study, Barrett-Connor E, Friedlander NJ, J Am Coll Nutr 1993;12:390-9

Dietary Fat Intake and Ovarian Cancer in a Cohort of US Women, Elizabeth R. Bertone, Bernard A. Rosner, David J. Hunter, Meir J. Stampfer, Frank E. Speizer1, Graham A. Colditz, Walter C. Willett and Susan E. Hankinson, Am J Epidemiol 2002; 156:22-31

Dietary fat intake and risk of epithelial ovarian cancer, Risch HA; Jain M; Marrett LD; Howe GR, J Natl Cancer Inst Sep 21 1994, 86 (18): 1409-15

Dietary fat reduction and plasma estradiol concentration in healthy postmenopausal women, Prentice R, Thompson D, Clifford C, Gorbach S, Goldin B, Byar D, The Women's Health Trial Study Group, J Natl Cancer Inst 1990 Jan 17;82(2):129-34

Dietary Fiber and the Risk of Colorectal Cancer and Adenoma in Women, Fuchs CS, Giovannucci E., Colditz GA, Hunter DJ, Stampfer MJ, Rosner BR, Speizer FE, Willett WC, N Engl J Med 1999;340:169-76

Dietary fiber intake in Japan, Minowa M, Bingham S, Cummings JH, Human Nutr Appl Nutr 1983;37A:113-9

Dietary Fiber, Vegetables, and Colon Cancer: Critical Review and Meta-analyses of the Epidemiologic Evidence, Bruce Tock, Elaine Lanza, and Peter Greenwald, Journal of the National Cancer Institute 82:650-661, 1990

Dietary flavonoids and the risk of lung cancer and other malignant neoplasms, Knekt P, Jarvinen R, Seppanen R, et al., Am J Epidemiol 1997;146:223-30

Dietary habits and prognostic factors in breast cancer, Holm LE, Callmer E, Hjalmar ML, Lidbrink E, Nilsson B, Skoog L, J Natl Cancer Inst 1989;81:1218-23

Dietary influences on bone mass and bone metabolism: further evidence of a positive link between fruit and vegetable consumption and bone health?, Susan A New et al., American Journal of Clinical Nutrition, 2000; 71: 142-151

Dietary lipids and colon cancer, Giovannucci E, Willett WC, Principles and Practice of Oncology 1994;9:1-12

Dietary Monounsaturated Fatty Acids Promote Aortic Atherosclerosis in LDL Receptor-Null, Human ApoB100-Overexpressing Transgenic Mice, Lawrence L. Rudel, Kathryn Kelley, Janet K. Sawyer, Ramesh Shah, Martha D. Wilson, Arterioscler Thromb Vasc Biol. 1998;18:1818-1827

Dietary phytoestrogens and cancer: in vitro and in vivo studies, Adlercreutz H; Mousavi Y; Clark J; Hockerstedt K; Hamalainen E; Wahala K; Makela T; Hase T, J

Steroid Biochem Mol Biol Mar 1992, 41 (3-8) p331-7

Dietary Protein level and aflatoxin B1-induced preneoplastic hepatic lesions in the rat, Dunaif, GE, Campbell TC, Nutrition 117 No. 7, 1987: 1298-302

Dietary Reference Intakes for Calcium, Phosphorus, Magnesium, Vitamin D and Flouride, National Academy of Sciences, Institute of Medicine, 1997

Dietary salt, nitrate and stomach cancer mortality in 24 countries, Joossens JV, Hill MJ, Elliott P, et al., Int J Epidemiol 1996;25:494–504.

Eat Healthy First, Ask Questions Later: Diet's Link to Cancer Risk Obvious, Yet Controversial, WebMD, 9/12/02

Eat to live, not live to eat, Weisburger J. Nutrition 2000; 16:767-73.

Eat Your Veggies, but Don't Forget Fruit: Eating Lots of Fruit as a Kid May Prevent Cancer as an Adult, WebMD, 2/19/03

Eating 20% Less May Prevent Aging Damage, WebMD Medical News, 10/28/02

Eating Lots of Tofu May Prevent Breast Cancer: High-Soy Diet Linked to Low Breast Cancer Rate in Asians, WebMD Medical News, 10/2/02

Effect of Diet on Vascular Reactivity: An Emerging Marker for Vascular Risk, Sheila G. West, Current Atherosclerosis Reports, Vol 3.6, pp. 446-455

Effect of Diet and Lifestyle on Bone Mass in Asian Young Women, Takako Hirota et al., American Journal of Clinical Nutrition, 1992; 55

Effect of low-fat diet on female sex hormone levels, Ingram DM, Bennett FC, Willcox D, de Klerk N, J Natl Cancer Inst 1987;79:1225-9

Effect of a High-Fat Ketogenic Diet on Plasma Levels of Lipids, Lipoproteins, and Apolipoproteins in Children, Peter O. Kwiterovich, Jr; Eileen P. G. Vining; Paula Pyzik; Richard Skolasky, Jr; John M. Freeman, JAMA. 2003;290:912-920.

Effect of a low-fat diet on the incidence of actinic keratosis, Black HS, Herd A, Goldberg LH, et al., N Engl J Med 1994;330:1272–5

Effect of risk factor values on lifetime risk of and age at first coronary event, Fraser GE, Lindsted KD, Beeson WL, The Adventist Health Study. Am J Epidemiol. 1995;142:746-758

Effects of a low calorie vegan diet on disease activity and general conditions in patients with rheumatoid arthritis, Fujita A; Hashimoto Y; Nakahara K, Tanaka T; et al., Rinsho Byori 1999;47(6):554-60

Effects of a Very Low-Fat, Vegan Diet in Subjects with Rheumatoid Arthritis, John McDougall, M.D., Bonnie Bruce, Ph.D., Gene Spiller, Ph.D., John Westerdahl, M.P.H, R.D., C.N.S, J. Alternative and Complementary Medicine, Vol. 8, No. 1, 2002, pp. 71-75

Effects of human growth hormone in men over 60 years old. New England Journal of Medicine, Rudman, Daniel, et al., Vol. 323, July 5, 1990, pp. 1-6

Epidemiologic and Dietary Evidence for a Specific Nutritional Predisposition to Esophageal Cancer, S. J. van Rensburg, Journal of the National Cancer Institute 67:243-51, 1981

Epidemiology of breast cancer with special reference to the role of diet, Hirayama T, Prev Med 1978;7:173-95

Epidemiology of rheumatoid arthritis, Alarcon GS, Rheumatol Dis Clin N Am 1995; 21:589-604

Estimation of the renal net acid excretion by adults consuming diets containing variable amounts of protein, Remer T, Manz F, Am J Clin Nutr. 1994; 59:1356-1361

Evidence that a low-fat diet reduces the occurrence of non-melanoma skin cancer,

Black AHS, Thornby JI, Wolf JE Jr, et al., Int J Cancer 1995;62:165–9

Excess dietary protein can adversely affect bone, Uriel S Barzel and Linda K Massey, Journal of Nutrition, 1998; 128: 1051-1053

Exercise Builds Strong Bones, Los Angeles Times, 11/25/02

Famine Symposium – Physiology of acute starvation in man, Cahill GF, Ecology of Food and Nutrition 1978;6:221-30.

Fasting: the history, pathophysiology and complications, Kerndt PR, Naughton JL, Driscoll CE, Loxterkamp DA, Western Journal of Medicine 1992;137(5):379-99

Fasting-A review with emphasis on the electrolytes, Weinsier RL, The American Journal of Medicine 1971;50:233-40

Fat and calories in colon and breast cancer: from animal studies to controlled clinical trials, Macrae FA, Prev Med 1993;22:750–66

Fatty acid proportions in cholesterol esters and risk of premature death from cancer in middle aged French men, Zureik M, Ducimetière P, Warnet JM, Orssaud G, BMJ 1995;311:1251–4

Fish consumption and breast cancer risk: an ecological study, Kaizer L, Boyd NF, Kriukov V, Tritchler D, Nutr Cancer 1989;12:61–8

Fish consumption and cancer risk, Fernandez E, Chatenoud L, La Veccjoa C, et al., Am J Clin Nutr 1999;70:85–90

Fish Intake Is Positively Associated with Breast Cancer Incidence Rate, Connie Stripp, Kim Overvad, Jane Christensen, Birthe L. Thomsen, Anja Olsen, Susanne Møller and Anne Tjønneland2, J. Nutr. 133:3664-3669, November 2003

Flavonoid intake and long-term risk of coronary heart disease and cancer in the Seven Countries Study, Hertog MGL, Kromhout D, Aravanis C, et al., Arch Intern Med 1995;155:381–6

Food Consumption Statistics 1955-1971, Organization for Economic Cooperation and Development (O.E.C.D.) , Paris, 1973

Food, Nutrition and the Prevention of Cancer: a global perspective, World Cancer Research Fund / American Institute for Cancer Research, Fox Chase Cancer Center Study Links Oxygen Levels And Angiogenesis In Prostate Cancer, ScienceDaily Magazine, 10/25/00

Fractures, calcium, and the modern diet, Hegsted DM, Am J Clin Nutr. 2001 Nov;74(5):571-3

Fruit and vegetable intake and incidence of bladder cancer in a male prospective cohort, Michaud DS, Spiegelman D, Clinton SK, et al., J Natl Cancer Inst 1999;91:605–13

Fruit and vegetable intakes are an independent predictor of bone size in early pubertal children, Frances A Tylavsky, Katherine Holliday, Robert Danish, Catherine Womack, John Norwood and Laura Carbone, American Journal of Clinical Nutrition, Vol. 79, No. 2, 311-317, February 2004

Fruit, vegetables, and cancer prevention: a review of the epidemiological evidence, Block G, Patterson B, Subar A, Nutr Cancer 1992;18:1–29

Fruits, Veggies Do a Tummy Good as Cancer-Fighters, Reuters Health, 12/23/02

Galactose consumption and metabolism in relation to the risk of ovarian cancer, Cramer DW, Harlow BL, Willet WC, Lancet 1989;2:66-71.

Genetic engineering and the use of bovine somatotropin, Grossman, Charles J., Journal of the American Medical Association, Vol. 264, August 22/29, 1990, p. 1028

Calcium and fructose intake in relation to risk of prostate cancer, Giovannucci E., Cancer Res. 1998 Feb 1;58(3):442-7.

'Good' cholesterol helps very old keep their smarts, Journal of Gerontology 2002;57A

Growth of vegetarian children: The Farm Study, O'Connell JM, Dibley MJ, Sierra J, Wallace B, Marks JS, Yip R, Pediatrics. 1989;84:475-481

Gymnastics Strengthens Girls' Bones: Study, Journal of Pediatrics 2002;141:211-216

Hazel said 'No' to chemo: Determined ... Hazel fought disease with fresh vegetables, London Times, 6/15/02

Health & Healing, Julian Whitaker, M.D., October, 1998, Volume 8, No. 10

Health aspects of vegetarian diets, Dwyer JT, Am J Clin Nutr. 1988;48(suppl):712-738

Health implications of the n-3 fatty acids, Odeleye OE, Watson RR, Am J Clin Nutr 1991;53:177-8.

Heart Disease in Children, American Journal of Medical Science, 1995, Volume 310, page 22

High cholesterol linked to Alzheimer's, MSNBC, 3/14/02

Higher Intake of Dairy Products May Be Linked to Prostate Cancer Risk, Harvard School of Public Health, Press Release, 4/4/00

High-meat diets and cancer risk, Bingham SA, Proc Nutr Soc. 1999 May;58(2):243-8

Hormones and diet: low insulin-like growth factor-I but normal bioavailable androgens in vegan men, Allen NE, Br J Cancer. 2000

How Well Do Their Dietary Patterns Meet the Healthy People 2010 Objectives?, Cheryl L. Perry, PhD, Maureen T. McGuire, PhD, Dianne Neumark-Sztainer, PhD, RD, Mary Story, PhD, RD, Arch Pediatr Adolesc Med. 2002;156:431-437

Huge Study of Diet Indicts Fat and Meat, J. Brody, NY Times, May 8, 1990, Science Times Section, p. 1.

Human breast milk contains bovine IgG. Relationship to infant colic?, Clyne PS, Kulczycki A, Pediatrics 1991;87(4):439-44

Hypervitaminosis D associated with drinking milk, Jacobus CH, Holick MF, Shao Q, et al., N Engl J Med 1992;326(18):1173-7

Hypocholesterolemic Effects of Oat-Bran or Bean Intake for Hypercholesterolemic Men, J. Anderson, American Journal of Clinical Nutrition 40:1146-55, 1984

Immune complexes containing food proteins in normal and atopic sunjects after oral challenges and effect of sodium chromoglucate on antigen absorption, Paganelli R, Levinsky RJ, Brostoff J, Wraith DG, Lancet 1979;1:1270-72

Impact of dietary fiber on colon cancer occurrence, Kim Y., Gastroenterology. 2000 Jun;118(6):1235-57.

Impact of Westernization on the Nutrition of Japan, Preventive Medicine 7:205-17, 1978

Incidence of cancer in men on a diet high in polyunsaturated fat, Pearce ML, Dayton S, Lancet 1971;I:464–7

Increased fish consumption may be risky, Foran, J., JAMA 262:28, 1989

Inhibition of tumor cell kinetics and serum insulin growth factor I levels by octreotide in colorectal cancer patients, Cascinu, S., et al., Gastroenterology, Vol. 113, September 1997, pp. 767-72

Insulin-like growth factor 1 in relation to prostate cancer and benign prostatic hyperplasia, Mantzoros, C.S., et al., British Journal of Cancer, Vol. 76, No. 9, 1997, pp. 1115-18

Insulin-like growth factor binding proteins in neoplasia (meeting abstract), Rosenfeld, R.G., et al., Hormones and Growth Factors in Development and Neoplasia, Fogarty International Conference, June 26-28, 1995, Bethesda, MD, 1995, p. 24

Insulin-like growth factor-I receptors are overexpressed and predict a low risk in human breast cancer, Papa, Vincenzo, et al., Cancer Research, Vol. 53, 1993, pp. 3736-40

Insulin-like growth factors (IGFs), IGF receptors, and IGF-binding proteins in primary cultures of prostate epithelial cells, Cohen, Pinchas, et al., Journal of Clinical Endocrinology and Metabolism, Vol. 73, No. 2, 1991, pp. 401-07

Insulin-like growth factors in health and disease, LeRoith, Derek, moderator, Annals of Internal Medicine, Vol. 116, May 15, 1992, pp. 854-62

Intake of flavonoids and lung cancer, Le Marchand L, Murphy SP, Hankin JH, et al., J Natl Cancer Inst 2000;92:154–60

International comparisons of mortality rates for cancer of the breast, ovary, prostate, and colon, and per capita food consumption, Rose DP, Boyar AP, Wynder EL, Cancer 1986;58:2363-71

Intolerance of cow's milk and chronic constipation in children, Iacono G, Cavataio F, Montalto G, et al., N Engl J Med 1998;339(16):1100-4.

Is there a time bomb in your diet? Exploding the myths about milk, The Sunday Times Magazine (London), July 21, 2002

Mammary secretion of oestrogens in the cow, Janowski T., Domest Anim Endocrinol. 2002 Jul;23(1-2):125-37.

Jogging builds better bones in men, American Journal of Public Health as reported by the Associated Press, June 28, 2002.

Lawyers See Fat Payoffs in Junk Food Lawsuits, 1/23/02, NY Times

Long-term effect of dietary marine omega-3 fatty acids upon plasma and cellular lipids, platelet function, and eicosanoid formation in humans, C von Schacky, Fischer S, Weber PC, J Clin Invest 1985;76:1626-31.

Low protein intake: the impact on calcium and bone homeostasis in humans, Kerstetter JE, J Nutr. 2003 Mar; 133(3):855S-861S

Lupus erythematosis and nutrition: A review of the literature, Brown AC, J Ren Nutr 2000; 10(4):170-83.

Lycopene is a more potent inhibitor of human cancer cell proliferation than either a-carotene or ß-carotene, Levy J, Bosin E, Feldman B, et al., Nutr Cancer 1995;24:257–66

Lymphomas and Animal-Protein Consumption, Cunningham AS, Lancet.1976;Nov.27:1184-86

Macronutrients, energy intake, and breast cancer risk: implications from different models, Decarli A, Favero A, La Vecchia C, Russo A, Ferraroni M, Negri E, Franceschi S, Epidemiology 1997 Jul;8(4):425-8

Mammary secretion of oestrogens in the cow, Janowski T, Domest Anim Endocrinol. 2002 Jul;23(1-2):125-37

Maternal diet during pregnancy and risk of brain tumors in children, Bunin GR, Int J Cancer Suppl 1998;11:23–5

Meat consumption and its association with other diet and health factors in young adults: the CARDIA study, Slatter ML, Jacobs DR, Hilner JE Jr, Caan BJ, Van Horn L, Bragg C, Manolio TA, Kushi LH, Liu D, Am J Clin Nutr. 1992;56:699-704

Meat consumption, cancer risk and population groups within New Zealand, Ferguson

LR, Mutat Res. 2002 Sep 30;506-507:215-24

Meat intake, heterocyclic amines, and colon cancer, Maric R, Am J Gastroenterol. 2000 Dec;95(12):3683-4

Medically Supervised Water-Only Fasting in the Treatment of Borderline Hypertension, Alan C. Goldhamer, D.C., Douglass J., et. al., The Journal of Alternative and Complementary Medicine, Volume 8, Number 5, 2002, pp. 643–650

Medically supervised water-only fasting in the treatment of hypertension, Goldhamer AC, Lisle DJ, Parpia B, Anderson SV, Campbell TC, Journal of Chiropractic and Manipulative Therapy 2001

Mediterranean Diet Keeps Arthritis Symptoms at Bay, Reuters, 2/19/03

Men who eat soy and tomatoes reduce their risk of prostate cancer, study shows, Environmental News Network, 6/7/01

Micronutrients and Immune Function, A. Bendich and R.K. Chandra, NY Academy of Sciences, Vol. 587

Milk and Diabetes, Jürgen Schrezenmeir, PhD and Alexandra Jagla, PhD, Journal of the American College of Nutrition, Vol. 19, No. 90002, 176S-190S

Milk Dietary Calcium and Bone Fractures in Women: a 12-Year Prospective Study, D. Feskanich, W.C. Willett, M.J. Stampfer and G.A. Colditz, 1977, Am. J. Public Health 87: 992-97

Milk hormone data bottled up for years, Coghlan, Andy, New Scientist, October 22, 1994, p. 4

Milk intake and bone mineral acquisition in adolescent girls: randomised, controlled intervention trial, Cadogan J, BMJ 1997;315:1255-1260

Milk intake and bone mineral acquisition in adolescent girls: randomised, controlled intervention trial, Cadogan J, Eastell R, Jones N, Barker ME. BMJ 1997;315:1255-60.

Milk may raise prostate cancer risk, AP, 4/4/00

Milk, dietary calcium and bone fractures in women: a 12-year prospective study, Diane Feskanich et al., American Journal of Public Health, 1997; 87: 992-997

Minimum Protein Requirements of Adults, D. Hegsted, 1968, Am. J. Clin. Nutr. 21:3520

MS: A case-control study of milk-drinking and ovarian cancer risk, Mettlin CJ, Piver, American Journal of Epidemiology 132(5): 871-876, 1990

Mortality in vegetarians and nonvegetarians: detailed findings from a collaborative analysis of 5 prospective studies, Timothy J Key, Gary E Fraser, Margaret Thorogood, Paul N Appleby, Valerie Beral, Gillian Reeves, Michael L Burr, Jenny Chang-Claude, Rainer Frentzel-Beyme, Jan W Kuzma, Jim Mann and Klim McPherson, American Journal of Clinical Nutrition, Vol. 70, No. 3, 516S-524S

Natural killer cells, vitamins, and other blood components of vegetarian and omnivorous men, Malter M, Schriever G, Eilber U, Nutr Cancer 1989;32:271–8

New research links meat with cancer: Double or triple the risk for some forms, Reuters, 12/20/01

New Scientific Thinking Implicates Body Fat as Cancer Promoter, Press Release July 11, 2002, American Institute for Cancer Research (AICR)

Nutrient intakes and eating behavior scores of vegetarian and nonvegetarian women, Janelle KC, Barr SI, J Am Diet Assoc. 1995;95:180-189

Nutrition and Coronary Heart Disease Epidemiology, Nutrition and Biotechnology in Heart Disease and Cancer, Herman A. Tyroler, ed. John Longenecker, David

Kritchevsky, and Marc Drezner, 1995, pp. 7-19.

Nutrition and Health: The Conclusions of the B.I.R.N.H. Study, H. Kesteloot, Acta Cardiologica 44, No. 2, 1989, pp. 183-194.

Nutrition and subsequent hip fracture risk among a national cohort of white women, Huang Z, Himes JH, McGovern PG, Am J Epidemiol 1996;144:124-34

Nutrition, and the Prevention of Cancer: A Global Perspective, World Cancer Research Fund. Food, American Institute of Cancer Research. Washington, DC: 1997

Nutrition, immune response, and outcome, Chandra S, Chandra RK, Progress in Food and Nutrition Science 1986;10:1-65.16

Nutritional characteristics of wild primate foods: do the diets of our closest living relatives have lessons for us?, Katharine Milton, Nutrition, 1999; 15: 488-498

Nutritional influences on bone mass, Reid DM, New SA, Proceed Nutr Soc 1997;56:977-87

Obesity and body fat distribution and breast cancer prognosis, Schapira DV, Kumar NB, Lyman GH, Cox CE, Cancer 1991;67:523-8

Omega-3 polyunsaturated fatty acids and skeletal health, Bruce A Watkins et al., Experimental Biology and Medicine, 2001; 226: 485-497

Oxidative damage and defense, Jacob RA, Burri BJ, Am J Clin Nutr. 1996;63(suppl):985S-990S

Pesticide Exposure and Cancer in Children, Marion Moses, M.D., March 21, 1997, Pesticide Education Center,

Phytoestrogen content of foods--a compendium of literature values, Reinli K, Block G., Nutr Cancer 1996;26(2):123-48.14

Plant Compound Kills Lung Cancer Cells, Reuters Health, 2/21/03

Plant proteins in relation to human protein and amino acid nutrition, Young VR, Pellett PL, Am J Clin Nutr. 1994; 59 (suppl 5):1203S-1212S

Plasma androgens, IGF-1, body size, and prostate cancer risk: a synthetic review, Kaaks R, Prostate Cancer Prostatic Dis. 2000

Plasma insulin-like growth factor I and prostate cancer risk: a prospective study, Chan, June M., et al., Science, Vol. 279, January 23, 1998, pp. 563-66

Position of The American Dietetic Association: Vegetarian diets, 1999, The American Dietetic Association

Potassium, magnesium, and fruit and vegetable intakes are associated with greater bone mineral density in elderly men and women, Tucker KL, Hannan MR, Chen H, Cupples LA, Wilson PWF, Kiel DP, Am J Clin Nutr 1999;69:727-36

Potbelly may increase stroke risk: Link found even among people of normal weight, MSNBC, 4/16/02

Potential public health hazards of biosynthetic milk hormones, Epstein, Samuel S., International Journal of Health Services, Vol. 20, No. 1, 1990, pp. 73-84

Premenopausal Fat Intake and Risk of Breast Cancer, Eunyoung Cho, Donna Spiegelman, David J. Hunter, Wendy Y. Chen, Meir J. Stampfer, Graham A. Colditz, and Walter C. Willett, J Natl Cancer Inst 2003; 95: 1079-1085.

Prevalence of low femoreal bone density in older U.S. women from NHANES III, Looker AC, Johnston CC, Wahner HW, et al., J Bone and Mineral Research 1995;10:796-802

Preventing and arresting coronary atherosclerosis, Roberts WC, Am Heart J. 1995;130:580-600

Processed meats and risk of childhood leukemia, Peters JM, Preston-Martin S, London SJ, et al., Cancer Causes Control 1994;5:195–202.

Prospective study of dietary protein intake and risk of hip fracture in postmenopausal women, Munger RG, Am J Clin Nutr. 1999

Prostate cancer in relation to diet, physical activity, and body size in blacks, whites, and Asians in the United States and Canada, Whittemore AS, J Natl Cancer Inst. 1995 May 3;87(9):652-61

Protective effects of raw vegetables and fruit against lung cancer among smokers and ex-smokers: a case-control study in the Tokai area of Japan, C.M. Gao, K. Tajima, T. Kuroishi, et al, 1993, Japan J. Cancer Res. 84 (6): 594-600.

Questions and answers on synthetic bovine growth hormones, Epstein, Samuel S., International Journal of Health Services, Vol. 20, No. 4, 1990, pp. 573-82

Racial bias in federal nutrition policy, part I: the public health implications of variations in lactase persistence, Bertron P, Barnard ND, Mills M, J Natl Med Assoc 1999;91:151-7

Randomized trial of intake of fat, fiber, and beta carotene to prevent colorectal adenomas, MacLennan R, The Australian Polyp Prevention Project. J Natl Cancer Inst. 1995 Dec 6;87(23):1760-6

Rarity of colon cancer in Africans is associated with low animal product consumption, not fiber, O'Keefe S, Am J Gastroenterol. 1999 May;94(5):1373-80

Relationship of animal protein-rich diet to kidney stone formation and calcium metabolism, Neil A Breslau et al., Journal of Clinical Endocrinology and Metabolism, 1988; 66: 140-146

Relationship of Soybean Paste Soup Intake to Gastric Cancer Risk, T. Hirayama, Nutrition and Cancer 3:223-33, 1981

Relative Weight, Weight Loss Efforts and Nutrient Intakes among Health-Conscious Vegetarian, Past Vegetarian and Nonvegetarian Women Ages 18 to 50, Susan I. Barr, PhD and Terri M. Broughton, BScD, Journal of the American College of Nutrition, Vol. 19, No. 6, 781-788

Resolving the Coronary Artery Disease Epidemic Through Plant-Based Nutrition, Caldwell B. Esselstyn, Jr., M.D., Preventive Cardiology, Fall, 2001

Revolution in Diet and Medicine, Spectrum #24, May/June 1992

Risk factors for hip fracture in Asian men and women: the Asian Osteoporosis Study, E M C Lau et al., Journal of Bone and Mineral Research, 2001; 16: 572-580

Risk factors for hip fracture in white women, Cummings SR, Nevitt MC, Browner WS, et al., N Engl J Med 1995;332:767-73

Risk factors for prostate carcinoma in Taiwan: a case-control study in a Chinese population, Sung JF, Cancer. 1999 Aug 1;86(3):484-91

Risk of death from cancer and ischaemic heart disease in meat and non-meat eaters, Thorogood M, Mann J, Appleby P, McPherson K, BMJ 1994;308:1667–71

Risk of death from cancer and ischaemic heart disease in meat and non-meat eaters, Thorogood M, Mann J, Appleby P, McPherson K, BMJ. 1994;308:1667-1670

Role of Dietary Fat in the Causation of Breast Cancer, Greenwald, P, Prev 8: 3-7

Role of dietary fiber in colon cancer: an overview, Reddy BS, Am J Med. 1999 Jan 25;106(1A):16S-19S

Role of fat, animal protein and dietary fiber in breast cancer etiology: a case control study, Lubin F, Wax Y, Modan B, et al., J Natl Cancer Inst 1986;77:605-12

Role of lifestyle and dietary habits in risk of cancer among Seventh-day Adventists, Phillips RL, Cancer Research 1975;35:3513-22

Role of the insulin-like growth factor family in cancer development and progression, Yu H, J Natl Cancer Inst. 2000 Sep 20;92(18):1472-89

Safety of bovine somatotropin, Brunner, Eric, The Lancet, September 10, 1988, p. 629

Safety of milk from cows treated with bovine somatotrophin, Mepham, T.B., et al., The Lancet, Vol. 344, July 16, 1994, pp. 197-98

School Lunch Program Fails to Make the Grade, A Report by the Physicians Committee for Responsible Medicine, Fall 2001

Screening for prostate cancer with prostate-specific antigen. An examination of the evidence, Woolf SH, N Engl J Med. 1995 Nov

SEER cancer stastics review, 1973-1997, Ries L, Bethesda, MD.: National Cancer Institute, 2000

Serum insulin-like growth factor-I levels and prostate cancer risk—interpreting the evidence, Cohen P., J Natl Cancer Inst 1998;90:876-9.

Similarities of prostate and breast cancer: Evolution, diet, and estrogens, Coffey DS, Urology. 2001 Apr;57(4 Suppl 1):31-8

Single nutrients and immunity, Beisel WR, Am J Clin Nutr 1982;35:Feb(suppl):417-68

Soybean phytochemicals inhibit the growth of transplantable human prostate carcinoma and tumor angiogenesis in mice, Zhou JR, J Nutr. 1999 Sep;129(9):1628-35

Studies of Japanese Migrants, W. Haenszel and M. Kurihara, Journal of the National Cancer Institute 40:43-68

Studies Say Vegetables Good Against Alzheimer's, Reuters, 2/17/03

Study links red meat to some cancers, CNN, 4/30/96

Study Says Portions, Like Our Waistlines, Have Been Growing Eating in or out, food servings have increased since 1977, research concludes, LA Times, 2/3/03

Study Suggests Western Diet Tied to Prostate Cancer, Reuters, 4/28/03

The Causes of Cancer: Quantitative Estimates of Avoidable Risks of Cancer in the United States Today, R. Doll & R. Peto, Journal of the National Cancer Institute 66 (1981): 1191-1208

The contribution of vegetarian diets to health and disease: a paradigm shift?, Joan Sabaté, American Journal of Clinical Nutrition, Vol. 78, No. 3, 502S-507S

The crisis in U.S. and international cancer policy, Epstein SS, Int J Health Serv. 002;32(4):669-707

The development of biological therapies for breast cancer, Lippman, Marc E.. Science, Vol. 259, January 29, 1993, pp. 631-32

The Dietary Environment and Cancer, Wynder EL, J Amer Dietetic Assoc. 1977;71:385-92

The effect of dietary supplementation with n-3 polyunsaturated fatty acids on the synthesis of interleukin-1 and tumor necrosis factor by mononuclear cells, Endres S, Ghorbani R, Kelley VE, et al., N Engl J Med 1989;320:265-71

The effect of high-protein diets on coronary blood flow, Fleming RM, Angiology 2000;51(10):817-826.

The effect of milk supplements on calcium metabolism, bone metabolism and calcium balance, Recker RR, Am J Clin Nutr. 1985

The effects of acid on bone, David A Bushinsky and Kevin K Frick, Current Opinion in Nephrology and Hypertension, 2000; 9: 369-379

The effects of calcium supplementation (milk powder or tablets) and exercise on bone mineral density in postmenopausal women, Prince R, Devine A, Dick I, et al., J Bone Miner Res 1995;10:1068-75

The effects of long chain free fatty acids on human neutrophil function and structure, Hawley HP, Gordon GB, Lab Invest 1976;34:216-22

The Famine of Youth: Severely restricting diet may increase life span, but few will be able to follow such a harsh regimen, Gary Taubes, Scientific American, June, 2000

The genesis and growth of tumors. II. Effects of caloric restriction per se, Tannenbaum A, Cancer Res 1942;2:460–7

The impact of vegetarian diets on renal disease, Pagenkemper J, Top Clin Nutr. 1995;10:22-26

The Influence of Diet on the Appearance of New Lesions in Human Coronary Arteries," D. H. Blankenhorn; R. L. Johnson; W. J. Mack; H. A. el Zein; L. I. Vailas, JAMA, 1990, Vol. 263, pp. 1646-52

The incidence of dementia and intake of animal products: preliminary findings from the Adventist Health Study, Giem, P. et al (1993), Neuroepidemiology v. 11 p.28-36

The nature and significance of the relationship between urinary sodium and urinary calcium in women, Nordin BEC, Need AG, Morris HA, Horowitz M., J Nutr 1993;123:1615-22.

The Prime Cause and Prevention of Cancer - Part 1, Ottow Warburg, ed. Dean Burk, National Cancer Institute, Bethesda, Maryland, USA, 2nd Ed. Rev. 1969

The Rationale for Controlling Dietary Lipids in the Prevention of Coronary Heart Disease, Buletin of PAHO 24, No. 2, 1990, pp. 197-209

The relationship among adiposity, diet and hormone concentrations in vegetarian and nonvegetarian postmenopausal women, Barbosa JC, Shultz TD, Filley SJ, Nieman DC, Am J Clin Nutr. 1990;51:798-803

The Relationship Between Dietary Cholesterol and Blood Cholesterol, Dept. of Health and Human Services; Dept. of Agriculture.

The role of soy products in reducing risk of cancer, Messina MJ, Barnes S, J Natl Cancer Inst 1991;83:541-6.36

The role of the insulin-like growth factor-I receptor in cancer, LeRoith, Derek, et al., Annals New York Academy of Sciences, Vol. 766, September 7, 1995, pp. 402-08

The skeleton crew: is calcium enough?, Finn SC, J Women's Health 1998;7(1):31-6

The use of calcium in the management of osteoporosis, Kanis JA, Bone. 1999 Apr;24(4):279-90

Tomatoes, tomato-based products, lycopene, and cancer: review of the epidemiologic literature, Giovannucci E, J Natl Cancer Inst 1999;91:317–31.

Treatment failure and dietary habits in women with breast cancer, Holm LE, Nordevang E, Hjalmar ML, Lidbrink E, Callmer E, Nilsson B, J Natl Cancer Inst 1993 Jan 6;85(1):32-6

Twenty-year follow-up of a randomized trial comparing total mastectomy, lumpectomy, and lumpectomy plus irradiation for the treatment of invasive breast cancer, Fisher B., N Engl J Med. 2002 Oct 17;347(16):1233-41

U.S. Department of Health and Human Services. Surgeon General's Report on Nutrition and Health. DHHS Publ No. 88-50210, 1988, p. 1

Unlabeled milk from cows treated with biosynthetic growth hormones: a case of regulatory abdication, Epstein, Samuel S., International Journal of Health Services, Vol.

26, No. 1, 1996, pp. 173-85

Update on the Biological Characteristics of the Antioxidant Micronutrients: Vitamin C, Vitamin E, and the Carotenoids, Journal of the American Dietetic Assn 96 (July 1996): 693-702.

Updating a 12-year Experience with Arrest and Reversal Therapy for Coronary Heart Disease, Caldwell B. Esselstyn, Jr., M.D., The American Journal of Cardiology, Vol. 84, August 1, 1999

Vegan diet in physiological health promotion, Hanninen O; Rauma AL; Kaartinen K; Nenonen M, Acta Physiol Hung 1999;86(3-4):171-80

Vegan Nutrition, a Survey of Research, Langley G, The Vegan Society, 1988

Vegetable consumption and risk of chronic disease, La Vecchia C, Decarli A, Pagano R, Epidem 1998;9:208-10

Vegetables, fruit, and cancer prevention: a review, Steinmetz KA, Potter JD, Journal of the American Dietetic Association, Oct 1996;(10)

Vegetarian and other complex diets, fats, fiber, and hypertension, Beilin LJ, Am J Clin Nutr. 1994;59(suppl):1130-1135

Vegetarian Diet May Protect Against Breast Cancer, International Journal of Cancer 2002;99:238-244

Vegetarian diets and children, Sanders TAB, Reddy S, Am J Clin Nutr. 1994;59(suppl):1176S-1181S

Vegetarian diets and colon cancer: the German experience, Frentzel-Beyme R, Chang-Claude J, Am J Clin Nutr 1994;59(suppl):1143S–52S

Very Low Rate of Fat in Diet Is Advised to Fight Cancer, Boston Globe, 4/23/91

Vitamin D and bone health, Holuck MF, J Nutr. 1996;126 (suppl):1159S-1164S

Western Culture May Be Culprit Behind Acne, Reuters Health, 12/20/02

What Causes Cancer?, Trichopoulos D, Li F, Hunter D, Scientific American, 9/96

Who is Susceptible to Cancers of the Breast, Colon, and Prostate? Walter Willett, Annals of the New York Academy of Sciences 768 (Sept. 30, 1995): 1-11.

Whole-grain intake and cancer: an expanded review and meta-analysis, Jacobs DR Jr, Marquart L, Salvin J, Kushi LH, Nutr Cancer 1998;30:85–96.

Whole-grain intake and insulin sensitivity: the Insulin Resistance Atherosclerosis Study, Liese AD, Roach AK, Sparks KC, Marquart L, D'Agostino RB Jr., Mayer-Davis EJ, Am J Clin Nutr 2003;78:965-71

With increasing ageing in Western populations, what are the prospects for lowering the incidence of coronary heart disease?, A.R.P. Walker, Q J Med 2001; 94: 107-112

Worldwide incidence of hip fracture in elderly women: relation to the consumption of animal and vegetable foods, Lynda A. Frassetto et al., Journal of Gerontology: Medical Sciences, 2000; 55A: M585-M592

Footnotes

Introduction

1. Attwood, Charles, M.D., "Enter the 'Zone': A Giant Leap Backwards" (1998) www.vegsource.com/attwood/zone.htm. Many people, from the Mayor of New York City to other doctors who have known him for decades have all said that Atkins was overweight. Re Mayor Michael Bloomberg, Daily News, January 21, 2004. Dr. John McDougall estimates Atkins was 40 to 60 pounds overweight. Deborah Norville on MSNBC, Wednesday, 2/11/04.
2. Barry Sears, Enter the Zone, p. 47.
3. Barry Sears, Enter the Zone, pp. 3. 96, back cover.
4. Barry Sears, Enter the Zone, pp. 67, 69.
5. See Protein in Notes for more discussion on protein.
6. New York Times, 10/27/03.
7. Doctor Wants 'South Beach' to Mean Hearts, Not Bikinis, New York Times, 4/14/04
8. This is based on using the dubious glycemic index. For more on this index, see *Problems With the Glycemic Index* under Notes.
9. New York Times, 10/7/03.
10. Bravata DM, Sanders L, Huang J, et al., Efficacy and safety of low-carbohydrate diets: a systematic review. JAMA. 2003;289:1837-1850.
11. Studies Link High-Fiber Carbs, Low Weight, WebMD Medical News, 3/5/04; American Heart Association Annual Conference on Cardiovascular Disease Epidemiology and Prevention, San Francisco, 2004.
12. Foryet, J. Limitations of behavioral treatment of obesity: review and analysis. 1981, J. Behav. Med. 4:159-73.
13. As quoted in The Food Revolution, John Robbins, p. 61.

Diet, Disease & Weight Loss

1. Eat Right, Live Longer, Neal Barnard, M.D., p. 35.
2. There are all kinds of bone diseases, e.g., rickets, but none are the result of a deficiency of calcium in a diet. In other words, any natural diet will provide enough calcium for the human body. The McDougall Program, John A. McDougall, M.D., p. 48, McDougall's Medicine, John A. McDougall, M.D., p. 70; Calcium Requirements in man: a critical review, C. Paterson, Postgrad Med J. 54:244, 1978; The human requirement of calcium: should low intakes be supplemented? A. Walker, Am J. Clin Nutr, 25:518, 1972; Symposium on human calcium requirements: Council on Foods and Nutrition, JAMA 185:588, 1963; Modern Nutrition in Health and Disease, 5th ed, Goodhart and Shils, 1973, p. 274.
3. Calcium could be key to weight loss, The Seattle Times, 4/21/04.
4. As related in Fasting and Eating for Health, Joel Fuhrman, M.D., p. 56.
5. Caldwell B. Esselstyn, M.D., as stated in the film Eating, The McDougall Program, John A. McDougall, M.D., p. 17.
6. Eat To Live, Joel Fuhrman, M.D., p. 51. In this estimate, oils constitute 11% of total calories. Oils are considered a refined food.

7. Estimates vary somewhat, depending on the authority, but according to world-renowned paleontologist Dr. Richard Leakey, animal foods were a very rare part of the human evolutionary diet. The five percent used here is hypothetical and may be lower. [Dr. Richard Leakey, as quoted in The Power of Your Plate, Neal Barnard, M.D., p. 170.] When ancient man did eat meat, he probably walked, ran and jumped 20 miles to get it. And, aside from a very few areas where meat was plentiful, ancient man ate meat only a few times a year. In addition, the composition of wild game was a far cry from our grain-fed, domesticated, high-fat, hormone-laced meat that almost all Americans eat today. There were, of course, some populations late in our evolution that ate higher amounts of meat. They did, however, suffer the consequences. Autopsy studies of meat-eating specimens, such as the Iceman, have shown advanced stages of heart disease in 25 year olds.

8. Meat and dairy foods account for over 90 percent of the population's intake of pesticides. This is due to the heavy pesticide use on crops destined for consumption by farm animals. Far lower levels of pesticides are used on crops destined for human consumption. These pesticide-laden crops are fed to farm animals and they end up in the tissues and fat that we eat. The higher on the food chain you eat, the more concentrated the pesticides. John Robbins, Diet For A New America, p. 343.

9. The use of hormones in cattle is so great that Europe has banned American beef from it's shores. Stephany, R.W., Hormones in meat: Different approaches in the EU and in the USA, APMIS 109:S357. And dairy is essentially a hormonal factory, containing dozens of active hormones to fuel the growth of a calf that will weigh up to 500 pounds within a year of its birth. Here are some of them: Pituitary hormones (PRL, GH, TSH, FSH, LH ACTH Oxytocin); Steroid hormones (Estradiol, Estriol, Progesterone, Testosterone, 17-Ketosteroids, Corticosterone, Vitamine D); Hypothalamic hormones (TRH, LHRH, Somatostatin, PRL-inhibiting factor, PRL-releasing factor, GnRH, GRH); Thyroid and Parathyroid hormones (T3, T4, rT3, Calcitonin, Parathormone, PTH peptide); gastrointestinal peptides (Vasoactive intestinal peptide, Bombesin, Cholecystokinin, Gastrin, Gastrin inhibitory peptide, Pancreatic peptide, Y peptide, Substance P and Neurotensin); Growth Factors (IGF's (I and II), IGF binding proteins, Nerve growth factor, Epidermal growth factor and TGF alpha, TGF beta, Growth Inhibitors MDGI and MAF, and Platelet derived growth factor; Others... (PGE, PGF2 alpha, cAMP, cGMP, Delta sleep inducing peptide, Transferrin, Lactoferrin, Casomorphin and Erythropoietin.

10. These additives were all FDA approved at the time. Ershoff, BH, J. of Food Science, vol. 41, p. 949, 1976.

11. New Study Suggests Chemicals Could Trigger Disease, AP, 11/6/00.

12. Japanese J. Cancer Research, Rao, AR, et al., vol. 81, p. 1239.

13. Lessons From the Miracle Doctors, Jon Barron, p. 54

14. Tomatoes May Be Better Against Cancer Than Lycopene Alone, LA Times, 11/10/03.

15. Eat To Beat Cancer, J. Robert Hatherhill, p. 17, 50.

16. As told to Neal Barnard in The Power of Your Plate, Neal Barnard, M.D., p. 23.

17. J Am Diet Assoc. 2003 Jul;103(7):867-72.

18. New England Journal of Medicine, July 4, 1985.

19. The effect of high-protein diets on coronary blood flow, Fleming RM, Angiology 2000;51(10):817-826.

20. Serum lipids and conjunctival circulation after fat ingestion in men exhibiting type-A behavior pattern, Friedman, M., Circulation 29:874, 1964 ; Effect of unsaturated fats upon lipemia and conjunctival circulation. A study of coronary-prone (pattern A) men., Friedman, M., JAMA 193: 882, 1965; John A. McDougall, M.D., A Challenging Second Opinion, p. 157. Citation: The effect of lipemia upon coronary and peripheral arterial circulation in patients with essential hyperlipemia, Juo, P., Amer J Med 26:68, 1959 Re 40% Fleming RM. The effect of high-protein diets on coronary blood flow. Angiology 2000;51(10):817-826.
21. As shown in the film, Eating.
22. Breaking the Food Seduction, Neal Barnard, M.D., 160.
23. Due to genetics, there is a small percentage of the population that can achieve total cholesterol levels below 150 regardless of their diet.
24. Dr. Joel Fuhrman, http://www.drfuhrman.com/cholesterol.html
25. Eat To Beat Cancer, J. Robert Hatherhill, p. 59. Of course, this hardly implies the Japanese have an ideal diet. Their high rates of stomach cancer have been blamed on the high sodium content of their diet. Corroborating evidence has recently been gathered by studies showing vegetable intake reduces the risks of smoking-related cancers. Veg-eating smokers 'cheat illness': Increasing fruit intake may boost your chances," BBC News, 7/31/02; "Veggies cut smokers' cancer risk," MSNBC, 4/8/02; Protective effects of raw vegetables and fruit against lung cancer among smokers and ex-smokers: a case-control study in the Tokai area of Japan, C.M. Gao, K. Tajima, T. Kuroishi, et al, 1993, Japan J. Cancer Res. 84 (6): 594-600.
26. Genetics accounts for only a small percentage of our common cancers. In the case of breast cancer, for example, genetics accounts for only 5% of all cases. In terms of other external factors, air and water pollution only account for 5%, alcohol and radiation account for 3% each, and medications account for only 2% of cancers. Tobacco use accounts for 30% and the balance is due to dietary factors. For many individuals, genetics may make a contribution in subtle ways, e g , it may determine one's susceptibility to carcinogens, the strength of the immune system, body weight, and other factors. But each of these is also influenced by diet and such weaknesses can be offset by dietary habits, as illustrated in the Japanese smoker example. For more discussion on this topic, see Genetics, Notes. Sources: Minamoto T, Mai M, Ronai Z. Environmental factors as regulators and effectors of multistep carcinogenesis. Carcinogenesis 1999;20(4):519-27; Cummings JH, Bingham SA. Diet and the prevention of cancer. BMJ 1998;317:1636-40.
27. Health implications of the n-3 fatty acids, Odeleye OE, Watson RR., Am J Clin Nutr 1991;53:177-8; Reply to O Odeleye and R Watson, Kinsella JE, Am J Clin Nutr 1991;53:178.
28. Effects of fish oil and corn oil diets on prostaglandin-dependent and myelopoiesis-associated immune suppressor mechanisms of mice bearing metastatic Lewis lung carcinoma tumors, Young MR, Cancer Res. 1989 Apr 15;49(8):1931-6; Influence of lipid diets on the number of metastases and ganglioside content of H59 variant tumors, Coulombe J, Clin Exp Metastasis. 1997 Jul;15(4):410-7.
29. Cancer, January 2002;94:272-281; Cancer, March 2002; 94:1867-75.
30. Diet For A New America, John Robbins, p. 343.
31. J U.S. Department of Health and Human Services. Surgeon General's Report on Nutrition and Health. DHHS Publ No. 88-50210, 1988.

32. Lifestyle Changes and the 'Spontaneous' Regression of Cancer..., Foster, H, Inter. Jnl Biosocial Research, 10(1), 1988, pp. 17-33, as quoted in Reclaiming Our Health, John Robbins, p. 283.
33. The Pleasure Trap, Douglas Lisle, Ph.D. & Alan Goldhamer, D.C., p. 130; The McDougall Program for Women, John A. McDougall, p. 131.
34. Patient No More, Sharon Batt, p. 82.
35. Triumph Over Cancer, Agi Lidle.
36. Eat To Live, Joel Fuhrman, M.D., p. 6.
37. John A. McDougall, M.D., http://www.drmcdougall.com/science/diabetes.html
38. Acne vulgaris: a disease of Western civilization, Cordain L., Arch Dermatol. 2002 Dec;138(12):1584-90; Acne diet reconsidered, Rosenberg EW, Arch Dermatol. 1981 Apr;117(4):193-5; Western Culture May Be Culprit Behind Acne, Reuters Health, 12/20/02; Diet may trigger acne after all, Los Angeles Times, 1/6/03.
39. Eat To Live, Joel Fuhrman, M.D., p. 51.
40. Trends in Intake of Energy and Macronutrients --- United States, 1971—2000, Centers For Disease Control, February 6, 2004 / 53(04);80-82.
41. Food Politics, Marion Nestle, Ph.D., p. 3.
42. Ibid, p. 113
43. Dr. Dean Ornish's Program for Reversing Heart Disease, Dean Ornish, M.D., p. 262.

The RAVE Diet

1. Breaking the Food Seduction, Neal Barnard, M.D., p. 46
2. Fast Food Nation, Eric Schlosser, p. 121
3. Ibid, p. 129
4. Stable behaviors associated with adults' 10-year change in body mass index and likelihood of gain at the waist, H.S. Kahn, L.M. Tatham, C. Rodriguez, et al, Am. J. Public Health 87 (5): 747-57 and American Heart Association Annual Conference on Cardiovascular Disease Epidemiology and Prevention, San Francisco, 2004. American Heart Association news conference; participants: Robert H. Eckel, MD, University of Colorado Health Sciences Center; Randal J. Thomas, MD, Mayo Clinic, Rochester, Minn.; Deborah J. Toobert, PhD, Oregon Research Institute, Eugene, Ore.; Kristie J. Lancaster, PhD, RD, New York University, N.Y.; Alison Jane Rigby, PhD, MPH, RD, Stanford University, Palo Alto, Calif.; and Linda Van Horn, PhD, Northwestern University, Chicago.
5. The Pritikin Program for Diet & Exercise, Nathan Pritikin, M.D., p. 93.
6. Dietary Protein level and aflatoxin B1-induced preneoplastic hepatic lesions in the rat, Dunaif, GE, Campbell TC, Nutrition 117 No. 7, 1987: 1298-302.
7. Inhibition of hepatocellular carcinoma development in hepatitis B virus transfected mice by low dietary casein, Cheng, Z, Hu, J., King, J., et al., Hepatology 26 No. 5 (1997: 1351-54.
8. Eat To Live, Joel Fuhrman, M.D., p. 91.
9. Dr. Dean Ornish's Program for Reversing Heart Disease, Dean Ornish, M.D., p. 256-257.

10. Eat To Live, Joel Fuhrman, M.D., p. 121.
11. The Influence of Diet on the Appearance of New Lesions in Human Coronary Arteries, JAMA, 1990, Vol. 263, pp. 1646-52.
12. Dr. John A. McDougall, M.D., http://www.drmcdougall.com/vegetable_fat.html
13. Young MR. Effects of fish oil and corn oil diets on prostaglandin-dependent and myelopoiesis-associated immune suppressor mechanisms of mice bearing metastatic Lewis lung carcinoma tumors. Cancer Res. 1989 Apr 15;49(8):1931-6; Coulombe J. Influence of lipid diets on the number of metastases and ganglioside content of H59 variant tumors. Clin Exp Metastasis. 1997 Jul;15(4):410-7
14. Lyon Diet Heart Study.
15. European Journal of Clinical Nutrition 2002;56:715-722.
16. The Influence of Diet on the Appearance of New Lesions in Human Coronary Arteries, JAMA, 1990, Vol. 263, pp. 1646-52.
17. The Influence of Diet on the Appearance of New Lesions in Human Coronary Arteries," D. H. Blankenhorn; R. L. Johnson; W. J. Mack; H. A. el Zein; L. I. Vailas, JAMA, 1990, Vol. 263, pp. 1646-52; Lancet 344:1195, 1994); Aterioscler Thromb Vasc Biol 15:2101, 1995; Dietary Monounsaturated Fatty Acids Promote Aortic Atherosclerosis in LDL Receptor–Null, Human ApoB100–Overexpressing Transgenic Mice, Lawrence L. Rudel, Kathryn Kelley, Janet K. Sawyer, Ramesh Shah, Martha D. Wilson, Arterioscler Thromb Vasc Biol. 1998;18:1818-1827; Combined Intense Lifestyle and Pharmacologic Lipid Treatment Further Reduce Coronary Events and Myocardial Perfusion Abnormalities Compared With Usual-Care Cholesterol-Lowering Drugs in Coronary Artery Disease, Stefano Sdringola, MD, FACC, Keiichi Nakagawa, MD, Yuko Nakagawa, MD, S. Wamique Yusuf, MBBS, MRCP, Fernando Boccalandro, MD, Nizar Mullani, BS, Mary Haynie, RN, MBA, Mary Jane Hess, RN, K. Lance Gould, MD, FACC, Journal of the American College of Cardiology, JACC Vol. 41, No. 2, 2003, 263–72; Effect of Diet on Vascular Reactivity: An Emerging Marker for Vascular Risk, Sheila G. West, Current Atherosclerosis Reports, Vol 3.6, pp. 446-455; Effect of a High-Fat Ketogenic Diet on Plasma Levels of Lipids, Lipoproteins, and Apolipoproteins in Children, Peter O. Kwiterovich, Jr; Eileen P. G. Vining; Paula Pyzik; Richard Skolasky, Jr; John M. Freeman, JAMA. 2003;290:912-920; Rudel LL, Parks JS, Sawyer JK. Compared with dietary monounsaturated and saturated fat, polyunsaturated fat protects African Green Monkeys from coronary artery atherosclerosis. Arterioscler Thromb Vasc Biol 1995;15:2101- 2110; de Lorgeril M, Salen P, Martin JL, Monjaud I, Deloye J, Mamelle N. Mediterranean diet, traditional risk factors, and the rate of cardiovascular complications after myocardial infarction. Circulation 1999;99:779-785.
18. Supersize Me, Roger Ebert, Chicago Sun-Times, 5/7/04.
19. American Chemical Society Press Release, 3/3/03, printed in Journal of Agricultural and Food Chemistry, 2/26/03.
20. Biological Effects of Dietary Flaxseed In Patients With Breast Cancer, Thompson LU, Li T, Chen J, Goss PE Nutritional Sciences, University of Toronto, Toronto, ON, Canada; Medical Oncology, Princess Margaret Hospital, Toronto, ON, Canada, San Antonio Breast Cancer Symposium 2000.
21. Breaking The Food Seduction, Neal Barnard, M.D.
22. Ibid, p. 90.

23. AP, "Diet Trends May Broaden Demographics," 3/30/04.

Sex, Booze, Rock 'n Roll

1. Feldman HA. Erectile dysfunction and coronary risk factors: prospective results from the Massachusetts male aging study. Prev. Med. 2000 Apr;30(4):328-38.
2. Bodie J. Laboratory evaluations of erectile dysfunction: an evidence based approach. J Urol. 2003 Jun;169(6):2262-4.
3. See Footnote #8, *Diet, Disease & Weight Loss*. John Robbins, Diet For A New America, p. 343.
4. Rozati R . Role of environmental estrogens in the deterioration of male factor fertility. Fertil Steril. 2002 Dec;78(6):1187-94.
5. Sexual Function in Men Older Than 50 Years of Age: Results from the Health Professionals Follow-up Study, Constance G. Bacon, ScD; Murray A. Mittleman, MD, ScD; Ichiro Kawachi, MD, PhD; Edward Giovannucci, MD, ScD; Dale B. Glasser, PhD; and Eric B. Rimm, ScD, Vol. 139, Issue 3, 161-68.

Notes

Protein

1. Minimum protein requirements of adults, Hegsted, D., Am. J. Clin. Nutr. 21: 3520; The amino acid requirements of man. XIII The sparing effect of cystine on methionine requirement, Rose, W.C. and Wixom, R.L., J. Biol. Chem., 216, 763-773.
2. Kofranyi, E., Jekat, F. and Muller-Wecker, H. (1970). 'The minimum protein requirements of humans, tested with mixtures of whole egg plus potatoes and maize plus beans', Z. Physiol. Chem., 351, 1485-1493; Clark, H.E., Malzer, J.L., Onderka, H.M., Howe, J.M. and Moon, W. (1973). 'Nitrogen balances of adult human subjects fed combinations of wheat, beans, corn, milk, and rice', Am. J. Clin. Nutr., 26, 702-706; Edwards, C.H., Booker, L.K., Rumph, C.H., Wright, W.G. and Ganapathy, S.N. (1971). 'Utilisation of wheat by adult man; nitrogen metabolism, plasma amino acids and lipids', Am. J. Clin. Nutr., 24, 181-193; Lee, C., Howe, J.M., Carlson, K. and Clark, H.E. (1971). 'Nitrogen retention of young men fed rice with or without supplementary chicken', Am. J. Clin. Nutr., 24, 318-323; Kies, C., Williams, E. and Fox, H.M. (1965). 'Determination of first limiting nitrogenous factor in corn protein for nitrogen retention in human adults', J. Nutr., 86, 350-356.
3. Eat To Live, Joel Fuhrman, M.D., p. 52.

Problems With the Glycemic Index

1. Fad Diets Versus Dietary Guidelines, American Institute for Cancer Research, 02/11/02:12.

Osteoporosis and Acidic Diets

1. The Pritikin Program for Diet & Exercise, Nathan Pritikin, M.D., p. 44.

2. McDougall's Medicine, John A. McDougall, M.D., p. 70; The McDougall Program, John A. McDougall, M.D., p. 48, Calcium Requirements in man: a critical review, C. Paterson, Postgrad Med J. 54:244, 1978; The human requirement of calcium: should low intakes be supplemented? A. Walker, Am J. Clin Nutr, 25:518, 1972; Symposium on human calcium requirements: Council on Foods and Nutrition, JAMA 185:588, 1963; Modern Nutrition in Health and Disease, 5th ed, Goodhart and Shils, 1973, p. 274.

3. JAMA. 2002;288:2300-2306 (41% difference in hip fractures between those women who exercised and those who did not); Aloia, J., Exercise and skeletal health. Journal of American Geriatric Society 29:104, 1981., Smith, E., Physical activity and calcium modalities for bone mineral increase in aged women. Med Sci, Sports Exercise 13:60, 1981, Gymnastics Strengthens Girls' Bones: Study Journal of Pediatrics 2002;141:211-216, Journal of Pediatrics 2002;141:211-216, Smith, E.L., 1982. Exercise for prevention of osteoporosis: A review. The Physician and Sportsmedicine 10(3):72-82.

4. Study: Exercise Important for Strong Bones, Associated Press, 6/9/04.

Recipe Index

Index